# Palm Springs
## á la Carte

# Palm Springs
## á la Carte

The Colorful World of the Caviar Crowd
at Their Favorite Desert Hideaway

## MEL HABER
### with
### Marshall Terrill

BOOKS

Fort Lee, New Jersey

Published by Barricade Books, Inc.
185 Bridge Plaza North
Suite 308-A
Fort Lee, NJ 07024

www.barricadebooks.com

Library of Congress Cataloging-in-Publication Data
A copy of this title's Library of Congress Cataloging-in-Publication Data is available on request from the Library of Congress.

ISBN 13: 978-1-56980-353-0
ISBN 1-56980-353-6

10 9 8 7 6 5 4 3 2 1

Manufactured in the United States of America

# DEDICATION

I dedicate this book to all the wonderful people of the Coachella Valley who made this thirty-three year trip such an incredible ride.

To my beautiful wife, Stephanie, who kept me together during the many "ups & downs."

To all my employees who always made me look like I knew what I was doing and without whom I would still be selling women's shoes.

Last but not least, to Marshall Terrill, my co-author who made this so easy.

I am one lucky guy!

*Mel Haber*

# Table of Contents

# FOREWORD

# Frank M. Bogert,
## Former Mayor of Palm Springs

**M**el Haber came to Palm Springs in 1974. The next year he bought the Ingleside Inn and soon became one of the village's leading citizens. He added rooms and refurbished the Inn keeping the same ambiance that made it one of the most exclusive hotels in the valley; with Melvyn's, a gourmet restaurant. Everything Mel does is a huge success. He opened five more restaurants in Palm Springs.

His marriage to Stephanie in 1982 has been very successful. In 1988, they had a daughter named Autumn who, at twenty, is as beautiful as her mother.

In his spare time, Mel wrote a book called *Bedtime Stories*, which is a great read and huge success. I'm hopeful this second literary endeavor is even more successful.

Mel's biggest success has been as president of the Angel View Crippled Children's Foundation. Twenty-five years ago, he joined the board of directors, becoming president in 1995. Mel spends most of his time working with the organization.

I am proud to call him my friend.

*Frank M. Bogert was a twice-elected mayor and is Palm Springs's most prominent citizen. He is immortalized in bronze riding a galloping horse outside the steps of city hall.*

# FOREWORD

# Andrew Neiderman

nyone drawn to or given this book will initially wonder, "Why read any biography if it's not the biography of a famous politician, government leader, famous celebrity, inventor or billionaire businessman?"

In Mel Haber's case, this is an easy question to answer, for in a real sense he embodies and personifies a true renaissance man—a man who has broad interests and accomplishments in seemingly quite different areas, such as business and the arts. In truth, he is comfortable with movie stars and with small businessmen, laborers and entrepreneurs, bankers and athletes. His thirst for knowledge is never ending, and his compassion and interest in all men and women, regardless of their wealth and power, makes him a star on the human stage.

Besides, this isn't just Mel Haber's story. It's a wonderful prospective of American history from the 1940s to the present, for in following Mel's journey, you live through the changes in style and fashions, the economic ups and downs, and the American entertainment scene. Written with an honesty capable only of someone comfortable with who he is, Mel Haber's story offers wonderful insights into the struggles, successes, and failures many of his contemporaries experienced. In an age when everything is spun, it's refreshing to read the words of a straight shooter who is willing to expose his own weaknesses and failures to portray himself three-dimensionally. Be ready to sit beside him on this ride when you read this book.

In telling us how he arrived in Palm Springs and what drew him to remain there, and how he built his Ingleside Inn into a world famous hotel and restaurant, Mel turns us into the perennial "flies on the wall," witnesses to the private and personal comings and goings of some of the world's most famous people. With his New York sense of humor and his never-ending youthful, impish view of the world, Mel weaves the most delectable anecdotes into his own story and clearly shows us why he is a terrific raconteur.

If you dine at Melvyn's when he is there, you will inevitably find yourself laughing and reminiscing with him when he stops at your table. His is an ongoing, always developing and expanding life story, and just being a patron of his restaurant makes you a character and participant in it. Few people you meet can perform that magic.

But perform it he does, and especially in this memoir. His journey from east New York to Europe to Palm Springs is not bloated with travelogue data meant to serve as filler. Mel's story needs no filler. It is peppered instead with tidbits of the sort of personal information that entertains while it informs. You will leave these pages feeling as if you weren't reading, but listening, you weren't alone, but with him, right there beside you. Believe me, few autobiographies, no matter how great the subject and accomplishments, succeed that well.

To open any restaurant is a prodigious task. Most fail within the first three years, if they last that long. The tenacity and determination Mel exhibited in his earlier life and ventures; however, supported him well in this grand battle. What makes this particular story fascinating is the range of celebrities who frequented his establishment even during the early formative days when most would stay away. Something drew them and has drawn them back repeatedly.

It won't take you long to figure out what that something is. Any business built out of the blood and guts of a single entrepreneur is bound to reflect him and take on his personality. What is Melvyn's today? Besides the excellent food and service, Melvyn's has an atmosphere that merges the New York style of personal contact with the flash of Hollywood, the glamour of Palm Springs, and the personal touch of someone who never forgets a face or a name and is able to reach into memories and come up with some story to make any first-time listener feel he's known Melvyn and his customers a long time. You're at home at Melvyn's because of Melvyn, and that didn't just happen.

There is no better example of this than Melvyn's reconstruction of his Sinatra experiences. Because of the excitement and the power of this American icon, it is difficult for anyone to re-tell an experience and not sound too foolish. Melvyn's story will surely bring a smile to any reader's face, but most importantly, it depicts what it was like to move in these spotlights and still hold on to your own identity, as Melvyn did and does.

Another highlight of his story is his creation of the word and concept palimony. The events that led up to it and its subsequent legal ramifications are again both entertaining and informative.

Beyond all the great stories involving celebrities of all walks of life, this is still at heart the personal journey of a man who has enjoyed successes, suffered defeats and tragedy, and found his own identity and happiness at an age when most men and women farm themselves out to pasture. One can clearly see that Mel Haber is not a man meant for retirement, and even if he were, he would turn the retirement community into a theater.

We read to learn, to enjoy, and to find some commonality with our fellow man and woman. This story succeeds on all those levels, and when you put it down, you will have met and gotten to know a most interesting man. It will enrich your own life.

Enjoy the ride.

I did.

*Andrew Neiderman, who is also known as V. C. Andrews, is the author of thirty-eight novels. Many of his books have been adapted into films, the most known being the Warner Bros. The Devil's Advocate. Andrew Neiderman and his wife Diane have been residents of Palm Springs since 1989.*

# INTRODUCTION

*I believe a man has three fantasies: to play the piano, to write the great American novel, and to own a restaurant that caters to the beautiful people.*

—Mel Haber

**H**ow does a man define success?

I've spent my life trying to figure that one out. Perhaps success is a work in progress based on working hard and enjoying the fruits of your labor, tinged with the sweet nectar of friends and family. It can't simply be money or fame—those tend to be tenuous, fleeting or mired in loneliness. I've found success is living the best quality of life that you can while giving back to others.

This book chronicles the hills and valleys of my life's work, my legacy to my children and others. When you get into your seventies, you've learned a few lessons and tricks along the way. You also tend to look at life with a fine-tuned eye, a little smirk, and a great big sigh for a job well done despite your best efforts to the contrary at times. This is my opportunity to reminisce, grimace, and laugh at myself, to marvel at the friendships and acquaintances I've made through the years, and perhaps to pass along a few well-earned tidbits of life to the next bevy of entrepreneurs out there.

You've got to find your opportunities; don't sit around waiting for opportunity to find you. I've seen too many people in life who just walk up to the proverbial door when opportunity presents itself and then just stand there, dumbfounded, not knowing what to do next, when all they had to do was knock and stride right in to the land of hard work and hard knocks.

Sure it's a risk. But when you don't risk, you can't capitalize on the returns. If I hadn't plunged into buying the Ingleside Inn, I would have missed the opportunity to meet some of the most famous people on the planet, as well as a lot of other colorful people. And I would not have met my loving wife, Stephanie, nor had my lovely daughter, Autumn.

No man is an island, it's true. I'd never have made it without my longtime staff and those who've worked and helped me along the way. Take care of those who take care of you. The good times are good, but there are those who will stand by your side through fear, quandary, and loss. I've been fortunate to have people in my life that grounded me in reality when the licentiousness of the good life nearly intoxicated me.

Balance hard work with enjoying the rewards of your labor and giving back to your community. This has been tough through the years, but again, I've been fortunate to have people around me to help me learn the true meaning of entrepreneurship and the spirit of giving, especially through the Angel View Crippled Children's Foundation.

I hope that as you read you will find inspiration in that youthful tenacity that eventually landed me in Palm Springs, Melvyn's, and the Ingleside Inn. Sure, maybe some of the time I didn't know what the heck I was doing, but that didn't stop me from trying to create my own success. Enjoy my book, laugh out loud, learn from my mistakes, and find a way to adapt it and give back.

At the beginning of this introduction, I quoted what I believe are a man's three fantasies: "to play the piano, to write the great American novel, and to own a restaurant that caters to the beautiful people."

With this book, I've finally accomplished all three. My family is by my side, my work with Angel View serves my spirit, and Melvyn's and the Ingleside Inn with all its glory is my home.

I think I've defined my success.

# CHAPTER 1

# Native New Yorker

Crack open any decent atlas or road map, and it will show you that Palm Springs is about 2,700 miles from Brooklyn. With that sort of distance, the oasis in the desert might as well have been a foreign country as far as I was concerned. Not that I had anything against the West Coast, but Brooklyn had everything a kid could ever want—a famous bridge, a thriving metropolis of three million people, authentic delicatessens, Nathan's hot dogs and, of course, the best baseball team in the world—the Brooklyn Dodgers.

Over the years, scores of well-known personalities were born and raised in Brooklyn, including television personality Larry King; actors Danny Kaye, Eli Wallach, Elliot Gould, Rita Hayworth, Susan Hayward, and Lauren Bacall; singers Barbra Streisand, Neil Diamond, and Barry Manilow; and former New York City mayor Rudy Giuliani.

There's a charm to the area, no question, and it was especially strong during the era in which I grew up. It was a time when "going out" meant a jaunt to the corner candy store for a chocolate egg cream, Coney Island was the place to impress a date, and Walter Winchell was every Brooklynite's main news source. I guess those kinds of proclamations sort of date me.

To take the mystery out of my age, I'll be forthcoming: I was born on October 24, 1936, the youngest of four children and the only boy of Louis and Mary Haber. My sisters Gloria, Alyce, and Phyllis, better known as "Franky," preceded me in birth.

As the only boy, I was naturally spoiled. Almost all the Jewish mothers I've ever known are overprotective of their children, but my mother took it to another level as a result of a medical condition I suffered at the age of two after falling down a flight of steps and hitting my head hard, which affected my vision. As a result, my eyes deteriorated to the point where I was taken to the Mayo Clinic. Doctors there told my father that in order to save my life they had to remove both eyes. My father's reaction was extreme.

"I'm not going to have a blind child," my father told doctors. "I'd rather let him die."

Fortunately for me, my mother and father found an eye doctor in Brooklyn who told them that he could save my left eye.

As a result of my losing my right eye, my mother became my protector. If I got in a fight or a tangle with a neighborhood kid, my mother came down on my transgressor like a landslide.

Our family was equally protected by my father, in a financial sense. Even though I'm technically a child of the Great Depression, I can't say that I really experienced the hardships that millions of Americans did when Wall Street crashed. My father was a button and zipper salesman in the garment district earlier in his life but because of a bad heart never worked when I was a kid. He wore monogrammed shirts, smoked cigarettes out of the corner of his mouth, and had a taste for the finer things in life. When I became older, I suspected he might have had a little something going on the side.

You see, my father received five checks every Friday until the day he died. Somehow we were able to live in a lovely two-bedroom apartment overlooking Ocean Parkway in the Flatbush section of Brooklyn. For those of you not familiar with Ocean Parkway, it was Brooklyn's equivalent of the Champs-Élysées in Paris. It was no small wonder the parkway was drawn up by city planners who were influenced by boulevards in Paris and Berlin. Begun in 1874 and completed by 1880, the six-lane parkway was 210 feet wide. The six-mile road runs from Prospect Park to the southeastern edge of

Coney Island and had a four-lane central roadway with two malls, one a bike path and the other a horse path, and two side roads. Ocean Parkway was lined with trees, benches, and playing tables. This was the hub of my youth.

We spent all of our winters in Miami Beach, Florida, at a time when only three kinds of people visited there: gangsters, movie stars, and garment center people. Needless to say, our family of six never wanted for anything. Perhaps even more impressive than our comfortable lifestyle was the heavy-duty company my father kept.

Our family went out to dinner almost every night, which was almost unheard of back in that era. My mother hated it because my father seemed to work the room, stopping at almost every table to schmooze with fellow diners. He seemed to know everybody, and I mean everybody. When I was eleven, he introduced me to Al Jolson and Al Capone on the same day.

One of my father's best friends when he was younger was Louis "Lepke" Buckhalter, a notorious member of Murder Incorporated, who was part of the enforcement machinery for a nationally known labor leader. Word got around that he shot and killed a garment manufacturer named Guido Fererri in the street and that he gunned down another man, Joseph Rosen, in a Brooklyn candy store.

But the long arm of the law caught up with ol' Lepke when police found out he was the mastermind of a $10 million narcotics ring. Uncle Sam said they'd go easy on him and even enlisted the help of journalist Walter Winchell, who arranged for Buckhalter to turn himself in to his custody in Miami Beach. But instead of giving him a nice cozy cell that they promised in a federal penitentiary, the government gave him the electric chair.

Dad kept fast company but also liked living in the fast lane. He was a big-time gambler who didn't always come out on the winning end. My Uncle Mike, a very wealthy dress manufacturer, once told me that he gave my father $10,000 to gamble with and Dad immediately put it all down on the crap table. My uncle couldn't believe that he lost it all on one roll of the dice.

"What'd you want me to do, Mike? Nurse it all night?" my father said, shrugging his shoulders.

My father's lifestyle caught up with him when he suffered his first heart attack at age forty-two. He then had a heart attack every year for the next decade. What rendered his heart virtually useless? I think it was a combination of several things—he smoked, he drank, he gambled, and he devoured my mother's Jewish cooking.

Almost all of his meals were deep fried in chicken fat. From what we now know about chicken fat, you could sink a battleship with that stuff. His cholesterol levels must have been off the charts. But he wasn't the only member of the family who had heart problems. My father was one of seven children—five brothers and two sisters—and not one of them made it past the age of fifty-two. They all died of heart attacks.

Three different times I remember the doctor telling my mother at the hospital in Florida that we needed to "say good-bye" to my father, who just waved it off. Ironically, he woke up on October 1, 1949, which happened to be "Joe DiMaggio Day" at Yankee Stadium. He confessed, "Mel, I'm not going to live to see Yom Kippur"—which was the very next day. Like the trooper he was, he placed and lost a $3,000 bet on the Yankees and then sent me out for Chinese food. When I got back with the delivery, he was dead. It was twenty-three days before my thirteenth birthday.

Those five checks he received every Friday mysteriously disappeared, which meant our upper-middle-class status and our way of life was about to get a serious downgrade.

My mother, who was fifteen when she met my father and forty-two when he died, had never worked a day in her life. She was forced to hit the pavement in search of gainful employment. My three sisters were already married and out of the house and weren't a financial burden, but that meant I was the new man of the house. I needed to find work as well.

While the workplace was a major shock to my mother (she wound up working as a retail clerk in a dress shop) I didn't mind at all. In fact, I loved it. In addition to delivering groceries, I sold peanuts and beer at Ebbets Field for a concessionaire named Harry M. Stevens. In those days, you had to be fourteen to obtain work papers. Since I was a year younger than the state requirement, a friend named Shelley Smith allowed me to work under his name.

Did I say work? It was one of the best jobs I ever had. The money was decent, the atmosphere was electrifying, and I got to see every Brooklyn Dodgers home game for free, which included watching the great Jackie Robinson play ball.

Perhaps even more enjoyable were the summers I spent in the Catskill Mountains in upper New York State. Known as the "Borscht Belt" or "Jewish Alps," the Catskills were frequented by prominent New Yorkers.

It was almost a rite of passage for every Jewish kid to work in the Catskills during that era. It was there that I really established my indefatigable work ethic while having the time of my life.

My work as a busboy required fifteen-hour days for ten weeks straight with no days off. I bussed dirty dishes from morning until midnight and literally fell down in my bunk at the end of each day.

I rotated shifts at the Swan Lake Hotel in Swan Lake, the Plaza Hotel in South Fallsburg, and Grossingers in Ferndale, which was the swankiest and best known resort in the area. The tips were good, and if you really hustled, you could rake in close to $1,000 over the course of the summer, which was serious money back then.

The most important business skill I learned as a busboy that I apply to my life today is "motion efficiency," or what is commonly referred to as "working smart." If someone asked me for bread, butter, or more water, I didn't dash off to the kitchen after each individual request. I waited until I had several requests and a full tray of empty dishes. The same applied when I left the kitchen: I waited until I had a full tray of food. This work ethic and philosophy served me well over the years when I oversaw an assembly line in a manufacturing business, and much later, to set up six restaurants. I devised a system where my waiters didn't waste any steps and my customers received quick and efficient service.

I also learned restraint. Upper management insisted that the employees dance with the women guests to the sounds of the great mambo bands every night at the casino to keep them entertained while their husbands were back in the city during the week. Of course, that often lent itself to trouble. Sometimes the husbands came up unexpectedly and caught their wives with a young turk. Fortunately for me, my business and street smarts kicked in and I knew I could look but not touch. A beautiful woman could be dangerous, but a powerful man was a person you didn't want to cross.

I derived most of my pleasure from watching headlining comics that came through the Catskills. I saw many of the greats in person, including Henny Youngman, Rodney Dangerfield, Milton Berle, Alan King, Shecky Greene, Jackie Mason, Jack Carter, and Phyllis Diller.

Sadly, the Catskills scene pretty much died in the late sixties when airfare became affordable and Miami Beach and Puerto Rico became the new Jewish hotspots. However, the work ethic, the experiences, the friendships, and the business skills I learned in the Catskills were a significant part of my growing up, and will always remain very special to me.

Life back in Brooklyn was harder. After my father died, we moved from our lovely apartment overlooking Ocean Parkway to a one-bedroom unit in the same building, which had a view of a concrete courtyard. My mom worked all day while high school and my part-time jobs kept me occupied.

I was a very bright student (I hardly worked at my schoolwork and yet won a scholarship medal) but not so bright when it came to picking high schools. I had two educational opportunities back then—Brooklyn Technical High School or Erasmus. Both were quality schools, but Brooklyn Tech was harder to get into. The school heavily concentrated on courses in math, science, and drafting, and groomed students for a technical career in engineering. Several graduates went on to become PhDs in math and science, astronauts, CEOs, Nobel Laureates, and technology pioneers.

The only reason I chose Brooklyn Tech over Erasmus was that a friend of mine issued a direct challenge to me—he said there was no way in hell that I could ever get admitted into Brooklyn Tech.

*We'll see about that*, I said to myself.

I think I surprised everyone, including myself, when my test scores were good enough for admittance. In hindsight I might have gotten a little more than I bargained for—the school was a major schlep from home. I woke up at 6:30 in the morning, took two trains to get to school, and didn't get home until 5 p.m. I noticed that my friends who attended Erasmus took a taxi to and from school, got out at one o' clock in the afternoon, and hung out afterward in a nearby cafeteria chatting up the opposite sex. Jealous, I marched into the school counselor's office and asked to be transferred. He was flabbergasted by my request.

"But you can't transfer," he told me. "We've never had a student leave Brooklyn Tech who is doing well." I took care of that little problem in a hurry. I cut school for the next forty days and was shown the door by school officials.

Good-bye Brooklyn Tech and hello Erasmus!

Erasmus High School was nothing to sneeze at, either. Built in 1786, the institute was the second oldest high school in America and considered the "mother of all local high schools" in the area.

The school also boasted a healthy roster of famous and important people throughout the years. Some of its alumni included actors Jeff Chandler, Moe Howard, Bernie Kopell, and Barbara Stanwyck; singer Barbra Streisand; author Micky Spillane; chess player Bobby Fischer; football owners Al Davis (Oakland Raiders) and Bob Tisch (New York Giants); and Sid Luckman, the famous quarterback for the Chicago Bears.

I wish I could say my academic career in high school was as stellar as theirs, but I'd be lying. The only career path that interested me was the path of least resistance. I did just enough to get by. I did like math, but only applied my knowledge in poker and crap games.

One time my mother left me the rent money, which was around $65 a month. Unfortunately, before I paid the rent, I took in a game of craps and lost the entire amount. I had planned a nice weekend in Atlantic City with some of my friends, and stashed some money away for the trip. Once I lost it all in craps, my plans dramatically changed and couldn't go to Atlantic City. I decided I was going to sleep in the basement of our apartment house for the weekend and wash up when my mother went outside to sit on the park bench, which was her usual routine until dusk.

I slipped into the apartment to grab a bite to eat while my mother was outside. Unbeknownst to me, she thought she saw a light go on in her apartment and asked a neighbor to intervene. While I was munching away at the refrigerator door, I felt a poke in my back.

"Stick 'em up," said a voice. I lifted my hands and slowly turned around. The neighbor had a gun pointed right to my head. I quickly made up a lie about how the Atlantic City trip didn't work out and came back early. I was lucky I didn't roll snake eyes and get shot.

I burned the candle at both ends—going to school during the day, delivering groceries after school, and selling peanuts at Ebbets Field on certain nights and weekends. I later worked for a neighborhood businessman by the name of Arthur Schifrin, who made bicycle accessories. I assembled hub shiners, locks, chains, and raccoon tails for the handlebars for the minimum wage of seventy-five cents an hour. But the part-time description soon changed. As time went by, orders dried up and business slowed down considerably. Artie turned to me, all of sixteen, to save his small empire.

"Mel, I can't pay you unless you bring in some business," Artie told me.

I added "salesman" to my job title and went to work. I picked up the Yellow Pages and pulled out a list of all the bicycle shops in the five boroughs of New York. I bought a city street map and cross-referenced the addresses and plotted my daily routes.

After school I went from store to store taking their orders, then shuffled back to our little store at night and assemble the accessories. I would deliver the orders the next day, collect the money, and start the process all over again. This kept us in business for a few months, until I realized it was a hand-to-mouth existence.

Upon graduation, I was forced to take a good look at my life. It was then I had an epiphany: I had no money and no connections, and I realized that all I had to work with was whatever brains God gave me. Traditional college wasn't in the cards, and hard labor was absolutely out of the question. Many things were out of my control with the exception of my ability to control how hard and the amount of hours I was willing to work. I figured that if I was only half as good as the guy next to me, then I would have to figure out a way to work twice as hard just to keep up with him.

Taking a step back, I looked at the biggest industry in New York City at the time, which was the garment business. Even though my father had been gone for several years, I would once again try to follow in his footsteps.

# CHAPTER 2

# Successes and Failures

By the age of seventeen I had been inside many crazy places, but I never thought a fashion institute would be one of them.

There were only two colleges in the country at the time that catered to the garment industry: Lowell Textile in Lowell, Massachusetts, and the Fashion Institute of Technology on the west side of Manhattan. The former was expensive and I would have to pay out-of-state tuition, so that pretty much left the latter, which was free if I passed an entrance exam. At that time F.I.T. was only two floors on top of Central Needle Trades High School. More than 500 people interviewed for sixty openings, and much to my surprise and delight, I was accepted.

Today the school is a New York City institution and is as much a part of the Gotham landscape as the Empire State Building or Times Square, taking up an entire city block. Now an international leader in career education, F. I.T. was founded in 1944 as a bold experiment. Founder Mortimer Ritter envisioned an "MIT for the fashion industries" and his experiment was and continues to be an amazing success more than six decades later, even offering a satellite program halfway across the world in Florence, Italy.

It was a very interesting experience. Most of the students who attended F.I.T. were either females who wanted to become designers or male veterans putting their G.I. Bill to use. I fit neither category.

In the fall of 1954, I started my college career. The school offered seven courses in design and one in management, which is the course I enrolled in. I found the work stimulating, especially the management and international trade classes, but the homework was a little strange to say the least. My friends got a big kick when they came to my apartment and watched me try to drape muslin fabric on a body form with pins, copying the latest fashion craze.

But the school wasn't a diploma mill. Many students got big-time jobs because college graduates in the garment district were virtually nonexistent and large corporations recruited heavily from the school. Several of my fellow classmates shot to corporate stardom. One of my classmates became the president of BVD (they made Jockey Shorts) while another was a major contractor for FILA sportswear. As for me, I was never much of a company man. I guess you could say I had leanings toward being an entrepreneur.

Two months after I enrolled at F.I.T., Artie Schifrin called me with an offer I couldn't refuse. In December 1954, ABC aired a three-part series called "Davy Crockett, Indian Fighter." The coonskin hat worn by actor Fess Parker set off a craze with the nation's youth. Artie was already in the raccoon tail business packaging them for bicycle handlebars. He was convinced that this fad would make him rich and keep me out of the poorhouse. And for a while, I believed him.

"Quit college and I'll make sure you clear $85 a week," Artie said. The offer was tempting and sounded like a great idea at the time. So I quit F.I.T. to work full-time for Wallfrin Industries.

Over the next three months, *Time* magazine estimated more than $100 million worth of coonskin hats were bought and an additional $200 million in Crockett merchandise was sold.

The demand was so great that Disney's merchandising division worked fourteen-hour days, seven days a week to keep up with the demand. It was so great in fact that several manufacturing companies like Artie's jumped on the bandwagon and began producing the same items.

Stores across the country had special Crockett clubs where kids could find everything from a Davy Crockett peace pipe, bath towels, rifles, and powder horns.

Artie's tiny store in Brooklyn wasn't nearly big enough to handle all the business for raccoon tails. I quickly enlisted the help of my friends and we were working sixteen hours a day to try and fill the orders, which was for about 1,000 units a day.

The craze lasted longer than anyone thought, and as each month passed the price of raccoon tails went up from twenty-five cents each to five dollars a pound by May 1955. The price continued to surge as the demand increased. It got to the point where manufacturers were gobbling up raccoons so fast that they were about to be added to the endangered species list! The raccoon tails became virtually non-existent after six months.

But Artie was a resourceful fellow. He thought by substituting possum tails, which were similar to raccoon tails, no one would know the difference. Without permission, we started filling orders for raccoon tails with the possum tails. Turned out that Woolworth's, our main buyer, smelled a "rat."

Within three months, twenty-foot trailers were pulling up to our storefront with returns from Woolworth's 2,200 stores from around the country. We had no room at all to take back all the possum tails and had to call a cartage company to get them off the street. We were out of business overnight, flat busted!

While Artie tried to figure a way how to salvage his business, I was still trying to figure out what I was going to do with my life. I had turned nineteen, and for some strange reason, I felt *my* biological clock ticking. Now that I was technically a "man," I should do grown-up things, say for instance, like getting married.

A friend had introduced me to Pat Meyers, a very sweet, nice-looking Jewish girl from Forest Hills. For those of you who aren't familiar with New York, Forest Hills is a swanky suburb where girls don't normally date outside the social pecking order. For a Brooklyn guy like me, Pat was a major catch.

While my logical mind worked well in business, it didn't work so well when it came to personal relationships with the opposite sex. I had always prided myself on being a romantic. For some reason I had always gone steady when I was single and never dated around much. It was always my theory that there was no bargain in playing the field. If you liked one girl more than another, why would you spend any time with number two when you could be with number one? A friend always used to say that if you spend all your time with just one person, you'd burn the relationship out. But I really didn't give it that much thought. If I wanted to see someone, then that's what I did. I had gone steady a handful of times before I met Pat.

I told Pat that if we were still together after a year, we'd get married. It wasn't the most romantic proposal in the world, but she went along with the plan.

Her parents also didn't oppose the idea. They told me if I married their daughter, they'd make arrangements for a wedding at the Essex House, a very elegant hotel in Manhattan. On January 13, 1955, Pat and I exchanged our wedding vows. I kept up my end of the bargain but her parents did not. We got married in their second-story walk-up apartment with approximately twenty people present. What the hell happened to the Essex House? Well, it turned out that Pat's father was the only man in all of Forest Hills who barely made a living. Just my luck.

I was pretty much in the same boat. I was out of work for the first time in my life, newly married and had no idea what to do. I managed to get a job from my then brother-in-law, whose family owned Ansonia Shoes, a six-store upscale chain of designer women's footwear. But there were strings attached.

My brother-in-law, Morty Unger, came from a very prominent family who felt that he married down when he took my youngest sister Franky's hand in marriage. Suffice it to say, his family didn't want to have anything to do with ours. Morty gave me a job as a salesman at their store on 5<sup>th</sup> Avenue and 53<sup>rd</sup> Street in Manhattan, but I was under strict orders not to ever reveal that we were related by marriage. At times it was a hard rule to follow. Whenever his wife, my sister Franky, came into the store, she couldn't even say hello or act like she knew me.

My clientele included gorgeous debutantes, beautiful socialites, and very important people. Even better was the money—about $150 a week, which was mostly commission. It wasn't that bad for a nineteen-year-old kid in 1955. One day, after I had been on the job a few months, a veteran salesman took me aside and dispersed some of the best advice I ever received.

"Kid, one day you're going to be sixty years old like I am and still be a shoe dog," he whispered. "Get out now while you can." He didn't have to tell me twice.

By then Artie Schifrin was back on his feet and began looking at stability rather than get rich quick schemes. He had changed Wallfrin Industries from bicycle accessories to an automotive accessories business and appeared to be on to something.

Following World War II, the greatest and longest economic boom in world history was launched, and by the mid-fifties, approximately ten million cars were sold on an annual basis.

It was an era when American teenagers (the Baby Boom Generation) did everything in their cars. They ate at drive-in restaurants, watched movies at a drive-in theater, cruised up and down Main Street, and drag raced, and many even lost their virginity in the backseat. Cars were a symbol of these kids' independence and coolness, and they wanted accessories to show off their most treasured possession. That's where we came in.

We're not talking flashy hubcaps and bumpers here, but items such as hula dolls that gyrate in rear windows, religious statues for the dashboard, fuzzy dice for the rearview mirror, and tiger tails to hang on the gas tank, plus 750 other kitschy trinkets that did absolutely nothing. Nothing that is, except to make Artie Schifrin wealthy beyond his dreams.

When I quit the shoe business I became Artie's right-hand man, running the automobile accessory plant in Coney Island, Brooklyn.

We were a great business team because we complemented each other so well. I was the inside man who ran the factory, and crunched the numbers while he was the outside salesman who came up with great ideas. He got up late, I got up early. He was mechanical, I was athletic. I was everything he was not and vice versa. We were the total antithesis of each other, but as a team, we were hell on wheels.

When I first went to work for Artie, I consciously made the effort to make myself so indispensable that if I went to the bathroom, the company would stand still. The penalty was that I could never take a day off or go on vacation. But the protection I had was that Wallfrin Industries couldn't function without me.

I had worked tirelessly for two years when Pat gave birth to our first child, Lonny, who was born June 11, 1959. She felt, rightfully so, that it was time for me to ask for a raise now that we had another mouth to feed. I was making $100 a week and asked Artie for an additional $10 a week. He turned me down flat. However, he offered to pay me a certain percentage if we went over the amount of business we did the previous year, which was about $100,000. I did the math and figured out that the previous year was as good as it was going to get. I told Artie I was leaving and gave my two weeks' notice. I needed to look around and see what options were available to me.

I came up with the ingenious idea of buying my own taxicab after a friend told me it could be a very lucrative opportunity. I found out that the license, called a taxicab medallion, was $25,000, and could easily be financed. I figured I could work 100 hours a week to pay off the medallion, then sell it, and I would have a $25,000 stake to go into any business I wanted. I was so excited that I woke up my wife early the next morning and told her about my grandiose plans to make us rich.

I went right down to the taxi licensing board early next morning only to find out that I couldn't get a license to drive a taxi because I had only one eye.

Totally dejected, I wandered over to visit my wife's cousin, Stanley Levine, who owned a stock brokerage firm, S.P. Levine and Company. It was right down the street from the licensing board. I was pretty sure I didn't need two eyes to sell stocks.

Stanley said he could put me to work immediately since the market was booming at the time. He gave me 400 shares of a $4 stock called Land Equities, and asked me to see if I could sell them. So I called my mother, who immediately bought 100 shares. I called my best friend, Barry Eisner, and he promptly bought 100 shares as did my other good friend, Marvin Schnapp. Then I dialed Artie's number, who was a soft touch in my time of need. I was four for four. I sold all 400 shares in fifteen minutes and told Stanley what I had just done.

"You sold all 400 shares?" he asked.

"Yeah," I said, acting as if it were no big deal.

"Well, you just made $100," Stanley said.

"Really? You have to be kidding me?" I said. "You just got yourself a stockbroker."

The next morning I went down, took the test and I got my stockbroker license. Instead of getting up at 7 a.m. and working until all hours of the night, I now got to work at 10 a.m. I wore a suit and tie, got my shoes shined every morning, had coffee delivered to me by a pretty secretary, and made a few phone calls. Piece of cake.

The market was booming and I was making $1,500 a week, hanging out with big shots, brokers and traders. And, I might add, I was having the time of my life. But I found out that the stock market was cyclical and I was riding the crest of the wave. I had yet to experience a downturn. From April when I started to October 1961, the market went straight down. Every stock that I had sold was virtually worthless. I sold fifty different stocks and they all tanked. I buried everybody, including myself because I bought all the same stocks that I sold. I became "gun shy"—a sales euphemism for being afraid to answer the telephone when customers called to check on how their stocks were doing. In those days prices of over-the-counter stocks were not readily available to buyers and were only listed in the "pink sheets." You had to call a broker in order to get quotes. It was easy to tell customers when they were making money and holy hell when they were not. I felt like I was robbing everybody and actually, I was. I eventually learned that I was working for a "boiler room" and was selling everybody fly-by-night stocks.

But fate intervened once again.

Right around this time Artie had been involved in a serious car accident and needed someone to run his company while he was out of commission. He begged me to come back and offered me $200 a week. But by now my whole philosophy had changed. Now I was looking for the home run. I had left before because I wanted a $10 a week raise. I paused for a moment and decided I would take him up on his original offer of $100 a week plus a percentage over the business we did the previous year. It turned out to be one of the smartest moves I ever made. Over the next few years we grew the business to the point where my salary was still $100 a week but I was earning $20,000 a month in bonuses.

The years 1961 to 1968 were a time of great prosperity for Wallfrin Industries. Artie was the "Hot-Rod King," and had a great pulse on what the kids were doing with their cars. He would observe the new trends with the kids and come up with the original item, and then I would build a whole line around the idea. For example, he noticed that many of the hot-rodders hand-painted pin stripes on their cars and then I developed a line of fifteen different self-adhesive pin stripes in various widths and colors.

We also developed stickers, decals, and patches, but the first big product that really put us on the map was our Amber Lens Dye.

In the early sixties, all the new automotive models were manufactured with amber lenses on the headlights and taillights. Our product allowed the consumer to mimic the newer cars by allowing older car owners to paint their own lenses with an amber dye we created with a nail polish manufacturer. It cost us nine cents a bottle to create the amber lens dye and we wholesaled them for twenty-one cents apiece. Oh, did I forget to mention we sold more than one million units?

From there business just took off. We came out with several hundred fad items over the next seven years, including hula dolls, chromed lug nuts, mirror muffs, tiger tails for the gas tank, and religious statues for the dashboard. We produced the Sacred Heart, the Crucifix, and the Madonna. We even received letters from buyers asking us if the statues were blessed at the factory. We left that one up to their imagination.

Artie and I also made sure we had a lot of fun. Whenever we did a big trade show, we pulled out all the stops. We'd rent a huge suite at the hotel and hire several beautiful women to entertain our best customers. Our suite was always party central. We became famous in the industry for this. As a result, we always wound up selling at least $100,000 in merchandise.

While my professional life was booming, my personal life at home was deteriorating. Pat was everything a wife should be: kind, tender, patient, understanding, and nurturing. Unfortunately, I was not a great husband or father. Free time was my enemy because I didn't know how to relax. I was a workaholic and that was all that mattered to me. Pat and I even adopted two children (Gary and Shani) thinking it would help save our marriage. It didn't.

My life wasn't working, so I spent a lot of time philosophizing why I was so unhappy. I used to think that if I made $200 a week, I'd be the happiest man alive. When I started making $20,000 a month, I couldn't figure out why I was so unhappy.

I even tried to fill the void through some serious retail therapy. When you start to make big money, there are holes inside of you that you try to fill. You buy a bigger house, move to a nicer neighborhood, purchase a fancy car, or buy your wife a new mink coat or diamond ring. We now lived in a large house on Long Island, on the water with three boats in the back and even a live-in maid. I bought my first Rolls Royce the day before my thirty-sixth birthday. I couldn't believe it. I almost wanted to sleep in the garage at night with my new trophy. But no matter how much money I made, how big my house was, or how many material things I had, material things didn't make me happy.

In fact, everyone I knew was going through the same confusion, raising a family and running into walls. My friends and I were all looking for some direction, but we all kept going in circles.

My world was strangely upside-down despite all my success. I had all the money in the world, but I was emotionally bankrupt. I had a great job, but I hated going home. I had fallen out of love with my wife, but I wanted love more than anything else in the world. I was an incredible success, but I was also an immense failure. Something had to give.

# CHAPTER 3

# Searching for Mel Haber

They say misery loves company, and by the late sixties, the only constant company I was keeping was a cold bottle of Beefeater Gin.

By this point I knew I had fallen out of love with my wife Pat, but I didn't see a way out. You just don't walk up to a spouse, especially one who has always been so nice to you, and say, "See ya later."

And Pat was clever, too. Instead of arguing with me or giving me a hard time about being away so often or being an emotionally vacant husband, she gave me an extra-long leash.

There was one time when I told Pat that I was leaving her, and she literally begged me to stay. She told me that she'd rather have one percent of Mel Haber rather than 100 percent of someone else. It was a heartbreaking statement to hear, but one that made me stay in the marriage for a few more years.

At times, I couldn't understand how I got to this point. I hadn't hurt anyone, I hadn't done anything wrong; I was in my thirties and no longer willing to live in a loveless marriage. I wanted to be out in the world and have the freedom to come and go as I pleased. I couldn't fathom why I couldn't have it all. What kind of sentence was I serving? What kind of punishment was God dishing out to me? I just wanted the pain to go away.

I began to drink to cope with my problems. Though I was not a seasoned drinker, the liquor shut out all my guilt so that I was able to concentrate on what was in front of me with no thought of my wife and kids in the background. But sometimes I was forced to face the inevitable.

One morning while hungover, I stood over our new adopted baby in his crib: "You poor bastard, I don't believe it," I'd say to him, shaking my head. "Your father and mother gave you away, and now maybe I'm going to walk out." I was absolutely tormented.

Still, I stayed in the marriage and looked for new toys or experiences to give myself renewed enthusiasm. I had a lot of money to invest in new toys. I made $250,000 in 1968. But that wasn't going to last very long.

The stock market was up the entire year, and almost everything was inflated. Companies went on frenzied buying sprees, several mergers took place, and corporations acquired new subsidiaries with their new inflated stock. Boston-based Automatic Radio heard about Wallfrin Industries and fell in love with Artie and me because we were two crazy guys who had a lot of fun and made a lot of money. Automatic Radio wanted to buy us for $3 million in 1968, but our company, like many others, looked very attractive on paper but was only worth about half of that amount. However, Automatic Radio was going to pay with inflated stock anyway, so they really didn't care. Artie asked me for advice on what he should do.

"The object in the financial world is to lock up enough money so you won't ever have to worry about money again," I said. "This deal would set you up for life. You have to take it." Based on my advice Artie sold the company and gave me 10 percent, which equaled about $300,000 in inflated stock. That was a nice chunk of change back then, but it didn't guarantee me the financial security that he was going to get from the deal. I was still looking to make my own big score.

Automatic Radio insisted that Artie and I stay on as president and vice president, respectively. They paid me a salary of $45,000 a year to run the company. Artie told them if they needed any information or wanted anything done, just talk to Mel Haber. It was as if he wanted absolutely no responsibility. I turned to Artie at that point and cried foul.

"Artie, that's not fair," I told him. "You've cashed in as the boss of the company and now you're just the guy at the next desk." I was now in the precarious situation where I had to work twice as hard and got paid 20 percent of what I was making before. When I ran the company for Artie, I didn't have to answer to anybody and ran the company the way I saw fit. Under the acquisition, I had a new set of bosses back in Boston that I had to answer to while Artie was never around.

Artie had decided that since we could no longer make big money, we should buy a business in California for the sole purpose of being able to spend a lot of time there on the company expense account. He felt it was a perk to which he was entitled.

In 1969, we purchased a company called LaCal Manufacturing, which was located on Slausen Avenue in the Watts area of Los Angeles. The company manufactured luggage racks and gas cans for cars.

We convinced Automatic Radio that it would be a very prudent business decision because we would then have warehouses and manufacturing on both coasts. It could also benefit distribution and with LaCal's line of products, open doors to new accounts that were previously unavailable to us and open new accounts for them as well.

After we purchased LaCal, Artie and I began spending about ten days a month at the Century Plaza Hotel in Century City, right next to Beverly Hills. We would eat every night at the trendiest restaurants and party in the best clubs in Beverly Hills on the company expense account. I got up every morning and drove to Watts to attend to business while Artie hung out at the hotel pool.

This arrangement went on for several years and worked somewhat to my advantage, especially where my marriage was concerned. Pat could hang on to the illusion that I was still committed to her and the kids while I only had to be a family man a portion of the time. Not a bad deal for either of us. I lived each month for those ten days that I spent in California.

Financially I was treading water. The salary I received from Automatic Radio covered my monthly nut and a few other things, but not much else. I was really at a dead end as far as making big money or becoming financially independent. I decided it was time to find *my* Mel Haber, as Artie had done with me. I needed to find a young workhorse who would help me become financially successful based on their hard work.

Over the next few years, I started several new businesses on the side. I took friends and young people I knew, and put them in the various businesses. I gave them a salary and a percentage of the profits. I fronted the money to get the business off the ground and was the brains behind the operation. Let me tell you, my brains took a beating.

I launched a boiler-cleaning business, a front-end wheel-alignment franchise, a company factoring medical centers, an import business, a vacuum forming business, and an automotive-chemical manufacturing business.

I thought I had found the answer to economic success and felt like quite an entrepreneur because I had all of these companies. However, all I ended up doing was spinning my wheels.

The truth was that almost all of my money was going to pay the people who were running these different businesses. As soon as one company started to turn the corner, another business developed a problem, which required money to fix. I was plugging holes and fixing problems, but not seeing any profits. It was terribly frustrating, because making money had been so easy for me before. As soon as I heard one company calling with a problem, I would gear my head into that business. Then I would get a call from another business with a different type of problem. I would have to clear my mind of the business that I had just geared up for, unwind, then gear up again for the other business. I spent all of my time gearing up only to gear down. I kept running into walls.

Around that time I had read a brilliant business book called *Up the Organization Chart* by Robert Townsend, the president of Avis. The book changed my life. At the time, Avis was the number two rental car agency, just behind Hertz. Townsend's profound statement that "Concentration is the key to economic success" stuck with me. If I was in a business part-time, how did I think I could compete with someone who's been in that business for a long time, doing it full-time? I was like the little mouse in a maze, constantly running in circles.

Now I had a serious dilemma. I wanted to succeed in the business world, but I was doing everything wrong. I had started all of these businesses, but I was running around like a headless chicken. I was not concentrating on my real goal to achieve economic independence; instead, I was just in action all the time. I realized I had to refocus. I had my secretary needlepoint the saying "Concentration is the key to economic success" and put it on the wall right in front of my desk so I would stare at it every day and not forget my purpose. I even created a mental illustration to make the point: if you put a pot of water on a thousand different stoves for two minutes each, you will not get one bubble. But if you keep the pot in one place for three minutes, you will get all the bubbles you wanted. Like Robert Townsend wrote, "Concentration is the key to economic success."

As quickly as I set up all of my businesses, I shut them down and regrouped. I didn't make any money during my short stint as a business mogul, but I didn't lose a fortune either.

In 1971, I decided to try a separation with Pat and moved into an apartment I had kept in a building I had co-owned with Artie in Brooklyn.

I finally confessed to Pat that I had not been in love with her for a long time and I was sorry for having to say it, but it had to be said. I wanted to be in love with her, for she was a wonderful person. But the truth was, I stayed for many years without loving her. Had she not been such a terrific person, I would have left years ago. I told her that I had gotten married too young, and it was time for me to go out and find my own way. Pat was a wreck. She admitted that she knew I was not totally committed to our marriage but she loved me unconditionally. It took all of the strength I could muster to leave, but I knew deep down that I had to in order to keep my sanity.

Sensing my sadness and knowing about my current marital status, one day a friend of mine told me that he and his wife had met an adorable lady named Barbra Kahn and wanted to fix us up. My friend described Barbra as gorgeous and interesting. He insisted that I take her out. I almost took a pass because I was nursing a cold, but she did sound intriguing.

I decided to tough it out and meet Barbra. I pulled up to her swanky eastside Manhattan office address at the appointed time and waited for about half an hour, and finally she walked out to greet me. My initial impression was that she was definitely not my type. Barbra had the blond, cheerleader "Waspy" look, which was never my type.

We went out and had a few drinks, and I discovered that Barbra was definitely different from any other lady I had known before. She had traveled the world, lived in Europe for a time, clubbed at famous nightspots like 21, and lived in a lovely brownstone on a great street in Manhattan.

I guess the initial attraction for her to go on a date with me was that she had never been out with a "Jewish guy" before. Throughout the night I think she kept looking for my horns.

I'm not even sure why we had a second date, because there was not much chemistry between us on the first night. We went out again, and I was even more firmly convinced that we were miles apart. That all changed when we became intimate.

Instead of the cool, aloof person that she had been, she became warm, sensitive, and passionate, and within a short time, she had me hooked. I felt as if I was in love, but I was only basing that at this point on our sexual experience. We started to spend a lot of time together, and Barbra turned out to be an incredible woman.

I learned over time that she was from a small Seventh Day Adventist family but had left home at an early age and rebelled against her conservative background. Barbra had lived in Europe, gotten married, and lived in Aspen, Colorado, where she became a ski bunny. She had moved to New York after her divorce and was living well. When I met her she was carrying Louis Vuitton when everyone else was first discovering Gucci. She was always ahead of the curve when it came to the next big fashionable thing.

Looking back, my biggest attraction to Barbra was that there was no way to dominate or own her. I never had the feeling that I had made an impression on her one way or the other. It was all very strange, and it was the first time I had run up against a formidable lady like her. When we first started dating, she told me something I never forgot: "As bad as you are as a man, I am as a woman."

Even though I had fallen in love with Barbra, she constantly reminded me that I was still in "Drawer C." She knew I was still legally married to Pat, and her rule was never to fall in love with a married man. Barbra was quite capable of not letting her emotions get in the way. She let it be known that she didn't have anything better going on at the time, which is why she put up with me. We had dinner a couple of nights a week, and I spent all day Saturday with her. Sundays were reserved for Pat and the kids.

Pat and I were invited to a resort in the Catskill Mountains for New Year's Eve 1972, and for old time's sake, I thought I'd go to please Pat. It turned out to be our last hurrah.

When we got to the resort I spotted an old acquaintance whom I had never particularly cared for sitting in a restaurant booth cuddling and smooching his wife and enjoying a romantic dinner. It made me very depressed and jealous. Here was a guy who was really not nice, and he had what I wanted. He was with the woman he wanted to be with, and I wasn't. That made everything seem ten times worse.

The sight of the two threw me into a tizzy, and I called Barbra to complain: Why couldn't we be together? I got drunk and developed a serious headache. My close friend and confidante, Judy, spotted me at the bar and asked me to dance. It didn't take long for her to notice that I was miserable. She asked me what was wrong.

"Judy, how much longer is this going to go on?" I asked. "How much longer do I have to go through this?" Judy cut right to the chase.

"Just leave, Mel," she said. "You're not doing yourself any good, and you're sure not doing Pat any good. If you don't leave, you'll be standing here next New Year's Eve feeling the same exact way, only worse."

At midnight, Pat wanted me to kiss her and sing along to "Auld Lang Syne." As much as she wanted me to kiss her, I couldn't bring myself to do it. I was in love with Barbra, who was back in New York City, and I was tortured as to where and with whom she might be.

Pat and I went to sleep that night at the resort, and when we woke up, she suggested we make love. It was the furthest thing from my mind.

"I've gotta leave," I said. I then went downstairs to my car to retrieve a bottle of gin and brought it back to the room to wash away my guilt. It was like a scene right out of a movie as we both finished the bottle. Pat was sick, but did not put up the fight I had expected. It was almost as if she knew this scene was bound to happen and finally accepted the inevitable. An hour later we were both drunk, and we made the three-hour trek back to the city without exchanging a word.

I got back to the house, packed a suitcase, and said, "Until we see what happens, tell the kids I went to California." I walked out of the house and the marriage was over.

I called Barbra to tell her the news, and I remember how shocked she was when she learned that I had three children. We had never discussed my situation at home. Looking back, I guess you could say we had a bit of a communication problem.

I had suggested to Barbra we take a trip to Puerto Rico for the weekend to forget our problems for a while, but nothing really changed. I had walked out on my wife, but I was still very unhappy. I was drinking myself to death; I was bleeding from both my mouth and my rectum, and overall I was a wreck. To compound my grief I had just lost several thousand dollars gambling in the casino, and dramatically pulled out my "suicide list," which I always carried to the casino as a joke. I could never handle losing lots of money. I started reading from the list: Should I jump out the window, throw myself in front of a car, drown myself, inhale carbon monoxide, or just shoot myself?

I was completely miserable because my life was in shambles. I was feeling guilty over Pat and the kids and drinking myself into oblivion. I pictured myself as the guy who wanted to get from one side of the street to the other. He eventually did, but he got hit by several cars while crossing and ended up on the other side a quadruple amputee. I had been over on one side with my marriage and wanted to get on the other side where I could be single again, but I was becoming so emotionally scarred that by the time I got to where I wanted to be I would be a basket case.

With no pressure from home I was still a mess. Had there been any sort of pressure, I would have been back in a flash. One phone call from one of my kids saying, "Daddy, we need you," and it would have been all over.

Lying on the beach in Puerto Rico, Barbra and I decided that we should take a very long trip to Europe to get away and get my head straight. I didn't know if I could do that. I had never even taken a lunch break in twenty years and now I was going to run around Europe for a month. It turned out to be the best thing I could have done at the time. We rented a house in Spain and just hung out.

I got off the booze, and Barbra and I grew closer. When we came back to New York, I made her an offer. I was already paying half her rent, and we didn't have as much privacy as I would have liked because Barbra had a roommate. I told Barbra if she asked her roommate to move out and if I moved in, I would pay her entire rent. Her friend complied, and Barbra and I set up house.

For a while, it was fun. She turned me on to new things. She didn't like the way I dressed in spite of the fact that I had thirty suits and was known as somewhat of a fashion plate. She took me to Saks Fifth Avenue for a navy blazer with contrasting slacks and said, "That's all you need." I had never eaten cheese or drank wine in my life, but she turned me into a connoisseur. I began wearing khaki chinos and penny loafers, and tied my sweater around my neck to go bicycling through Central Park in the mornings. It was as if I were following a list that someone had written outlining how all WASPs should exactly dress and behave. But it was fun because it seemed cute and adorable, no matter how much it bordered on the ridiculous. It was a complete change, as if I had discovered a whole new world. I was being exposed to things I had never seen or done before, and I enjoyed every minute.

My relationship with Barbra also had me severing ties with most of my old friends, whom she wasn't afraid of putting down. Barbra would not have skied the best mountain in the world unless it was the "right" mountain and she had to live at the "right address." The same applied to my friends. If they weren't the right people, they simply did not exist to her. Unfortunately, I was too smitten to see clearly, and I let those friendships fall through the cracks.

I visited with Pat and the kids every Sunday, but always came loaded with guilt. Pat and I usually had a few drinks when I got there. We'd cry and hold each other. "I don't know what the penalty is for not loving you, and if I could push a button to be in love with you, I'd push it," I said through tears.

At the same time my friendship with Artie also took a tumble. We had a major falling out—the first in twenty years. I finally decided to leave the company. Since we had a plant in Los Angeles, I needed a change in scenery. I would try the West Coast before I officially left Wallfrin Industries.

Looking back, I was in the throes of a textbook midlife crisis.

# CHAPTER 4

# Go West, Young Man

They say that you can't run away from your problems, but I must say in all honesty, 3,000 miles will give you a pretty good head start.

Barbra and I arrived in Los Angeles on the July 4th weekend of 1974. We took a furnished apartment in the Marina Del Rey area, and I bought a used Fiat for $3,000 so that we could get around. I visited New York ten days a month to check on our factory there and see my children.

Sunshine is a wonderful thing and there's always plenty of it in California. It can change your outlook on things, boost your energy level, and improve your disposition immensely. It took leaving the East Coast permanently to realize what a hard and fast-paced lifestyle I had led. The pace in New York is much quicker than in California. The people move and talk faster, the climate is harsher, the clothes are more formal, and the cost of living at the time was much higher than in California. In New York I made $250,000 a year and thought I had it made if I got away for a weekend. Californians are more carefree and in a different gear. It seemed as if they were always on vacation.

The California lifestyle suited me well. I had been overweight from the booze and the long days I spent sitting behind a desk. From the day of my arrival on the West Coast, I began to slim down and exercise every day, although I still chain-smoked. (In my prime, I smoked five packs a day.) I loved living in the Marina because the emphasis seemed to be on health and outdoor activities.

I went on a health kick and changed my diet, although I doubt if any nutritional gurus today would have endorsed my meal plan. I became known as "Chicken Wings Haber" to everyone I knew because I only ate chicken wings and cantaloupe. But who was I to argue with success? I lost thirty pounds.

My workaholic days and nights of endless partying also fell by the wayside. I went to bed early and got up at 6 a.m. to swim and exercise. It was a radical change, but Barbra and I settled nicely into our new lifestyle.

We had been introduced to Palm Springs through Lenny Poncher, a sales rep at LaCal who worked for me. He owned a condominium there and let us use his place on the weekends when he wasn't there, and when he was home, we'd stay in a hotel. As on our trip to Europe, we just hung out in Palm Springs. I usually wore cutoff jeans, T-shirts, and sneakers without socks. The weather was gorgeous almost every day of the year, save for the hot summer months.

Because the United States was in a recession, interest rates were 17 percent. You couldn't give real estate away in Palm Springs. I decided to buy a condo for $27,000 in January 1975, and Barbra and I came down every weekend. Every Thursday night we'd make the two-hour trek from Marina Del Rey to spend three relaxing days in Palm Springs and return Monday morning to the LA area totally refreshed and invigorated.

Barbra grew to like Palm Springs so much that she would stay there for the week. All my life I hated to be alone, and her absence caused me to start drinking again. I had discovered that one of my friend's line applied to me: "When we're together, I'm together." At the time, I was really only happy when I was with Barbra.

I found out the hard way that Barbra and I shared a similar trait. I discovered through various friends who kept a watch on her for me that when I went to New York on business, Barbra liked to go out and play. Once while I was on the East Coast, I called Barbra at the condominium early in the morning. A man answered the phone and then quickly hung up. I went ballistic. I immediately called back and demanded to know from Barbra why a man was answering our phone at 5 a.m. She concocted some crazy, convoluted story that I never believed. She always made me feel like she could do better than me any time she wanted. Barbra implied that she was settling for me, just hanging out until somebody better came along. Besides, she wanted to be in California to be among "the beautiful people."

When I came back to Los Angeles, I decided to break up with Barbra, which I think threw her for a loop. A few days later, she came to the Marina Del Rey apartment to patch things up. We managed to talk everything out and decided to try and put the relationship back together. It was touch and go for a while. But my luck was about to take a turn.

I had become friendly with a gentleman by the name of Billy Irwin who was married to a former roommate of Barbra's in Aspen, Colorado. Billy was the manager of the Ocotillo Lodge, one of the nicer places to stay in Palm Springs at the time. It was owned by Dr. Jerry Buss, the business mogul who made millions as a real estate developer before he bought the Los Angeles Lakers basketball team. On a lazy Saturday afternoon in late March, Billy dropped by my condo and asked if I wanted to take a ride with him. I didn't have anything better to do, so I took him up on his offer.

Piling into his convertible, we drove through town, and he told me he was going to look at a piece of property as a potential investment for his boss.

After a five-minute drive down Ramon Road, we pulled up to the property, which was two blocks from the center of town and at the foot of the San Jacinto Mountains. It was called the Ingleside Inn. We entered through a pair of iron gates on a private drive and it was as if we had been warped back in time. The two-acre estate was secluded, almost hidden if you will, and oozed a certain charm.

We parked across from a Spanish-style hacienda, which had a tile roof and vines running down the walls. In addition to the main hacienda, several Spanish-style bungalows were scattered around the property. Three people were seated under a large veranda, bantering, sipping drinks, and enjoying the sunshine. It was like a scene out of old-world Spain, or perhaps even Mexico. Very surreal.

Billy asked if I minded if we stopped to take a look inside. I was all for it, thrilled to have something to do for a few hours. Even though the place was borderline derelict and in need of a great deal of rejuvenation, I was looking at it through rose-colored glasses. Something about the place was enchanting, and it instantly grabbed a hold of me.

When we stepped inside the main building, it was even lovelier than the outside. The lobby had high-vaulted ceiling, wooden floors and a beautiful chandelier that hung in the center of the room. There was also an old stone fireplace in the corner and antique furniture scattered about. It reminded me of a quaint little European inn with a style and charm all its own.

Not long after we stepped in to the lobby, a gentleman came out from behind the registration desk and introduced himself as the manager. His name was Fred Shapiro. He knew Billy was coming over and let it be known that the owner was totally inactive and anxious to unload the property. I recognized Mr. Shapiro as a fellow Easterner, whose accent and mannerisms immediately gave him away. Fred told me he was from the "Borscht Belt," and was, of course, Jewish. I immediately felt a kinship with him from the several summers I spent working in the Catskill Mountains.

The fact that Fred was Jewish was only significant in light of the history of the Ingleside Inn. He revealed to us that the place was originally built as a private estate in 1925 by the widow of Humphrey Birge, manufacturer of the elegant Pierce Arrow motorcar. Ten years later she sold the two-acre property to Ruth Hardy, a businesswoman from Indiana, who transformed the Spanish-style estate into a twenty-room hotel. In 1935 it opened for business to the blue bloods of the world and was strictly off-limits to anyone who wasn't a pure WASP. From the first day it was an anti-Semitic establishment—almost to an extreme. (I came to discover that most of Palm Springs was in those days.)

Hardy successfully ran the Inn for thirty years as an exclusive private club whose guests came by invitation only. The impressive clientele read like a *Who's Who* of the world. It included billionaire Howard Hughes; movie stars John Wayne, Greta Garbo, Spencer Tracey, Katharine Hepburn, Greer Garson, Elizabeth Taylor, and Ava Gardner; artist Salvador Dali; pastor Norman Vincent Peale; opera star Lily Pons; Bank of America founder Peter Giannini; and department store mogul J.C. Penney. Ms. Hardy also lured presidents, royalty, and captains of industry. The secret of her success was that she lived on the property and catered to everyone's special needs, making her clientele feel as if they were staying at someone's home rather than at a hotel. You almost had to be invited to stay. Fred explained that the hotel was loaded with antiques gathered by the original owner on special trips to Europe. He said later the value of the antiques were probably worth more than the asking price of the entire property. That really got my juices going.

After Ruth Hardy's death in 1965, one of her regular guests, Winston S. Cowgill III, a very wealthy man from a banking family in San Francisco, bought the Ingleside Inn in hopes of carrying on the same great tradition. However, the place fell into a state of disrepair due to his constant absence and the stardust from the old days had largely faded away. Over the next decade, the Inn's traditional blue-blood clientele had gradually been supplanted by a blue-haired crowd, and the Inn had the air of a senior citizen's home. Just one look around confirmed the fact.

Fred then asked us if we'd like to see the restaurant, which was called Orville's. We didn't even know it existed. He walked us over to a little house at the end of the property, and I couldn't believe my eyes. It was about 12:30 in the afternoon and the temperature, which unseasonably hot, hovered around ninety-five degrees. Inside the dining room, which, had no air-conditioning, were about twenty couples having lunch. All the guests were dressed to the nines and looked like they were attending a gala ball. The women were wearing formal dresses with long, white gloves, while all the men wore jackets and ties. The average age was about seventy-five years old.

It was a scene out of *The Twilight Zone*. It looked like they were all dead and forgot to fall over. I was wearing cutoff jeans, a T-shirt, and sneakers, while all of these very proper people were sitting there in formal attire with no air-conditioning, and nobody seemed to be hot. For a second I thought that I was on a soundstage watching a movie or that my friend was pulling a fast one on me. Any second now, Allen Funt was going to pop out and say, "Smile, you're on *Candid Camera!*" It was downright bizarre, and I never felt more out of place in my entire life.

We were then led down to two different basements (a rarity in Palm Springs) by Fred where we viewed old newspaper clippings and spotted several old and seemingly valuable pieces of furniture. Out of the corner of my eye I saw fifteen full drawers of index cards of former guests. When I glanced at a few of them, I got goose bumps. They weren't merely guests but legendary figures. Singer Hoagy Carmichael visited in 1938. Howard Hughes and Ava Gardner stayed in 1946 as "Earl Martyn" and "Mrs. Clark," and paid twenty dollars for their room. Opera star Lily Pons checked into the hotel in 1941 and stayed until 1954. Actor John Wayne was a guest in 1941. Movie star Robert Taylor and his wife, actress Barbara Stanwyck, came for a romantic weekend in 1942. Walter Pidgeon, 1943. Actress Gene Tierney, 1944. Olympian-turned-movie star Esther Williams, 1946. Actress Margret O' Brien, 1949. Writer Norman Vincent Peale visited frequently in the fifties and early sixties, and former president Herbert Hoover and his wife enjoyed a visit in 1960.

The comments on some of the cards were sometimes funny and not so funny. A registration for Salvador Dali read, "I believe he is a painter." Howard Hughes's card read, "Howard Hughes, wants no one to know." Child star Elizabeth Taylor's comment card from 1950 read, "Lovely young girl. Movie actress." The owner didn't think so highly of movie mogul Samuel Goldwyn and his wife. Their card read: "No good. They're Jewish."

By this time I was absolutely intrigued. Old world charm never meant a thing to me, and it was the last kind of place that I would stay. However, I thought of the Ingleside Inn more as a diamond in the rough rather than a derelict hotel.

The history alone was a good enough reason for anyone to buy the place—that and the priceless antiques and expensive furniture that were hidden in plain sight. I couldn't believe it, but I was chomping at the bit to buy this property. I was entirely convinced that after I owned it I would find the treasure of Sierra Madre buried somewhere in the ground or perhaps in a hidden safe.

It made me think of a story my father used to tell about a peddler on the east side of New York who owned a men's clothing store. One of his best tricks to lure customers was to take a few pieces of paper, fold it like money, and put it in one of the pants pockets among the suits he was trying to sell. When a customer tried on the suit and put his hand in the pocket he assumed that the person who tried on the suit previously must have left his money there by mistake. The customer would quickly buy the suit only to find when he got home he had been duped. I wasn't sure if I was being baited or if it was the real deal. The asking price for the property was $375,000, which I felt was very reasonable for the land value alone, not to mention the priceless antiques and furniture.

I am an impulsive person by nature, and my tendency is to act first and ask questions later. Billy left me alone with Fred, and I asked him to seriously consider my offer of $300,000, which was 25 percent below the owner's asking price. This lowball method always made me feel better because I always tried to get a bargain. Besides, most sellers usually mark up their asking price by 30 percent. If we made a deal, both of us could pat ourselves on the back and still think we won. But that wasn't the case here. Fred practically turned up his nose and huffed, stating my offer was ridiculous and that the property was worth every dime of the $375,000. He was right even though real estate was cheap at the time because of a depressed economy. He pointed out that there was an assumable $200,000 mortgage at the Bank of America at only 6 percent.

For some inexplicable reason, I wanted that property. I suggested to him that I come over again around 10 a.m. the next morning to see if we could work out a deal. He agreed to meet with me but said he didn't want me wasting his time. He said if I was seriously interested, I would have to move fast because there were several other prospective clients, and he most likely would sell it quickly. His comment had the desired psychological effect. My heart was racing and my head was swirling. I immediately went into a panic. I was gripped with anxiety over the prospect of losing out to someone else. To curry favor with Fred, I promised him a $5,000 commission if I got the property at my asking price. He said I was in luck since it was the weekend and nothing could transpire until we met again. I felt somewhat assured when I left he wouldn't sell out from under me, but I wouldn't rest easy until I had the deed in my name.

I did not get to sleep that night, contemplating the many possibilities of the Ingleside Inn. I started to scheme from every conceivable angle about what I could do with the property—the furthest thing from my mind was keeping it as a hotel. Fred had informed me that the entire overhead, including mortgage, utilities, gardeners, and payroll, including the chef, was approximately $5,000 a month.

The first idea that popped into my head was making the place a private haven for me and my friends. I had just joined a private club in Los Angeles called Pips. The establishment was owned by *Playboy* magazine founder Hugh Hefner. The club was very regal and attracted a very affluent clientele, save for yours truly. I went there almost every night when I was in town and made fast friends with a few of the members. I had this idea that if I could round up four partners, the five of us could easily buy the property for $300,000. We would each put down $20,000 and have a 20 percent investment in the property. Each of us would have four rooms. We could then do whatever we wanted with them—we could knock down the walls and make it one large private suite or keep them separate rooms and have girlfriends and relatives use them as they saw fit. In addition, for $1,000 per month each, we would have our own private dining room and our own chef. I'd have my very own Playboy mansion and I could be Palm Springs's version (or poor man's version) of Hugh Hefner.

I invited two friends from Pips as potential investors to drive down to Palm Springs to look at the property. Frankly, they didn't get it. All they saw was that the buildings were in a state of disrepair, the carpet in the lobby was threadbare, the gardening left much to be desired, and there was no air-conditioning on the entire property. But there was an intrinsic charm to the place, and I saw it as a potential goldmine. My friends begged to differ, comparing it more to a lemon. They tactfully declined.

That paved the way for my second idea—a fat farm for women. Two acres in a private setting in the heart of downtown Palm Springs was a novel idea. The women could shed a few pounds and shop at nearby boutiques while their husbands played golf on some of the best courses in the country.

The following morning I drove through the property at least a dozen times, and each time I had a different idea what to do with the place. At no point did I ever consider leaving it as a restaurant and hotel. At the appointed time, I was waiting anxiously for Fred on the veranda. He showed up at 10:05 a.m. and escorted me into the restaurant for a cup of coffee. We spent an hour structuring various offers for the owner. I mustered up all the charm and persuasion I could to ensure I got the property. The key to the deal was simply to promise Fred that he could stay on as manager and live on the grounds as long as I was the owner. With that, we shook hands and he offered to appeal to Mr. Cowgill on my behalf, which would be very important to my getting the deal.

Fred called Mr. Cowgill and made an appointment to see him that evening with the $300,000 offer—$100,000 down plus I would assume Mr. Cowgill's $200,000 mortgage with the Bank of America.

I assured Fred I would stay in Palm Springs until Monday so that we could open escrow if my offer were to be accepted. That evening around ten o' clock, I got the call from him that I had a deal. The butterflies kicked in and I instantly got a nervous headache. Once again, I had another restless night of sleep, but come Monday morning, I opened escrow to buy the Ingleside Inn. On April 15, 1975, I was officially the proud new owner.

Looking back, I had no idea as to how that purchase would

affect the rest of my life.

That day I went back to the house and shared with Barbra my good fortune.

"Now what?" she asked.

"I don't know," I told her. "I haven't thought that far ahead."

God's honest truth.

# CHAPTER 5

# The Ingleside Inn

**W**hat I knew about operating a hotel and restaurant was less than the average Palm Springs resident knows about digging ditches.

I knew that my impromptu investment carried a total overhead of $5,000 a month, and that I inherited a cast of characters straight out of an old Preston Sturges comedy. My staff of misfits included a day-to-day manager who sported a Buddha-like belly, a bad toupee, and a pronounced limp; a twenty-year-old man-boy with a thick Arkansas drawl who alternately served as bell captain, bellman, bookkeeper, and front desk clerk; a temperamental chef with a huge appetite for pornography; a housekeeper who had difficulty making beds because of a bad back; and four sixty-year-old waiters, including an Englishman who caused diners to gag on their escargot by addressing them as "Mum" and "Pops."

Despite the low overhead, the Ingleside Inn barely showed a profit. The hotel was operating on the American plan: $40 per day including three meals. The key was that the place wasn't losing money; therefore it bought me some valuable time to decide what I was going to do with the property. If it were operating in the red, I would have been forced to shut it down. However, that wasn't the case, so I decided to hire someone to watch over the hotel and restaurant until I could figure out what to do. Since I only knew a handful of people in Palm Springs at the time, I asked my friend Lenny Poncher, who had owned a condo there for many years, if he knew of anyone I could trust to watch over my investment.

Lenny and I were having coffee in his house one morning when he suggested a local Baptist minister as the ideal manager. It sounded like the perfect setup. I mean, how much more honest can you get than a Baptist minister? Talk about a godsend!

His name was Luther, and not only was he a man of the cloth, but he had a background as a general contractor. I hired Luther to oversee the entire operation, which included being in charge of construction and decorating, handling the money transactions, and relieving the other manager, Fred Shapiro, when necessary. The contrast between Luther—a tall, lean, slow-talking (with a drawl no less) Baptist minister, and Fred—a short, fat Jewish manager from upper New York State—was a sight to behold. It was also quite typical of the rest of the characters who ran the Ingleside Inn at the time.

My entire staff was rounded out, but the problem was that the crew of misfits would have been more appropriate in a slapstick comedy than in a hotel and restaurant. The troops were waiting for the general (me) to start giving the orders and take the hill, but I had no idea what to do next. It was a textbook example of the blind leading the blind.

My whole life, the pattern has been the same. First, I would spend a great deal of time and effort digging myself into a hole. Then I would spend a great deal of time and effort trying to dig myself out of the same hole. If successful, I would eventually wind up exactly where I started. Let's just say that the Hilton Hotel Corporation was not the least bit worried about my foray into the hospitality industry.

After all the crazy novelty ideas about what to do with the place left my head, I decided the most prudent thing to do for the time being was to use Luther's construction background to upgrade the Ingleside Inn with some minor improvements, perhaps increasing my profits until I had a few more concrete ideas. I didn't have a great deal of money to spend, and Lenny volunteered to help decorate the property using his artistic talents.

At the time, Lenny lived with his girlfriend Patty in Palm Springs. Like me, he was shuffling back and forth between Los Angeles during the week and Palm Springs on weekends. Patty was a nice lady, but not very ambitious or motivated. She would have been quite content to spend her entire life in their Palm Springs home shuffling from the bedroom to the kitchen and back to the bedroom to watch television. She could usually be found wearing a robe, and if she never had to venture outside, that would have suited her just fine.

When Lenny came down on Fridays, he would collect Patty, and they'd come over to the hotel. He reminded me of a drill sergeant because he went from room to room with Patty a step behind him. Then he started barking orders, "Patty, take these notes. Paint this trim. Buy new carpeting for this room. Put drapes on this window. Put a picture on this wall," and so on, and she would dutifully act the part of a secretary marking down everything he said.

Lenny would then march off, quite content with himself. It was as if he saw the complete vision of the place in his mind. I sat in awe, watching his creativity flow. After all these sessions were over, someone must have forgotten the part about execution. As they left, Patty would always shoot me this puzzled look like, "What happens now?" It would have almost been funny, had everything not been on my tab, which wasn't so funny. Whether Lenny's plans could be carried out, or whether they were even economically feasible, never seemed to enter his mind. This went on every Friday and Saturday for six weeks. On Mondays, Lenny and I returned to Los Angeles and Patty returned to her bedroom, exhausted from two days of taking notes.

Two months passed before Luther finally got around to implementing Lenny's ideas and began tearing the rooms apart. One day it dawned on me that I was worse off than when I started. Six rooms, which had been shabby but in rentable condition, were now totally demolished with a great deal of money going into the effort. Nothing had been planned or ordered, and there were no immediate plans to get them back into shape. The only thing we had going for us were about fifty pages of notes from Patty.

During that same time period, I was very busy in Los Angeles formulating other plans and ideas for the Inn. I started work on brochures, a logo, stationery, and where to purchase supplies, merchandise, and all the necessary items for running a hotel. Lenny had also put me in touch with a prestigious Beverly Hills public relations firm whose clientele could run the Academy Awards.

They took me on as a client (at $1,000 a month) as a favor to Lenny, and I was totally convinced they were going to make my establishment the next Waldorf Astoria in a very short time. I met with them at least twice a week and discussed the various items I would need. I was primarily looking for a color scheme, and a logo for stationery, napkins, matches, and so on, to brand my product into the public's consciousness. My personal contribution to the physical improvement of the Ingleside Inn was the idea that it was absolutely essential to add a Jacuzzi to the property. My establishment had very few amenities, and almost every other pool in Palm Springs had an accompanying Jacuzzi attached to it, so why shouldn't mine? Luther assured me that he could build it without any problem.

As the weeks progressed, I devoted more and more time and brainpower to improving the place. Things were happening at a very fast clip. Lenny and Patty were busy decorating, Luther was having the Jacuzzi built and tearing down rooms, and the PR firm was working on a logo and theme. Me? I was very busy writing orders for toilet paper and soap.

Over the course of the next few months, I traveled to Palm Springs every Thursday evening and spent Fridays and Saturdays with Luther and Fred reviewing whatever progress we made. Sundays were spent organizing my notes and making lists to be accomplished in Los Angeles during the coming week. Mondays I tried to conduct some of my regular business back in Los Angeles, where I was *making a living* running an automotive novelty business. This effort was interwoven with my meetings with the PR firm and different toilet paper salesmen.

My weekend meetings in Palm Springs were always held at a certain corner table in the restaurant. That was primarily because in every movie I had ever seen, the owner had his special table and there always appeared to be an endless flow of people to and from the man who called the shots. I must admit, I enjoyed playing this role to the hilt.

As the bills and invoices made their way to me, I felt it was time to regroup. I had planned a series of meetings with my two managers and the PR firm to see where everything stood. It seemed like time was standing still for the last few months—a number of things were in progress, but nothing was getting done. I had already gone through quite a sum of money, and I feared things were quickly getting out of hand. I had to sell my interest in an apartment building in Westwood that I owned, which gave me a much needed cash infusion of $100,000. But even that dwindled very quickly.

I had paid the PR agency for two months of work and so far had received zilch. From day one, I had insisted that in order to capture the charm of the place, they had to personally come down to Palm Springs and see what it was all about. Finally, after much cajoling, the head man agreed to drive down on a Saturday from Los Angeles.

Saturday morning at approximately ten o'clock, he arrived, and I promptly took him on a tour of the property. We spent about forty-five minutes looking at everything and then sat down for a cup of coffee to chat and exchange ideas. He said he put a lot of thought into making this project successful. I waited anxiously (and paid handsomely) to hear those great pearls of wisdom from the man who was going to make me successful beyond my wildest dreams. He spoke slowly for dramatic effect and said, "Mel, we've got to keep this property clean. I've noticed several things lying around that I could point out to you such as cigarette butts, discarded papers, and other garbage."

After regaining my composure, I assured him I was aware of the importance of what he was saying and the astuteness of his observation. I apologized and explained that we were in the process of renovating and therefore everything was in a state of flux. I was too frustrated to say anything else and simply told him I would call him next week. I thanked him profusely for coming down and especially for the profound piece of wisdom he offered. He left with a feeling of being truly appreciated. I guess some of their PR spin was rubbing off on me. I diplomatically told the firm, couched in Southern California niceties, that I no longer required their services and that I had run out of money.

For my next meeting, I would dispense with the spin and get right to the point with Fred. I noticed that the daily receipts for the hotel restaurant were about $700 but somehow only $350 wound up in the bank. I needed to know the answer to the million-dollar question: Where did the other $350 go? The meeting produced no answers, save for a hurt and confused look on Fred's face. He said he couldn't explain the missing money because Luther handled all the cash. It just so happened that Luther was next on my list of people to have a chat.

So far I had accomplished nothing and could hardly wait to have my one on one with Luther. I had about a half hour to kill, so I wandered around the property making notes. I made my way over to my new pride and joy, the new Jacuzzi. It was not quite finished, and to my horror, I discovered a big crack in the bottom.

Luther and I sat down for a cup of coffee, and reviewed some of the work in progress. Six rooms had been torn apart, but Luther didn't have any idea what to do next. His general contracting background was becoming suspect. The Jacuzzi was coming along, but so were the bills to have it finished. Luther told me between the electric and pool work, it would probably cost me somewhere in the neighborhood of $50,000 to get it up and running. When he saw my eyebrows furrow, he said that without his expertise, it would have run me closer to $65,000. I'm no rocket scientist, but I knew it didn't cost $65,000 to build a Jacuzzi, especially one with a big crack in the bottom.

My suspicions now fully aroused, I began questioning Luther about the missing revenue from the restaurant. Of course, he had a ready answer.

"Fred probably took it," he said, casually throwing him under the bus. I guess Luther didn't feel the commandment "Thou Shall

Not Lie," applied to him. Then he apologized for having to run, but he had some important business to take care of at the church, like perhaps tending to the collection plate at the end of service or starting up a ministry in Africa.

When Luther left, I felt gut-shot. I wanted to scream, but I didn't want to alarm the six customers I had in the restaurant. *What the hell had I gotten myself into?*

I stared into space for about an hour, then grabbed my car keys and drove back to Los Angeles. Later that night I went to Pips to have a few drinks to mull over my life. Ever since I moved to Los Angeles, I had been dropping out slowly but surely. Whereas I once had thirty suits, I now only had three sports jackets. I had driven a Rolls Royce but had traded that in for a used and unreliable Fiat that broke down more than it started. I went from a big house on the water to an apartment with rented dishes and furniture. All the original values of what made Mel run no longer existed. I was ready to try something totally different.

In order to make the Ingleside Inn a go, the first thing I applied was Robert Townsend's maxim that concentration was the key to economic success. No one was going to look over my investment better than me, and the place needed my full and undivided attention.

Barbra was now living full-time in Palm Springs and I missed her terribly. Even though we were an item, on occasion I would take a woman out to Pips. We'd have dinner, dance and play a little backgammon. I'd usually take my date home around 11 p.m. and escort her to her front door. Once there, I gave her a peck on the cheek and bid her good night. I was the perfect gentleman. In hindsight, these lovely ladies must have thought I was gay because I showed them a wonderful night on the town and never made a move. I had no interest whatsoever because I was so in love with Barbra.

If I were to move to Palm Springs, I could look after my property and be with Barbra full-time. In order to do that, I'd have to give up the regular paycheck that had been my security for twenty-three years. No matter what other business deals I had been involved in over the years, that regular paycheck had always been there. Not that my paycheck had been much after I paid spousal support to my former wife Pat and Uncle Sam took his cut of about forty percent. But at least it afforded me some peace of mind and had been a security blanket of sorts.

I finally made a decision to leave the automotive business and take a shot at running a hotel and restaurant. I felt if I could just grind out a living, I'd be happy. I had a condo, a car, a girlfriend, and a business to run, and they were all in Palm Springs. It seemed logical that that's where I should be.

The folks at Automatic Radio were taken aback, even a bit saddened, when I told them I was bowing out and moving on.

"Don't feel bad. Mentally I checked out a long time ago," I confessed. "You just felt more secure sending me a check. I feel bad for taking your money." The person I had trained in New York, Harvey Abikoff, was a quick study and had been doing a wonderful job under my tutelage. I assured them that Harvey could run the business just fine without me.

I had finally cut all ties. On July 4, 1975, one year to the day when Barbra and I first came to California, I packed my car and moved to Palm Springs to launch a new career and life. I was never more excited or scared.

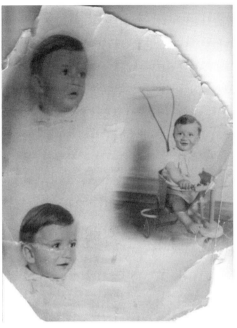

Me as a baby. Check out that stroller. It looks like it could chalk a baseball field.

The Haber women, my sisters: Gloria, Alyce and Franky, who is sitting.

My parents, Louis "Libby" and Mary Haber.

Brooklyn born buddies. Dizzy Davidson, me, Marvin Schnapp and Barry "Bo" Eisner.

My in-laws, Florence and Sam Meyers at mine and Pat's wedding. We were promised a lavish wedding at the Essex House, but ended up tying the knot in the Meyers' walk up apartment.

"A promotional brochure for Wallfrin Industries, circa late 1960s. That's my former business partner Artie Schifrin on the left."

The Ingleside Inn pool.

My three children, Shani, Lonny and Gary.

The entry way of the Ingleside Inn.

One of Melvyn's dining rooms.

An unbeatable combination: Me and my Rolls Royce in front of the Ingleside Inn.

Babs Rosen is an Ingleside Inn legend who ran the place with an iron fist.

Friday, May 18, 1984 — Page 3

CRITIC'S ACCLAIM — Elmer Dill (right), restaurant critic for ABC-TV, congratulates Mel Haber on his fine showing in this year's Palm Springs Life Restaurant Awards ceremony. Haber's three restaurants, Melvyn's, Doubles at the Tennis Club and Cecils — all in Palm Springs — took eight awards, including "outstanding wine list" at each establishment.

Receiving one of eight awards from Palm Springs Life magazine from restaurant critic Elmer Dills.

Sir John's arrival at the Ingleside Inn made local headlines.

Sir John in all of his glory. That's him in the white tux courting a beautiful lady in the wicker chair.

This is my vision of a man named Cecil and used it as my logo for my restaurant and disco.

No, this isn't Lynda Carter but my wife Stephanie, who is my Wonderwoman.

With my son Lonny, a wonderful kid who had a special zest for life.

Cecil's, the most gorgeous disco in the world.

Stephanie and me posing for wedding photos at the Hotel Del on Coronado Island. We now spend our summers on the island.

Movie producer Ron Samuels, his wife and the innagural Ms. Olympia, Rachel McLish, with me and Stephanie. My wife almost gave Ron a heart attack when she showed up for dinner.

Me, Stephanie and Autumn in front of Angel View Haber House, Palm Springs, 2002.

The entrance of Touché.

Touché was perhaps my greatest creation but also my biggest failure.

Receiving the prestigious Jefferson Award from Congresswoman Mary Bono.

Former Palm Springs Mayor Frank Bogert is 97 and still going strong. His inscription reads: "To Palm Springs' #1 citizen."

Receiving my Palm Springs Walk of Fame Star on my sixtieth birthday in 1996.

Posing with wife Stephanie and daughter Autumn. My hair is about as white as my shirt.

# CHAPTER 6

# Elegant Oasis

As I look back and reflect on the time when I opened the Ingleside Inn, it's hard to believe my good luck and fortune. I made every mistake in the book, and despite it all, the Inn became a success. In today's current competitive market, I would have been bankrupt in thirty days. But because nothing was happening in Palm Springs at that time, I was able to overcome all the obstacles and take a derelict hotel and restaurant and transform them into an elegant oasis. But it didn't happen overnight.

I learned the tourist season in Palm Springs was opposite from most other cities. The summer's almost unbearable heat brings tourism to a screeching halt from June to September. Because the Ingleside Inn had no air-conditioning at the time, I saw it as the perfect opportunity to shut down the place for renovations and refurbishment.

I also learned that every September for the previous twenty years a menswear convention called "Magic Bagic" came to Palm Springs and bought up every hotel room in the desert. They were going to take all the rooms at the Ingleside Inn, and it sounded like the perfect opening weekend—with every room occupied. With that in mind, I made it my mission to have the hotel open and ready for this convention by Labor Day. That might seem like a fairly reachable goal today, but two factors made it loftier than it sounds: I was financing everything out of my own pocket, and I had a construction crew almost as inept as my hotel staff.

Because there wasn't much building going on in Palm Springs, a good carpenter was about as hard to find in the desert as a ski instructor. In the absence of anyone else, I found a carpenter who hailed from Mississippi and hired him to be my foreman for the renovation work. Also, I engaged the services of two young lady decorators from Los Angeles, a decision based solely on their moderate fee rather than any proven ability in their profession.

Soon I was totally absorbed in the project and came to realize that there was a vast amount of work to be done before opening day. The major projects included installing air-conditioning with adequate electric power throughout the property; redecorating the dining room; remodeling the kitchen; building a bar and lounge area; renovating all the rooms; and restoring the exterior and grounds to a presentable condition. I also had to convert the servants' quarters into hotel rooms, which would give me a total of twenty-six rooms.

I had finally found a project that consumed all of my energy and time, and it was very satisfying. It also consumed almost all of my money, which was being spent at an incredible rate. I even had to sell my $300,000 worth of Automatic Radio stock, which was now worth only $30,000. One day I was grumbling to Barbra about the money situation, and she told me to start collecting unemployment. The suggestion stopped me dead in my tracks because it was so logical. I always liked logic.

"You've worked your whole life, Mel. You paid into the system for twenty-seven years. Now you don't have a job," she said. "Collect unemployment."

"Yes?"

"Yes."

I didn't know anybody in Palm Springs, so I didn't think it was a big deal, nor did I think it emasculating. The next day I visited the unemployment office in Indio, about twenty miles away. I stood in line with several people from all walks of life, including a few dishwashers who had worked for me before I shut the place down. After my embarrassment subsided, I spent a few hours with a clerk and was properly registered. Shortly thereafter I began receiving an $80 check every week. Not a bad deal.

Around the same time, the *Desert Sun*, the only newspaper in town, wrote a feature article on me, which made the renovation of the Ingleside Inn very big news.

They say dealing with the press can be a double-edged sword, and this particular article made that abundantly clear. The reporter mistakenly referred to Barbra as "Mrs. Haber," and I didn't bother to ask for a retraction when the article came out. I was just happy that he was giving my place a nice plug. Barbra seemed to like the new title, and from that point on began referring to herself as Mrs. Haber. At the time I didn't think it was that big of a deal, and I didn't bother to correct her. That later turned out to be a big mistake on my part.

The upside was that the article was read by many locals, giving the hotel and restaurant a big shot in the arm. The downside was that a representative at the employment office also read the article and called me on it the next time I went there.

"Are you Mel Haber?" asked the man across the counter.

"Yes."

"How can you collect unemployment? Why aren't you out looking for a job?" he said. The man seemed to know a lot more about me than I knew about him, which angered me somewhat. I thought I'd call his bluff.

"Mister, I'm thirty-nine years old and I've worked over twenty-seven years and I never collected unemployment," I said with a tone of authority. "Why can't I collect unemployment?"

"If you think it is okay to collect unemployment, that's fine," he said. "But I wonder how the public will react when I call the reporter who did that nice fluff piece on you and tell him the owner of the Ingleside Inn is collecting unemployment?"

I mulled this over for a moment, and while I might have had legal grounds in a court of law, there was the distinct possibility I might not have been right in the court of public opinion. The good publicity I had generated from the article would soon be forgotten with a juicy, scandalous tale about how I was taking advantage of the taxpayer's dime. I agreed to stop collecting unemployment.

"All right, I see your point," I said. "I won't cash another check. You have my word."

"That's fine," he said. "Did you want to send back the checks you've been collecting?"

I had only cashed three checks and immediately wrote a check out to the unemployment office, paying back the balance in full. I had avoided a scandal, but I had plenty of other fires to put out.

My ragtag construction crew was busy mucking up my establishment, but I had only myself to blame. They were hired mostly because they were the cheapest labor I could find. Some didn't even require money—just room and board. Or should I say diving board.

One of the people I hired was Jay, a nineteen-year-old kid who said he was capable of carpentry, painting, and some electrical work. He was illiterate and slept on the diving board over the pool because he claimed it was cooler outside. I did come to respect him in time because he literally worked around the clock. In time, he became my right hand despite the fact he couldn't read or write.

A friend in Los Angeles sent me two young guys named Larry and Skip who were willing to work as laborers for the summer in return for decent sleeping quarters and minimum wages.

Skip and Larry were as close as peas in a pod, and I could never figure out why they clicked. Skip was an intellectual but was attempting manual labor as one of life's great experiences. Larry was a simpleton who probably couldn't do anything other than manual labor, and he didn't do it that well. The two were nice enough fellows, even quite lovable, but I'm being kind when I say they were fumbling idiots.

When they painted a room, they painted themselves in a corner and could never figure out how to get out. It was impossible to explain to them to start at the back of the room and paint their way to the door. For some reason known only to them, they found it easier to start from the threshold of the door and paint their way into the room. Whenever they went to eat, they would simply walk across the freshly painted floor and across the property to a restaurant on Palm Canyon Drive. I never had to wonder where they were because I just followed their painted footsteps.

Paul, the architect, was another piece of work. He was obsessed with building dining room tables for the restaurant and worked at a feverish pace. He cut thousands of wood slats and nailed them together, believing with every ounce of his being that his tables were a work of art. That they would ultimately be covered by tablecloths, never to be seen by the public, did not deter him one bit.

The summer of 1975 had no days and no nights for me. It was one long blur where all I could see was work that seemed never ending. The norm was that every single project had to be redone three or four times. A combination of urgency and inefficiency resulted in everything costing twice as much as it should have. But ineptitude wasn't just limited to the construction crew. My restaurant and kitchen staff gave them a good run for the money, or should I say, my money, because unfortunately I was footing the entire bill.

My friend Billy Irwin introduced me to a young chef who was then living in Huntington Beach with his wife and baby. Charlie, who was in his late twenties, was a typical "beach bum." He had a walrus mustache, a jovial personality and a Buddha belly. Despite his quirks, Charlie was totally dedicated to the art of preparing fine foods. Once I hired Charlie full-time, he offered the services of two friends from the beach to help him renovate the kitchen. I took him up on the offer, only to regret it later.

Charlie and crew acted more like construction workers than like chefs and ended up ripping my kitchen apart and putting it back together three times. It wasn't necessary, but they had the idea that renovation meant pulling things apart so they could be put together again. Charlie and company had mistaken the kitchen for the beach and insisted on going barefoot. Consequently, they spent a good part of the day removing splinters and nails from their feet. I think they must have removed part of their brains because while they were busy ripping my kitchen apart and putting it back together, they forgot to put in a pantry—an essential element in a functional kitchen. But that was nothing compared to what happened in the bar.

One morning I was so wired that I showed up at the property around 3 a.m. There was so much going on that I went into the bar to check out my new bar stools, which had just arrived. Either I wasn't fully awake, or I was having a real-life nightmare. I was seated at the bar and for some reason I was forced to sit sideways rather than straight ahead. I had never been a "barfly," but I knew that whenever I sat at a bar, I had always faced the bartender. I was really confused and sat there for almost two hours wracking my brains as to what was wrong. Then it dawned on me—the carpenter forgot to put a ledge on the bar. There was no room to put your legs in front of you. But rather than being discouraged that someone had forgotten the overhanging ledge, I was excited because I had found the solution to the problem in only two hours!

As the month of August started to disappear, I held a pep rally to explain to the staff that we had to work harder as Labor Day and the Magic Bagic convention rapidly approached. For some reason, I had it fixed in my mind that Labor Day was the start of the season as it was back east. But someone forgot to remind me that September was still hot as Hades in Palm Springs, and the town was dead, or to tell me that Magic Bagic decided after twenty years that they had outgrown the desert and for the first time ever decided they would not be coming to Palm Springs. They held their next convention in San Diego. (Today they are so big they have to hold their convention in Las Vegas.)

The net result was that I spent a lot of extra time, money, and effort getting ready for September, when nobody would be in town. I had another meeting with the entire crew to rally the troops to get the site ready, but they looked more like the French Foreign Legion than like a battle-ready combat unit. As I looked at the entire crew assembled, all of whom I loved dearly by this time, I vowed that some day this story would be written. But just as I had my chest puffed out ready to deliver my victory speech, I was deflated by what I saw. Charlie the chef was busy picking his toenails while his two cohorts were picking splinters out of their feet; Paul the architect was noticeably anxious because he felt that precious time was being taken away from nailing his tabletops together; and Skip was almost invisible because he was covered from head-to-toe in white paint and literally blended into the wall. There was not one competent in the entire group, including me.

Although they did not inspire much confidence, they did swear their undying devotion and fullest energies to finishing the job in the next few weeks.

Almost magically, trucks and shipments started to arrive from the decorators, and certain finishing touches were finally being put in place. I cannot adequately describe the elation I felt at seeing all of the elements finally come to life after all our hard work.

Over the summer, many locals had stopped by to see what was happening, offering words of encouragement and some advice. Both were needed. The word was all over town that some "slick guy from New York" with plenty of money had taken it over. If only they knew I was literally down to my last dime.

I was so desperate for money that I had taken a box of silver coins I had collected over the years and given it to Barbra to take to a Los Angeles coin dealer and see what she could get. She brought back nearly $5,000, all of which I had to pay out immediately.

I also turned to Mark Owens, who was running an air freshener business for me back in New York called Medo. I told Mark he could buy the business from me because I was strapped for cash. I had an initial investment of $10,000 and just wanted to recoup my money. Mark agreed, and I even allowed him to pay me $100 a week with no interest for two years because I was desperate for cash. At first, times must have been tough for Mark because more than once his $100 checks didn't clear. But he stuck it out and made the business work big-time. (A few years ago, a friend of mine called me one day to say Mark had sold the air freshener business to Quaker Oil for $160 million—all cash. I sent Mark a fax that day and wrote, "I always knew one day one of us was going to make a big score, except that I thought it was going to be me!" He flew out the next day and spent a couple of days at the Ingleside Inn and we had a lovely reunion.)

I ended up spending every red cent I had on the restoration, which was about $250,000. I had barely enough money to advertise and zero cash to send out any personal invitations. But as it turned out, I didn't need to.

By opening night the whole town was waiting for me to open my doors. Back then the doyens of Palm Springs society were a small-knit group, but an informed one. I happened to open my place at a time when there was absolutely nothing else going on and I got lucky. Very lucky.

I also made a key hire—someone that could bring the stars to my hotel, bar, and restaurant, which I had renamed "Melvyn's" on the advice of a friend.

"I can't name it Melvyn's," I protested initially. "You'd have to be an egomaniac to name a place after yourself."

"Nobody has ever called you Melvyn," my friend said. He had a point. Nobody had ever called me "Melvyn," including my mother. Everyone simply called me Mel. But the trick was going to be trying to find a guy to be Melvyn—a suave, sophisticated front man who knew how to cater to powerful people. I knew I wasn't polished enough to pull it off.

As hard as this may be to believe, I'm basically pretty shy. I am not a very sociable person, but that doesn't preclude me from talking your ears off once I know you. It's never been my style to walk up to a stranger and strike up a conversation. I've always preferred my little space in the back office and pulling the strings. So the trick for me was to find someone who could be Melvyn, and be a face that the public would associate with my establishment.

Through a bit of good luck, I managed to lure Hank Van de Boer, who was the longtime maitre d' of the world famous Racquet Club. The historic hotel resort was founded by actors Charles Farrell and Ralph Bellamy in December 1934, and the opening and closing of the Racquet Club signaled the beginning and the end of each season in Palm Springs. Just about every major Hollywood star traipsed through the doors of the storied club, and now I had the maitre d' who'd befriended these stars. My timing couldn't have been better. The club had just been sold and was starting to lose some of its luster. The maitre d' saw it as the right time to make a move, and luckily for me, he did. He brought plenty of his former clientele to my new place, and for that I was very thankful.

August was drawing to a close, and the site was looking pretty spiffy. We were not completely finished, but I had come to the realization that it would never be and there would always be something to fix. My beach boy chef, Charlie, much to my surprise and delight, had put together a very ambitious yet traditional Old World menu. We decided to open the doors on September 15. I chose to have a quiet opening so that I could iron out the kinks before the season went into full swing. I placed a small ad in the *Desert Sun* announcing that Melvyn's was now serving dinner. I had also made up a critique sheet that I was going to use for customer feedback. It was presented at every table with the check, and the waiter was instructed to buy a round of drinks for every table that filled it out.

As I drove to Melvyn's for opening night, I honestly had no idea what to expect. Was it going to be a bust, or would my efforts be appreciated? I was stunned to find the bar full of people and every table in the dining room was taken. I mean, I couldn't believe my eyes. To say that I was nervous was a major understatement. The maitre d' informed me that we were sold out! Who knew? I thought maybe we might get some curiosity seekers, but to have a sold out crowd was beyond my wildest dreams. As I looked around the totally unfamiliar crowd, it appeared as if all the women were beautiful, and all the men were handsome and dashing, and everybody was impeccably dressed. I had argued with myself that day as to whether or not to wear a tie, but luckily I made the right decision. Had I guessed wrong, I would have been totally out of place because all the men were wearing jackets and ties.

The maitre d' pulled me into a corner in the dining room and gave me a run-down of the people in the room: actors Mary Martin and Tony Franciosa; Mousie Powell, wife of Dick Powell, who ran Four Star Studios; Mayor Frank Bogert; 21 Club owners Jerry and

Molly Berns; retired studio mogul Darryl Zanuck and his wife; the Florsheims, and several other movers and shakers. As he related their names and who they were, I felt flush. It seemed as if I had the *Who's Who* of the country in my establishment.

I circulated throughout the dining room and bar for about two hours, having no idea what to do with myself. As I walked around, several people stopped me to introduce themselves and wish me good luck. It seemed as if an angel had sprinkled some stardust on me because everything seemed to click. I had even hired a piano player for the lounge, and while he was tinkling the ivories in the back, that area began to fill up, too.

I had a college student named Danny Glick to thank for a lot of the patrons; Danny and I struck up an unlikely friendship over the course of the summer. He was a young, ambitious kid who parked cars at a well-known restaurant two blocks away. I immediately liked him. Perhaps I sensed in him the same work ethic and hustle that I had possessed at his age. His restaurant was closed over the summer, and he visited almost every day. Danny had assured me that when I opened he would recommend people to stop over and visit Melvyn's.

His word was good as gold, and several people dropped by Melvyn's on opening night, mentioning that Danny had sent them my way. At about ten o' clock, I walked outside to have a cigarette. Just at that very moment, a scruffy-looking guy dressed in dungarees and a T-shirt and sporting a heavy beard pulled up on a Harley-Davidson motorcycle. He had a very pretty lady on the back of the bike. *He's certainly not the Ingleside Inn type*, I thought, becoming a little full of myself. The guy said he had come to see the "new place."

"Please buddy, not tonight!" I begged him. "It's opening night and I don't want any trouble. Come back another night and I'll buy you a drink." He smiled at me, gunned the throttle on the motorcycle and drove off. I was pleased at how I handled a delicate situation so adeptly.

About an hour later, Danny showed up and asked, "Mel, have you been getting all the people I've been sending over?" I told him I had and thanked him profusely. He then asked how I enjoyed meeting Steve McQueen and Ali MacGraw, Hollywood's new golden couple. Startled and disappointed that I had not, I said they never showed. Danny said he was surprised because they assured him they would come right over to have a nightcap.

He said, "They were on a big, blue Harley-Davidson motorcycle and Steve McQueen was wearing blue jeans and a T-shirt." It turned out that I'd yanked the welcome mat from under the international box-office champion and his glamorous movie star wife. He never came back. Luckily for me, that was the only blunder of that night. However, it was the first of many faux pas that I eventually became famous for.

At the end of the night, Molly and Jerry Berns, who were the owners of the world-famous 21 Club in New York, bumped into me at the restaurant. Molly had been a great customer of mine in the shoe business when I was younger. The 21 Club was about a half block away from the shoe store on Fifth Avenue. Whenever she went on a cruise or long vacation, she'd call me up and ask me to select several pairs of shoes for her. She had enough faith in my taste to choose her shoes and was always happy with my choices. On this night, she was my customer again.

"Mel, what are you doing here?" she asked.

"This is my place," I said, beaming with pride.

"But you're a shoe salesman," she laughed.

"I got smart and switched from shoes to booze," I smiled. "But from the looks of it, I may have just become the hottest saloon owner in town."

# CHAPTER 7

# Bloops, Bleeps, and Blunders

F or all the grief Palm Springs gets for its reputation as a sugar-frosted society and the playground of the rich and famous, it is a very forgiving community. I mean, how else do you explain the fact that I've been in business for more than thirty years?

Not only did I make every mistake in the book, but a few of them were monumental. I made the kind of mistakes that can put someone out of business today in the snap of a finger. However, we were lucky to be able to overcome everything because we opened in a noncompetitive market because there weren't many white table-cloth restaurants in Palm Springs in 1975.

Being in the hospitality industry for more than three decades, you get every conceivable curveball thrown your way. Let me tell you, I've seen curveballs, knuckleballs, fastballs, sidearms, and a few pitches that I don't even know what to call.

One pitch that I didn't see coming was the night Debbie Reynolds called to say she wanted to book the entire hotel and restaurant to celebrate her fiftieth birthday at Melvyn's. The request wasn't a problem until the next day when ex-husband Eddie Fisher, who'd thrown Reynolds over for Elizabeth Taylor, called to say he would like to make a reservation for dinner that same evening. Another night, all three of actor Michael Landon's ex-wives ended up dining at the restaurant at the same time, creating a logistical nightmare the

Cartwrights never faced on the Ponderosa. We did some bobbing and weaving regarding both of those situations, and got through them without incident.

Some old lovers we just couldn't keep apart. Peter Cetera, lead singer of the group Chicago, often frequented the Ingleside Inn/Melvyn's with his wife Diane. They ultimately divorced and neither one of them had been back to the Inn for several years. As fate would have it, when he visited the place again with his new wife in tow, lo and behold the first person he spotted when he pulled into the driveway was his ex-wife with her new husband lounging by the pool. As if that was not enough of a coincidence, they wound up in adjoining rooms!

They also don't tell you in any textbook that I know of how to react when a skunk decides to take a casual stroll through your restaurant—on a busy Saturday night no less. That's exactly what happened to us, but we improvised by moving all of the tables outside to the pool area. Amazingly, none of our patrons left. They were all good sports and ate outside.

There were other animals as well. The desert is rife with raccoons, and on some nights, you can hear them tearing through the garbage or playing on the roof. By law you can't kill them, and you certainly can't intimidate the little creatures. A family of six raccoons frequented the pool area almost every night during one period. I'd try and throw a light on them to scare them off, but once the lights were switched off, they'd come back out. One night when a customer opened the front door of Melvyn's, three members of the raccoon family waltzed right through the front door and ran through the lounge, then changed their mind and ran back out. At least they behaved better than some of our personnel.

One busy Saturday night, our chef was drinking heavily during the dinner shift. The place was jammed and the chef actually passed out in the middle of the serving. The other cooks followed his lead and got drunk and started throwing steaks around the kitchen. It was total chaos. Customers had been served their drinks and appetizers, and were waiting for their entrees, which never came out.

I did what any reasonable owner would do—I picked up a bottle of Beefeater Gin, checked into one of the rooms, and drank myself silly. I was so traumatized that I didn't come out for two days.

When I opened the Ingleside Inn and Melvyn's, I had made up a critique sheet to pass out to customers seeking their opinion on what they thought about every aspect of the operation (such as decor, ambiance, food, service, and so forth). But that's tantamount to attending a movie premiere with the stars present and telling them it was a so-so flick—it just ain't going to happen. It was the same with our grand opening, and I found out very quickly people just didn't want to become involved. According to the critique sheets, everything at Melvyn's was absolutely great. *What an easy business*, I thought.

However, within a few weeks, I heard conversations around town about Melvyn's that drifted back to me and it wasn't pretty. Undercooked chicken had been served, hot food came out cold, cold food came out hot, and the service was painfully slow. It was tough to hear, but I knew that I had to make adjustments or I would be in trouble.

Because I was a novice in the industry, I wasn't familiar with the term "soft opening." That's when an owner invites family and friends to critique the food and service before the official opening for the public. A Broadway show usually opens out of town until the producer and director feel that it is ready for the big time. It takes time for a new restaurant to get the kinks out and establish the rhythm. Once again, I had to rely on my logic in order to figure it all out.

Every day I carried a pencil and piece of paper. I listened to everything the customer said. I was never accused of not listening to someone; I was accused of listening to everybody. I carefully watched how the staff operated and how the patrons reacted. I kept meticulous notes on what I observed. I hung out with the dishwashers for a few days to watch which food or entrees were coming back. If a lot of the same items were coming back to the dishwasher, I knew I needed to either eliminate it from the menu or ask the chef to prepare it differently.

One of the constant complaints we received in the early days was that the food was served cold. Common sense told me that when the food was cooked, it had to be hot. I had to figure out what happened between the time it was cooked and the time it got to the table. I discovered that the hot food was put on a cold plate, which dramatically changed the temperature of the meal almost immediately. I figured out that the dishes needed to be kept in a salamander to keep the plates burning hot, which in turn kept the food warm. Additionally, until the server picked up the food, it had to be kept under a heat lamp, and when the server picked up the food, it had to be covered for delivery to the guests.

Being the hot new operation in town from the day I opened, I had people waiting forty-five minutes to an hour and a half for a table. These were not just ordinary people, but very powerful people. I had the *Who's Who* not only of Palm Springs but of Beverly Hills as well. I had some of the most important people in Southern California clamoring to get into my establishment, and I didn't know how to solve the healthy problem of too much business. The goal was to keep the wait to a minimum while accommodating all the customers.

I had a manager who had been in the business for many, many years, and he explained that just like the airline industry, we had to "overbook" even if it meant keeping customers waiting. We had people with reservations screaming that they had been waiting for more than an hour, while people who were finished with their meal lingered at their table to see what celebrities might come in.

I could barely take the pressure of people screaming and hollering. Even though we were an upscale place, things could get heated and nasty. Looking back, the pressure was unbelievable.

One week I decided to take a different approach and not overbook. I only wanted to take the amount of people we could handle and seat within fifteen minutes of their reservation. That Saturday night I came to work and the restaurant was virtually empty. There was nobody in the bar waiting for a table, and a couple of people in the restaurant asked me what was wrong. Was I having problems? They were used to seeing the place jammed on a Saturday night. I found out the hard way that in the restaurant business you get a lot of no-shows. As a result, we had empty tables all night long. It was bad enough that it gave the impression that I was not doing well, and to top it off, this was going to hurt my pocketbook. So I decided to continue overbooking customers and live with the pressure.

One of the biggest problems I had was simply finding good help. I personally weeded through all the résumés to ensure I employed the most professional people I could. They didn't necessarily have to have a lot of experience, but they had to be attentive to customers' needs and yet know their place. They were there to serve the customers, not be their best buddy. Mostly, they had to be respectful and responsive and make sure the customer had the best possible experience that we could provide. It may sound easy, but it's not. It's a delicate balancing act that requires lots of common sense and a feel for the business. For some reason, being a server is considered a menial position in the United States while in Europe it is considered a proud profession. One restaurant in town proudly advertises some of their staff have been with them for fifteen years. I have been very lucky to have had many employees over thirty years. At Melvyn's and the Ingleside Inn, a fifteen-year employee is still considered a rookie.

Just as important as the service is the quality of the food. I quickly learned that if you buy the highest quality food and ingredients, you really have to go out of your way to mess it up. After all, if you buy the best steak, all you can do is undercook or overcook it. I remember one of the most sophisticated critiques I ever received was from Art Linkletter's son, Jack. He came up to me after a meal and said, "Mel, I just had your Veal Ingleside and I must tell you that the veal was excellent. I wasn't thrilled with the way it was prepared, but the veal was absolutely top-notch." 21 Club owner Jerry Berns once told me a patron told him after a meal that his food was horrible. Jerry said he replied, "I apologize sir, but I beg to differ with you. We buy only the finest product available. I apologize for not preparing it to your liking but the quality is absolutely the best."

Since we are on the subject, I must point out one of my biggest beefs (pardon the pun) is with food critics. Because Melvyn's was receiving an inordinate amount of attention, we became a magnet for every food critic in the region.

I don't have a problem with restaurant critics per se, but I do have a problem with someone coming into my restaurant, eating one item on a single day, and critiquing my entire restaurant career. That's just pure insanity. That's like judging a journalist's entire career based on one paragraph or an artist's career based on a single painting.

How can someone critique the quality of my food when they don't even know what I buy? I believe in addition to critiquing the ambiance, service, and quality of food, critics should ask the owner for the invoices for their food to see if they're buying the highest quality. How can they say a certain restaurant's food is great and mine is not when the other restaurant sells their food for less than I pay for mine?

I once had a long-running feud with a famous food critic who worked for the ABC affiliate in Los Angeles and had a column in a local newspaper. One night he strolled into Melvyn's for a cocktail but didn't eat a meal. I passed by him in the bar and told him jokingly that I was terrified of him.

"Why would you be terrified of me?" he asked.

"Because you can ruin my business in one night if you don't like it," I said, turning somewhat serious.

"Why would I do that? I'm a nice guy. Why would I want to hurt somebody?"

The very next day, his column appeared in a free local newspaper, and his review of Melvyn's was not particularly favorable. I went ballistic because I knew he hadn't so much as lifted a fork in my establishment, and yet he was critiquing my restaurant. I decided to respond in spite of the fact that I knew you can't fight city hall or the press.

I decided that I would write a letter to the president of ABC-TV, telling him that I knew for a fact that the critic had never eaten in my restaurant, therefore, how could he write a critique of my place?

Newscaster Jerry Dunphy and Dr. George the weatherman, both at the same station, were regular customers. They too were disappointed in the critique.

Two weeks later I received a correspondence from the president of ABC with a letter from the critic explaining that it was common practice for a food critic to send out stringers—people who work for them to write the critique so that the food critic doesn't have to visit every restaurant.

Several years later, *Palm Springs Life* magazine announced they were going to give out awards to various restaurants in the desert and as fate would have it, the critic would be one of the presenters of the awards. That night Melvyn's won seven awards. It got so embarrassing for me to constantly go up to the stage where he had to present me an award that I decided to send my maitre d' a few times. My adversary had to shake my hand on several occasions, have his picture taken with me, and act happy for me. Since he was a friend of mine, Dr. George told me he had a picture of the critic handing me an award, blown up to poster size. The poster hung proudly in his ABC office for years, and he told me that the food critic had to pass by that picture every day at the television studio.

My final word on the matter is this: I have been in the restaurant business for over thirty years. How many restaurants really last that long? Not many, I can tell you. It's obvious that the public votes with dollars on who should stay in business and who shouldn't.

While I did not deserve the bad critique, *Desert Sun* publisher Ted Grofer should have buried me for what I did to him over the years. I was only open for about a week when I was informed by the maitre d' that Mr. Ted Grofer, the publisher of the local newspaper, just made a reservation for a party of four. Needless to say, I was most anxious to make a good impression with the head of the only newspaper in Palm Springs. I told my maitre d' that the minute his party was seated to let me know so that I could personally meet him.

I was sitting at the bar chatting with a customer when the maitre d' motioned me over. He told me he had seated the Grofer party at table 20. I pulled myself erect, straightened my jacket, checked myself in the mirror (that night I had used an artificial face bronzer and I could have easily passed for George Hamilton's brother), and walked over confidently as I could. I reached across the table to shake his hand. Just as I said, "It's my pleasure to meet you, Mr.

Grofer," I knocked over the bottle of wine on the table. You could say I definitely made a splash.

My façade of confidence was immediately shattered, and my cover was blown. I turned into a blubbering idiot within seconds, and began apologizing profusely. I asked the guests if they would mind moving over to the next table so we could clean up the mess. The man sitting to the right of the gentleman whose hand I shook very casually said, "Number one, I am Mr. Grofer; and number two, don't you think it would be easier to change the tablecloth than switch tables?" I giggled nervously and explained to him that this was evidence of my long and distinguished background in the restaurant business, which at the time was one whole week.

I knew that I had accomplished part of my purpose, which was to make an impression on Mr. Grofer. I am not quite sure that this was the impression I had wanted to create, but I had made one nevertheless. I was rescued by a message that I had an urgent phone call. I figured that if my future in the restaurant business was going to be anything like that moment, my best solution would be to build a series of trap doors throughout the restaurant so I could exit gracefully.

Although my primary function at night is to circulate throughout the dining room with a big smile plastered on my face, I managed to avoid passing the Grofer table. I was absolutely new to the business and had no idea what it was I was supposed to do when I walked around. In all of the movies I had seen, a good owner always circulates and mingles with a very knowledgeable look on his face. But as I stated before, I'm basically shy unless you get to know me. I was grateful for the little pieces of debris and lettuce that fell on the floor during the evening so I could come in, swoop them up, and appear as if I knew what I was doing. At the very least, in my mind, it justified my existence.

On approximately my tenth tour of the dining room, about two hours after I had been to the Grofer table, he caught my attention. He motioned for me to come over.

"Don't be embarrassed, these kinds of things happen," Mr. Grofer graciously explained. I felt quite relieved. He then mentioned that he and his party would like to go into the lounge and listen to the night's entertainment, and asked if I would set them up with four seats. I promptly went back to the lounge and managed to secure the four best seats in the house. I escorted Mr. Grofer's party to the back of the lounge. I felt much better about the situation now that I had personally seated him.

Not wanting to impose, I kept my distance for a while and then decided to go back and see how Mr. Grofer's party was doing. As fate would have it, as I approached the back of the lounge, I saw the cocktail waitress slip and a bottle of wine fell over their table, soaking the entire party. The good news was that Mr. Grofer and his party got a nice sampling of our wine selection. The bad news was they never got to taste it, only to wear it. Being the stand-up guy that I was, I immediately turned on my heels and ran out of the front of the restaurant to let the waitress sort out the mess.

When I got outside, I realized I had no place to hide, and that sooner or later I would have to face the music. I sauntered back to the Grofer party and played dumb (a part that comes natural to me), acting as if I had not witnessed the accident. When I asked how everything was going, the publisher's wife informed me about the spilled wine and not so subtly hinted that her dress was very expensive. I offered to replace the dress—having no idea what I might be getting into. Fortunately, she said she would settle for a good cleaning. I apologized profusely, thanked them for their understanding, and assured them I would make it up to them.

About a week later, Mr. Grofer called me on the telephone and said he wished to entertain a group of very important people and wanted to make a reservation at Melvyn's. He asked if I would make the arrangements personally. Overjoyed that I could make amends so quickly, I marked on the reservation sheet, "GROFER VIP, party of six at 8 p.m." The reservation was scheduled for a Saturday night, which is always total chaos at any restaurant in Palm Springs. It is not unusual to wait a considerable amount of time on a Saturday evening, even if you have reservations. But for Mr. Grofer, I would clear my calendar to make sure he and his party was seated at 8 p.m. sharp.

Let me say that at this point, many things were happening to me at once. I was meeting so many new people because I was new to the business. I was still working out the kinks in my establishment, and so I was always in a constant state of confusion. Being one of the world's greatest list makers, and given that things were so hectic, I made notes to remind myself to take a shower and shave.

When Saturday night rolled around, I was in an advanced state of hysteria and nervous about fulfilling all of our reservations. We were a fine dining establishment and we couldn't give our customers the bum's rush once they finished their meals. Saturday was their big night out, and people wanted a five-course meal, dessert, and perhaps an after-dinner coffee. They wanted to linger, people-watch, and soak in the ambiance of being at an elegant, popular restaurant.

I arrived at Melvyn's around 7:45 p.m. to find a crowded foyer of people waiting to be seated. Several different patrons grabbed me to tell me they knew my Aunt Tillie back in Brooklyn or that they had gone to school with my cousin, Shelley. Everybody was trying to find a way to identify with me to make sure they got my attention and were seated promptly. The only thing it did was throw me off balance.

By the time I had worked my way to the back of the lounge, it was nine o' clock, and who should be sitting there but Mr. Ted Grofer with his VIP guests? He motioned me over and said, "We have already been waiting one hour. How much longer do you think it will be?" The tone of his voice would have kept ice cream frozen. I could not believe I had messed up his request. I had put on my list to check on the Grofer party but I forgot to make a note to actually *look* at my list. I ran back to the maitre d' and asked him what happened. I told him that I had marked the reservation "VIP." He promptly informed me that he could not read my writing and translated the name of the party as "G. Rofer VIP."

It took about ten minutes to get Mr. Grofer and his party seated. By this point, I figured the only article about me that would be printed in the *Desert Sun* would be my obituary or a bankruptcy notice, depending on which came first. My manager, a lovely man by the name of Alan Mald, who had been in the business for approximately thirty years, told me to relax.

"Mel, two o' clock in the morning will come and all the problems will be over for tonight," Alan would always say. Alan did, however, suggest that I should call Mr. Grofer on Monday morning and invite him and his wife to have an intimate dinner at Melvyn's as my personal guests. Taking heart that this might be my new salvation, I couldn't wait until Monday morning to right all of my wrongs.

They say time is a great healer, and I sincerely believe it because when I reached Mr. Grofer on Monday, the tone of his voice indicated that "fear is worse than fear itself." I told him that he would do me a great service if, at his convenience, he and his wife would give me another chance and be my personal guests at Melvyn's. He thanked me, said it was a very nice gesture and would see if he could coerce his wife into coming back. However, he made it clear he couldn't make any promises.

At this point, I was working seven days a week and six nights. I took off one weekday night in order to recoup my strength and sanity. When I went in Friday, my maitre d' called me over and said he had to talk to me.

"Mr. Haber, I don't know how to tell you this but I goofed with Mr. Grofer last night," he said in a nervous tone. I felt a stab in my chest. I didn't want to hear any more, but I had no choice. It seems I neglected to tell my staff that whenever Mr. and Mrs. Grofer came in, they were my personal guests and were to be "comped."

According to the maitre d', the Grofers had dinner on my one night off. As they were about to leave, Mr. Grofer thanked the waiter and gave him a tip. He then escorted his wife outside, but before he made it to the door, the waiter said, "Excuse me, sir, but you have neglected to pay the check." I gathered, knowing that particular waiter, that there might have been a little more to it than that. Maybe he had even "jumped" Mr. Grofer, as though he were trying to cheat the house. Having been confronted in front of several other customers, and rather embarrassed about the whole thing, it seems Mr. Grofer simply pulled out the money and paid the check. It was one of the few times in my life that I was capable of crying.

Trying to console me, my manager explained that in this business, every restaurant has what they called "jinxed customers." It just so happened that my jinxed customer was the head of the only newspaper in Palm Springs.

Not knowing what else to do, I sat down and composed one of the most apologetic letters in my oft-erring life. Even though I wasn't a very religious man myself, I reminded Mr. Grofer that to forgive is divine and that should he ever have the nerve to risk coming into my restaurant again, that I, personally, would be the doormat at the front door for him to walk on. I immediately set up a mental block about his name, and his newspaper, because the mere thought of him gave me cramps.

Approximately a month later, on a Wednesday night, I walked into the restaurant and lo and behold, there was Mr. Grofer with six other men. I tiptoed to the table since the whole situation was outrageous, and decided laughter was the best medicine in this case.

"I can't believe you came in here without a helmet, Mr. Grofer," I said. The comment drew a round of laughter, and a response from Mr. Grofer.

"Mel, I think maybe making the reservation under my name is bad luck, so I made it in someone else's name, and I thought maybe we could get away with it without incident," he said, clearly presenting a logical argument that even I could fully appreciate.

He went on to say that there wasn't a snowball's chance in hell that his wife would come back but that he had enjoyed living dangerously. Totally relieved, I went into my comic routine for his whole party, explaining that Mr. Grofer was my worst "jinxed customer" of all time, even though I had been in business for a very short time. I made myself the butt of every joke and a good time was had by all.

I must have been sitting there for twenty minutes telling my life story, of how I got into such an unlikely situation as the hospitality business, when Mr. Grofer suggested a toast to the new host in town. With that, he stood up to make the toast. At exactly that moment, the waiter was passing by with a tray and clipped Mr. Grofer's head with the tray and four hot entrees spilled onto the table. I am not quite sure whether he was serious or kidding when he picked up the knife and made menacing gestures toward me but I didn't wait to find out. My "fight or flight" instincts kicked in and I took off for the front door, got into my car and went home.

A few months passed and Mr. Grofer was nowhere to be seen. But, during lunch one weekday afternoon, I spotted Mr. Grofer sitting at a table with another gentleman. As much as I wanted to go over and greet him, my feet weren't cooperating. I just stayed put. I hid in the back of the restaurant when my manager said something that made me wince.

"You will not believe what just happened," Alan Mald said.

It seemed as if Mr. Grofer received an important phone call from his wife while he was having lunch. She informed him that her car would not start and was on her way to pick up their son at school. She asked him to drop whatever he was doing and pick up the child. As fate would have it, it was pouring rain that day, which was very unusual for Palm Springs. With that, Mr. Grofer headed to his car and discovered that after the parking lot attendant had opened the door, he had inadvertently hit the automatic lock control for the doors. Mr. Grofer's car had been sitting in the teeming rain, engine running, with all the doors locked. But wait, there's more—at the very moment Mr. Grofer went outside to get into the car, it ran out of gas!

As if that weren't bad enough, his car had been blocking the entrance to the restaurant, which forced the parking attendants to drive other customers' cars over my beautiful lawn in order to get the people out of the rain. I went into crisis mode and immediately offered to drive him to pick up his son but he very wisely declined. Not to be discouraged by his refusal of my help, I insisted he take one of my many cars. He accepted my offer and thanked me, and left.

Fifteen minutes later, my secretary informed me that Mr. Grofer was on the phone. Pleased that he had the courtesy to call and thank me, I picked up the phone and said, "Hello, Ted." In a voice that reeked of murder, he slowly and carefully explained exactly where he was—with a flat tire!

Over time, I had run into the Grofers at many social events, and we have been able to joke about their run of bad luck in my place. They joked that as long as we were on a neutral site, no harm could befall them and that we could remain friends. That was perfectly okay with me, because it was more important that I become their friend than they remain my customers. Mr. Grofer accepted the fact that this did not happen to everybody, and that his jinx only existed at Melvyn's.

At one party we both attended, he broke down and said that both he and his wife thought Melvyn's had the best atmosphere in town, that they absolutely adored my establishment. They wondered if they could celebrate their anniversary without any service catastrophes. I didn't offer them any promises in writing, but I did offer my personal supervision. I also told him that I would pray to the gods for help.

The following Friday night I watched their table carefully and the evening went smoothly, save for one glitch. I had arranged for the "Melvyn's Boys Choir," a group of waiters and busboys who sang on special occasions, to sing "Happy Birthday" to the Grofers on this very special night. Turned out I forgot it was not a birthday but their anniversary.

As they paid their check, they both let out a great sigh of relief, and were grinning from ear to ear as they motioned for me to come over. I stood at their table, feeling as if I had just taken the gold medal in the Olympics.

"I told you we could do it!" I boasted out loud. In my rare display of enthusiasm, while flipping my hand around to make my point more dramatic, you guessed it...I knocked a glass of water in Mrs. Grofer's lap.

By strange coincidence, I had discovered the Grofer's teenage son was my newspaper delivery boy. If they ever read this story, I want them to know I tried to make amends in my own small way. Do you think a $20 tip per week to their son was excessive?

# CHAPTER 8

# Mr. S

There was a Palm Springs saying I heard frequently when I opened Melvyn's: You weren't officially in business until Frank Sinatra visited your establishment.

The crooner's whereabouts was almost a daily topic in the desert. Being in the saloon business, you come into contact with certain people who seem to know everything going on around town. I felt important because I knew when "Mr. S" left for Vegas, when he got back into Palm Springs, or where he dined that night. I had a bartender working for me who was a friend of Frank's valet so I was able to keep tabs on him. Many of my customers had either been to his house or attended parties where he was present. Frank moved about Palm Springs rather easily and frequented almost every place in the desert. Several times during my first month in business, rumor had it that he would be visiting "my store" fairly soon. It hadn't happened, and I started to get the sinking feeling that it never would.

About six months after I opened, Larry Perino, who owned Perino's Restaurant, called to tell me Mr. S and his party had just left his place and was on their way to the Ingleside Inn. Larry's place was about ten blocks away, and that didn't give me much time to prepare for Sinatra's arrival. However, I didn't put too much stock into the phone call because I felt as if I were cursed and that Sinatra would never visit my place. About fifteen minutes later, three cars pulled up to the front of Melvyn's, and Ol' Blue Eyes and an entourage of about ten people walked into Melvyn's to have a nightcap.

I thought I would have a panic attack but calmed down when I realized that I knew three of the people in his group. As they entered the restaurant, I ran to the three familiar faces and greeted them as if they were long lost relatives. At the very least, they would be permanently placed on my Christmas card list for steering Sinatra to my neck of the woods.

I cannot possibly begin to describe the aura of being in Frank Sinatra's presence, but it was palpable to the entire room. Out of all of the celebrities I have ever met, he was the only man I was ever in awe of. You knew immediately that you were dealing with a man of great power and authority.

As private as Frank was, he placed himself at the front end of the bar, making himself quite accessible to everyone. However, Frank gave off a very strong vibe that said, "Look, but don't approach." Customers from the restaurant and bar passed by and glanced at him in wide-eyed wonder, but they didn't dare stop to chat or get an autograph. He and his entourage drank, told stories, and laughed heartily. They stayed for about two hours and then left.

Over the next few months, Mr. S returned at least five times, each time giving me an ulcer. His presence made me nervous as hell. Without thinking, I inevitably ended up in the storage room, the kitchen, the men's room, or any other place that was far away and inaccessible to his party. Which made it all the harder for me to get my picture taken with him.

Yes, I'm one of those people who like to have my picture taken with celebrities and proudly hang the photos on my walls. Usually celebrities don't mind having their pictures taken when it's a request from the owner. However, Sinatra was a different cat. On one occasion, the maitre d' asked Mr. S if he would be kind enough to pose for a picture with my son Lonny. Frank was very curt and even threw in a few expletives to make his point. He told the maitre d' that he didn't take pictures while he was out relaxing. He came to the restaurant as a customer and if he did not want to be disturbed, that was his right.

As one would expect, Frank always came in with a group of very interesting people. And while some members of the group would occasionally change, his girlfriend Barbara Marx was always included. One day, a Sinatra employee confided to me that Barbara and Frank were planning to get married in four weeks at the Annenberg Estate on July 11, 1976, a Sunday afternoon. He impressed upon me how confidential this information was. He didn't have to worry. Betraying a big Frank Sinatra secret was the last thing I would ever consider. Besides, I liked my kneecaps just the way God had made them—in one piece.

The following week Mr. S and his entourage visited Melvyn's, and during the course of the evening I was told that Mr. Sinatra wanted to see me personally. That could either be good or bad, and I didn't even want to ponder the latter scenario. I could not believe the butterflies in my stomach and this time, I couldn't hide in the storage room or kitchen. It was like being summoned by a mob boss—you came when called.

Mr. S was sitting in the back of the lounge by himself waiting for me to join him. I approached him like I was walking the plank. As I sat down, he told me that he wanted to throw a dinner party at Melvyn's on a certain date. Immediately I realized it was the Saturday night preceding his scheduled wedding date and it was going to be, in fact, his and Barbara Marx's pre-wedding dinner. He was meeting with me to make the arrangements. My mind raced at the thought of all the world-famous dignitaries and VIPs who would be there to help him celebrate the occasion. Then reality set in: I had no idea how to set up a party, least of all a fancy soirée like this. I sat there sweating it out, wondering how I was going to bluff my way through this. After a year in business, I still didn't know how to make a drink, cook a steak, or open the cash register. How in the world was I going to help Frank Sinatra, who was known for his fastidiousness, plan his pre-wedding dinner for eighty people at my restaurant?

The first question Frank asked was whether we had black or gray caviar. The way he posed the question, I had a fifty-fifty chance of guessing correctly. Normally I like those odds, but not when Frank Sinatra is pressing you for an answer. Before I could reply, he asked me another question about our wine selection—one I had no chance of answering. Frank grew up on the streets of Hoboken, New Jersey, and I knew his bullshit detector was probably perfectly fine-tuned to the point where he could see right through me. I saw it as the perfect excuse to suggest that I bring my manager into the conversation so he could help us plan the occasion. Frank was amazingly exacting in the details of how he wanted everything to be. He knew how he wanted the food to be cooked, how it should be positioned on the plate, what china pattern to use, and the order in which everything would be served. I could not believe this giant superstar had the ability or inclination to focus on the minutest of details. Then again, that's probably what separates people like him from us mere mortals.

The dinner party was to be held in July, and I asked Mr. S if he wanted me to close the entire restaurant to the public. He said that wouldn't be necessary as long as I could assure him that there would be complete privacy for his party. We had a separate patio, which we could open to the public and still maintain his privacy in the other two dining rooms. We went over all the details one more time and finalized all the arrangements.

Three weeks passed rather quickly, and the night of the big party was at hand. I had fortified myself with several shots of whiskey, primarily because the butterflies in my stomach were awful thirsty. As I waited anxiously by the front door, I saw that the first people to arrive were ambassador Walter Annenberg and his wife, Lenore. I had always hoped I would have the honor of meeting him one day as he was one of the world's great philanthropists. The door opened, and Ambassador and Mrs. Annenberg entered, but before I could open my mouth, the Ambassador extended his hand and said, "Melvyn, I've been looking forward to meeting you. I've read so much about you!" His words could have knocked me over. I've had many years to ponder his simple gesture and kind words. It isn't a person's status or job title that makes someone a great diplomat—it's how he treats people. The Ambassador made a lifelong indelible impression on me with that one thoughtful statement.

Mr. S followed soon thereafter, flanked by his own security to ensure that there would be no intrusions by anyone, especially the tabloid press. The party started around 8 p.m., and a half hour later, three people with cameras slung over their shoulders and looking very suspicious walked up the driveway entrance to the restaurant. The security detail confronted them, and they said they were from the *National Enquirer* and wanted to snap some pictures of the special occasion. I was absolutely shocked that they were so obvious, even more so that they admitted who they were. I wondered how they ever got any inside stories using this approach. But that was their business, and they were obviously successful at what they did. As expected, Frank's security guys promptly escorted them off the property, and not so nicely, I might add.

The patio was jammed with customers from the public, as it always was on a Saturday. In spite of my nerves, the party inside went without a hitch. Everybody seemed happy and in good spirits. Frank had given Barbara a new Rolls Royce, which they had driven to the restaurant.

The party broke up around one o' clock in the morning, and we still had a few customers lingering on the patio. Frank and Barbara were the last to leave with his best friend, Jilly Rizzo. My manager and I walked them out to the car, and they thanked us for a lovely evening as the valet brought up their sparkling new Rolls.

After Frank and Barbara were securely in their car, my manager and I walked back to the restaurant and breathed a huge sigh of relief. We congratulated each other on getting through the night without any major problems. Just then we heard a commotion and turned around to see the Rolls Royce stopped in the middle of the driveway and Frank screaming at two men while Jilly ran toward them. A camera hung around one of the men's necks, which Jilly immediately grabbed. He then opened the camera, took out the roll of film and threw the camera to the ground. With that, Frank told Jilly to handle the matter and drove off. One of the men screamed that Frank deliberately tried to hit him with the car. Jilly returned to the bar, and we tried to figure out exactly what had happened.

Twenty minutes later, Frank was on the phone asking to speak to me. He told me that he had not attempted to hit the two men with the car, but rather that when they jumped out from behind a tree and took the picture, the flash temporarily blinded him and the car veered off to the side toward them. He said if the police were to call about the incident, I was to tell them that was exactly what happened.

But what actually transpired was the following: the *National Enquirer* had sent two very well-dressed couples to have dinner at Melvyn's. They were seated on the patio with the rest of the public. The three people who had shown up earlier were deliberately obvious so that they could be tossed out and everybody would feel safe and secure. Essentially they were decoys. The two couples who dined on the patio waited the entire evening until Frank and Barbara were about to leave. Then the men positioned themselves behind a large tree that the Sinatras would have to pass to leave the premises. When the Rolls approached them, the men jumped out from behind the tree and took the picture through the car window from a special camera that one of the men kept inside his jacket pocket. The camera around the neck was a phony, because they knew that most likely one of Sinatra's security guys would rip the film out, which is exactly what Jilly did. The camera with the actual picture was hidden back in his jacket pocket. The picture of Frank and Barbara in the car appeared in the following week's edition of the *National Enquirer* along with a not-so-flattering story calling the encounter a "senseless brawl" and reporting that Sinatra acted like a "wild animal."

I guess I underestimated those guys—they really are good at getting the story. Now that the *National Enquirer* had its picture, it was time for me to get mine.

In the years after the pre-wedding dinner, the Sinatras occasionally visited Melvyn's. I had befriended an insurance broker by the name of Fred Wilson, who knew former president Gerald Ford and his wife Betty quite well. He was hosting a party in honor of their thirty-second wedding anniversary, to which I was invited. No rented tux for this occasion—I actually went out and bought one. Even better, a show business agent had arranged for actress Angie

Dickinson to be my date for the evening. Boy was I traveling in the right circles!

A week before the party, Angie was called for a job assignment and had to report to work on location. She was as classy as she was beautiful, and phoned to cancel our date. She did, however, offer me a rain check.

I had just met a beautiful lady at my club, who is now my wife, Stephanie. She was a schoolteacher from a very good family, and I casually asked her if she wanted to be my date for this party. It was an elegant black-tie affair that promised to be star-studded.

I must admit, I was going to this elaborate affair with a certain amount of trepidation. Not only was it a party for the former president of the United States, but every celebrity in Palm Springs would be there, including Frank Sinatra, Lucille Ball, Pearl Bailey, Tony Orlando, and Marvin Davis.

It was indeed an affair to remember. The cocktail reception took place in a large tent on the Wilsons' property, and as soon as I stepped foot in the tent, I was greeted by Palm Springs photographer Paul Popeil. By this time, I knew every photographer in the area, and all of them knew I salivated at the thought of having my picture taken with Frank Sinatra. But based on the one experience with my son, I never could work up the nerve to ask Frank to pose with me. Paul walked up to me and said discreetly, "Mel, tonight's the night you're going to get your picture taken with Frank Sinatra. Just position yourself next to him and I guarantee you a picture." I was torn between acting cool with my new date and getting a picture with Mr. S. But there really was no choice—I opted for the picture.

Mr. S just arrived as I walked past the front door.

"Hi, Mel," Frank greeted me. I suddenly went into a trance and became obsessed with the idea of getting my picture taken with him.

I walked Stephanie over to the buffet table and told her to remain there until I took care of an important business matter. She made herself at home and grabbed a few shrimp and a drink. I located Frank and sashayed right next to him. The photographer gave me the thumbs-up, and as he swooped in to take the picture, Mr.

S turned around to greet somebody. Every time I positioned myself next to him for the photographer to snap a picture, Frank turned to chat with somebody. If Sinatra would have stopped short, I would have broken my nose. This nonsense went on for thirty minutes. Stephanie must have eaten about a hundred shrimp by that point. Frank had engaged himself in a conversation with a gentleman and seemed as if he was going to stay there for a while. The photographer signaled to me where I should stand and as he counted to three with his fingers, I popped up in between them and he snapped the picture. Both Sinatra and the man he was speaking to looked at me like I was crazy, but they had no idea what was going on.

About a week later I received the picture, and it was better than I had imagined. If every picture tells a story, then this one told a big fib. It appears as if I'm holding a very serious conversation with Mr. S and this gentleman, making me appear more important than I really am. Today the picture hangs proudly in the lounge of Melvyn's.

After about an hour of this nonsense, the party moved to the backyard for dinner where the host had set up a tent with tables. As Stephanie entered the tent, she suddenly went ashen.

"Oh my God, look who's over there," she remarked. I assumed she meant one of the celebrities in attendance. But she had pointed to a trio of violinists, one of whom it turned out was her dear old dad. She had no idea he would be playing at the party, and he of course, had no idea she would be there, either.

The seating arrangement was three rows in a semicircle in order of importance. We, of course, were seated in the back row, and the most important VIPs were proudly on display in the front row. Naturally, Stephanie's father directed the trio to spend a lot of time serenading our table. It got to the point where it started to bug one guest in particular. The host, Fred Wilson, came over and discreetly mentioned that Sinatra had complained as to why "Melvyn" was getting all the attention from the violinists. I shrugged my shoulders and tried to brush it off. I never let on that one of the violinists was Stephanie's father. I figured in this crowd, I needed all the cachet I could get.

There are two interesting postscripts to my association with Sinatra.

One: For many years I have been the president of a local charity called the Angel View Crippled Children's Foundation. As such I met annually with one of the trustees of the Bob Hope Golf Tournament regarding a grant for my charity. As the trustee and I sat down to have lunch at my restaurant one day, he casually mentioned that he kept a picture of me in his office. I was flabbergasted.

"Why would you have a picture of me in your office?" I asked.

"Well, you should remember," he replied. "You, Frank Sinatra, and I were having a conversation at the party for Gerald and Betty Ford."

It dawned on me that even he was convinced that I belonged in the picture and that I was actually a part of the discussion. I figured it was more interesting to go with the legend rather than the truth and didn't bother to set the record straight.

Two: In the mid-eighties, I was contacted by author Kitty Kelley, who told me she wanted to meet with me regarding a biography she was writing about Frank Sinatra. I was really quite flattered that somebody of her stature thought I was that close to Mr. S and could recount any stories of significance. Miss Kelley (who has become world-famous for her stinging biographies of former First Lady Nancy Reagan, and Lady Diana and the Royal Family) and I met and chatted for quite a while. As I told her about events I recalled from my limited contact with the Sinatras, I was totally unaware of the type of book she intended to write and it turned out to be a stinging tell-all. I just assumed she was gathering anecdotes from locals about Mr. S. Needless to say, there was really nothing of interest or particularly juicy that I knew or could tell about the Sinatras. Much to my surprise, when the book came out in 1986, my cooperation was acknowledged, along with many other names in the book.

I'm just glad she didn't ask me anything about Nancy Reagan!

Soon enough, I would have another memorable guest waltz into the Ingleside Inn, and he was an entire book unto himself.

# CHAPTER 9

# A Royal Pain

While the patronage of the Palm Springs well-to-do and Hollywood elite restored the Ingleside Inn to its former glory, it was a member of English royalty that really put my establishment on the world map.

I had heard about this wealthy titled Englishman, who had just checked into a local Palm Springs hotel. Palm Springs was a much smaller community back then, and the rumor mill was very fast and effective. Somebody had mentioned to me that this Englishman was quite unhappy with his accommodations and was considering checking into the Ingleside Inn. Though he had only been in town for a few days, his reputation preceded him. He owned two rare old Rolls Royces, had a valet who waited on him hand and foot, and was supposed to be quite a colorful person. In time, I would find that to be a major understatement.

It was about ten o' clock in the morning when two gentlemen entered the lobby of the hotel. One stood about 6-foot-1, weighed around 200 pounds, had a mane of beautiful white hair, and appeared to be about seventy years old. Accompanying him was a short, stocky bald-headed man approximately the same age. The shorter man immediately reminded me of a World War II Nazi general; the only thing missing was the monocle and an armband with a swastika. They were both well dressed, but they made a very odd pairing. The taller of the two approached the desk, announced loudly in a very proper British accent, "My name is *Suh* John and I wish to see the *ownuh!*"

Overhearing this very regal voice in my office, I approached the two with outstretched hand and introduced myself. John introduced himself and then his cohort, Colonel Russell Hopf. This member of royalty said that he wished to rent my very best *villah* for approximately one year. At that point I hadn't rented this $160-a-day villa for one day. In today's dollars, that would be equivalent to about $500 a night. He explained that he was presently at another hotel and was leaving because they had the audacity to charge him for a plate of cheese and crackers. He felt that this should have been complimentary in view of the money he was spending there. I quickly summoned all my charm and manners in order to handle my first experience with "real nobility."

I immediately showed the two men the suite. Sir John said it would be fine with certain minor improvements. In a flash, Sir John whipped out twenty crisp $100 bills and requested that I credit his account $2,000. He then inquired if we could properly care for his two vintage Rolls Royces, feed his *drivuh*, and cater to the whims and demands made by royalty.

For that kind of money, I would have looked after his mother-in-law, cared for his children, and walked his dog. After assuring him that the entire staff was at his disposal, we returned to the registration desk. He signed in as Sir John Beech from London, England, informing me that he had been personally knighted by Queen Elizabeth. He casually mentioned that he would be doing his usual jet-setting around the world, but when his room was vacant, we should keep tabs on it for him. He said that he would gladly pay for the room when he was not there. Sounded like a pretty good deal to me.

Just at that moment, the bell captain informed me that the hotel limousine had just broken down. Overhearing the conversation, Sir John made a magnanimous offer that almost floored me.

"As long as I will be staying here, feel free to use my Rolls Royces for the convenience of your guests," Sir John said casually, as if it were nothing. At that very moment, I thanked my lucky stars for sending Sir John to me. After seeing to it that Sir John was moved from his former hotel, which was about ten blocks away, I immediately summoned my entire staff from the hotel and restaurant. I informed them that we had visiting royalty from across the pond and that he was to be accorded every courtesy and convenience humanly possible. That meant he was not going to get charged for cheese and crackers!

That evening I arrived at the restaurant at my usual time —7:30 p.m. I quickly scanned the dining room, looking for a familiar face. I spotted Sir John wearing a white dinner jacket with a black velvet bow tie. He was accompanied by Colonel Russ Hopf and a woman I judged to be about fifty years old. I must say that Sir John was a striking man because of his size and that flowing head of white hair. Add to the mix his distinct British accent, put him in a white dinner jacket in an elegant dining room, and you have a very dramatic atmosphere, to say the least. Central casting in Hollywood could not have done better. He looked like he belonged there.

As I approached Sir John and his company to say hello, I noticed a bottle of iced Dom Perignon nestled comfortably near the table. Sir John cordially shook my hand and introduced me to Irene, his personal secretary of twenty years. Sir John also extended an invitation for me to have a glass of champagne with them. I just happened to catch him in the middle of recounting his World War II experiences, in which he played an important part in the Central Intelligence Agency and had subsequently been decorated. (I eventually learned that during WWII, there was no CIA. The Office of Strategic Services served in that capacity.) I sat through the entire meal with them, where he regaled us of tales of the war, his Arabian horses, his turquoise mines in Arizona, his current acrimonious divorce, and his retreat to the desert. Everybody in the restaurant noticed Sir John because he spoke with such a loud and distinctive voice, and I felt honored to be sitting with a man of such accomplishment.

The next three days passed uneventfully with my illustrious guest despite the fact that he took all of his meals in the restaurant and never failed to make his presence known. He was hard to miss because he was usually accompanied by his dutiful secretary, Irene, and the distinguished Colonel Hopf. The third night he was there we were having a drink at the bar when Frank Sinatra walked in with his troops. Sir John bolted upright and immediately went up to Frank, shook his hand, and reminded him that they had once met at one of Frank's Royal Command Performances for the Queen of England. Frank acknowledged him, was unfailingly courteous, and proceeded with his party to the lounge area. Sir John then recounted for all of us all the brilliant details of that night, emphasizing the fact that whenever he was in England, the Queen invited him to all the Royal Command Performances.

In the few days that Sir John had been at the Ingleside Inn, he managed to make sure that everyone on the premises, both employees and customers, were aware of his story and his place in the world. His words and actions also drew a few raised eyebrows. Several times a day people would call me aside and ask, "Mel, is Sir John for real?"

I really couldn't answer that question based on my limited experience. The $2,000 cash he gave me upon check in was *real* green. It also felt *real* good when it was deposited into my bank account. And his two Rolls Royces looked *real* expensive to me. So yes, he was *real* as long as he paid his hotel bill on time.

During the first ten days, Sir John firmly established himself in town as visiting royalty and word spread quickly that the Ingleside Inn was playing host to this monarch. It didn't take long for Sir John to get acquainted with everybody. He even requested a hundred sets of hotel stationery so that he could inform all of his rich and famous friends that the Ingleside Inn was the only place for them to stay. I happily complied with his request.

Sensing that I was new to the business with no following, Sir John took a personal interest in my financial well-being and assured me that he would turn the Ingleside Inn into what I always dreamed it could be. Nobody could have been a better goodwill ambassador than Sir John. Wherever he went—shops, parties, gala events—he announced that he was permanently residing at the Ingleside Inn. If I could have afforded his price, I would have put him on salary as my public relations representative. Sir John, being the dashing and flamboyant character he was, completely took Palm Springs by storm and was invited to almost every social event in town.

Arriving to work one morning around six o'clock, I found Sir John swimming in the hotel pool. He informed me that by swimming every day he was able to maintain a body that belied his seventy-two years. The guy impressed me more by the minute. That morning I found a note on my desk to call Colonel Hopf. When I had a free moment, I called the colonel, who answered the phone, and in a rather apprehensive tone I might add. Hopf asked if I might be able to take a few minutes out of my busy schedule to have coffee with him. After assuring him that I was never too busy for him (any friend of a $160-a-day guest was a friend of mine), we arranged to meet at 10 a.m. at a local coffee shop outside the Ingleside Inn.

Obviously, my curiosity was piqued. At the appointed time, Colonel Hopf came striding into Sandy's coffee shop in full military regalia. After exchanging pleasantries, he bluntly asked, "Mel, do you think Sir John is for real?" There was the million dollar question again. Automatically, I reviewed in my mind my impressions and doubts about Sir John, and the fact that all my doubts were allayed because of the constant company of Colonel Hopf, whom I knew to be real because of his associations with various people around town over many years. His question of Sir John's credibility shook me to the core. It took about two minutes for me to regain my composure.

"That's a very strange question coming from you, Colonel," I said, treading lightly. It didn't take long for him to reply.

"Mel, if I wasn't at the point of total frustration, I wouldn't be here right now," he said. "Let me tell you what I know about Sir John."

The colonel went on to say that about three weeks previously somebody had told him about a titled Englishman who had arrived in Palm Springs and was looking to purchase a couple of Rolls Royces.

Colonel Hopf said he had two Rolls for sale and met with Sir John, who was living in a magnificent suite at the time at the other hotel. The Englishman looked at the cars, negotiated an $80,000 price and asked the colonel if he could drive the cars until he received the funds from overseas. Almost every day Sir John gave Colonel Hopf a different excuse about the funds. He also threw in the fact that he was going through a nasty divorce, which made his financial matters a bit complicated. The colonel said he was starting to have serious doubts about the entire situation and needed to blow off a little steam.

Despite the warning shot from Colonel Hopf, I found Sir John even more intriguing. However, I assured the colonel that I would now view Sir John from a totally different perspective.

When I got back to the hotel, I relayed the information to my general manager. He told me that since Sir John paid his money up front, our exposure to him was limited, and that we would just have to keep tabs on him.

Almost ten days had passed, and Sir John owed me approximately $2,500, which we requested, and he promptly paid. He informed us that he would be out of town for a few days, and that we should keep his villa intact.

When he got back, Sir John reappeared with a brand-new Mercedes 450 SL and a very polite young man whom he introduced as Tony, his new driver. He wanted to know if this young man would be able to take his meals with my staff. I assured him that he would be treated as one of our own. Sir John suggested that we have a cup of coffee together so he could fill me in on the details of his exciting trip.

We were seated in the corner of the dining room, and he told me that the main purpose of his trip was to receive an award for his Arabian horses and that I should come to his villa and see the beautiful crown that was bestowed upon him. He also explained that he was finally making progress on his messy divorce and was celebrating at Melvyn's for dinner.

Later that evening, Sir John strolled into the lounge, beautifully attired in an elegant white dinner jacket with a black velvet bow tie, making his usual grand entrance. He was carrying several gift-wrapped boxes and started passing them out like candy. He gave one to my manager, one to my son, and one to me, saying that he found a great men's shop in town that afternoon. Sir John had loved the merchandise and had indulged himself with a spending spree. He had purchased $3,000 worth of clothing on his good name. When Barbra appeared, he presented her with a gold goblet and dubbed her "Lady Barbra." His stock instantly rose in my book, and his benevolence was overwhelming.

After dinner we all went back to the lounge to listen to the night's entertainment. Sir John was seated in his regular seat, which had become known to employees as "The Throne." It didn't take long for people to gather around him because he was so charismatic. As fate would have it, a socially prominent couple from Newport Beach sat nearby and was absolutely thrilled over the experience of meeting Sir John. They struck up a fast friendship with our visiting royalty and promptly invited Sir John, Lady Barbra, my singer, and me to their daughter's wedding in two weeks. They would send a private jet to pick us up and assured us that the wedding would be the social event of the year. The entire evening was fascinating to behold, as people presented themselves to Sir John as if he were the Pope. Two weeks later, the Newport Beach paper ran an article on the wedding, but focused on that fact that visiting royalty was in attendance and paid little attention to the bride and groom.

The following morning I was summoned to the courtyard area of the hotel to witness the local pet store stocking the pond in my courtyard with the most magnificent fish I have ever seen in my life. Sir John was supervising to ensure that everything was perfect. It was the most breathtaking array of exotic fish I had ever seen in one place. I didn't know what to say and was rendered speechless. I was so full of gratitude that I wanted to plant a big one on Sir John's lips. I found out that Sir John had also purchased a 100-gallon aquarium from the pet store and had it installed in the living room of his suite. He had invited me to take a look, which I did out of curiosity more than anything else.

As I approached the villa, I was stunned to see seven different bird cages hanging in the front patio with various types of colorful birds. As I walked inside, I was overwhelmed at how beautiful the aquarium looked in the living room. I had not been to Sir John's villa since he moved in out of respect for his privacy, but in a matter of weeks he had literally transformed my peaceful hotel into the unofficial Palm Springs Zoo.

What really surprised me was that as I looked around the room I saw many pieces of antique furniture and artifacts that had been missing from around the hotel and were now in his villa. I was quite upset that he took these items without asking, but I figured the blessing of Sir John's presence far outweighed such trivial matters. He then took me into the bedroom and showed me a magnificent crown, which sat atop a red velvet pillow. The crown was supposedly the award for his champion Arabian horses. Scattered carelessly over the dresser, I noticed several large pieces of turquoise jewelry that Sir John informed me came from his turquoise mines in Arizona. Interestingly enough, I never saw him wear the same piece twice. Sir John excused himself and said that he had a luncheon date with someone in the restaurant and had to get ready.

Around one o' clock, as I was strolling about the dining room, I noticed Sir John sitting with a nice-looking lady. He motioned me over and introduced me to "Miss Jorgensen." She had a very deep, resonant voice that belied her soft looks. Sir John was quick to point out that she was Christine Jorgensen, who had received worldwide publicity as the first human being ever to have a sex-change operation. The company that man kept! There was no end to his surprises.

One day, we couldn't find the gardener, a full-time employee. I searched high and low for him until the bellman pointed out that he was in Sir John's villa. The gardener was a holdover from the sixties, a "hippie" with long hair and a very casual attitude about life. It turned out that he and Sir John were passing the "peace pipe" back and forth, and were getting stoned out of their gourds.

That evening in the lounge, Sir John was on a natural high. He entered Melvyn's in a red velvet robe and a crown on his head. I thought I was seeing things and did a double take. Everyone in the lounge turned around and stared, then spontaneously broke out in a loud, cheering applause. Sir John explained that every once in a while he liked to flex his royal muscles by donning the robe and crown.

The following day, word had spread around Palm Springs about Sir John's exploits, and I noticed we had several gawkers visit the Ingleside Inn just to get a glimpse of his "highness." The local newspaper devoted the entire second page of its edition to Sir John with a glorious article entitled, "Royalty Invades the Desert." He most certainly did. Sir John became the most sought-after guest in the city, and no party was complete without his royal presence. I have never been much of a partygoer, but Sir John was at the few I did attend in all his glory as the guest of honor. Naturally, he was always the center of attention. But I couldn't say I minded too much. He was a walking billboard for the Ingleside Inn, telling everyone within earshot where he was staying. Our relationship was really a two-way street—he added prestige to my establishment, and I gave Sir John credibility. Anyone who could afford to stay at my best villa on an indefinite basis certainly had to be substantial. Not only was he substantial—he knew how to get things done.

I had commissioned a couple of custom dune buggies to be built for me, and I was having a problem getting them registered with the Department of Motor Vehicles. Sir John said he was about to visit the governor of New Mexico and suggested that I jot down the serial numbers of the engines and he would "handle it." The governor, whom he insisted was a personal friend, would have them registered in New Mexico. He said then it would be easy to transfer the New Mexico registrations to California and all of my problems would be solved. I had nothing to lose, so I gave him the serial numbers on a piece of paper. Lo and behold, Sir John returned about a week later and brought back with him three New Mexico registrations and three sets of license plates. The guy was truly amazing.

I wondered about Sir John, but I always came to the same conclusion. Whatever game or scam he was running, I didn't see any harm in it as long as no one got hurt or burned. I was reasonably sure by now that he was a fake, but nonetheless, his bill was fairly current, and to my knowledge had not asked anyone for anything.

And with respect to me, he certainly gave more than he received. Besides, I had some of his collateral if he ever thought of pulling any funny business.

Sir John mentioned that he had produced several movies in Hollywood, and at one point asked me to store some very valuable film equipment in the hotel safe. I figured if he ever took off, I could sell the equipment for a nice chunk of change to offset any damages.

But then I got a little greedy. I had an inventory of about 3,000 elaborate belt buckles that I had manufactured in one of my previous businesses. The belt buckles sat in the basement, and for some reason I had opened my big mouth to Sir John, who graciously offered to unload them for me at $1.50 apiece. Hey, a member of royalty who knew how to wheel and deal with the best of them—he was beyond belief.

Sir John had mentioned to me that he was planning another trip to New Mexico and needed the camera equipment. That set off a red flag and I immediately went to check on his hotel bill. It showed he had an outstanding balance of $4,200. He was going to take the only security I had, plus the belt buckles. I had an ominous feeling this was the end. It was time to confront Sir John, but I didn't know how. He even approached me and asked me to take care of his two Rolls Royces while he was gone. Now I was really stuck because I knew the cars were not his.

About then I received a phone call from a local singer whom I had met and befriended in the restaurant. She called to invite Sir John and me to the opening of a new nightclub in Los Angeles. It was impossible for me to attend as it was going to be a very busy night in the restaurant, but I conveyed the message to Sir John, who was absolutely delighted. He begged me to go, but I excused myself on the pretext of business. He then lined up several other people whom he had befriended, and they planned to tear up the town.

His entourage left for Los Angeles in a limousine around five o'clock on the night of the grand opening. A couple of hours later, the Palm Springs police rolled up and walked into Melvyn's with an arrest warrant for Sir John. When I questioned them about the matter, I was told it was over a bad check charge from Michigan. I explained to them that Sir John was in Los Angeles for the night and would return the following morning. The police said they would wait in case he came back sooner. Their presence at the restaurant and word about the arrest warrant had spread through Palm Springs like wildfire.

Two hours later, Sir John called, saying that he had heard the Palm Springs police were looking for him. He asked me what they wanted. I told him about the bad check and he replied there must have been some mistake. Sir John then asked if I could find out more information for him and that he would call back in an hour. When I relayed our conversation to the police, they had advised me to keep him on the phone so that when he rang back they could trace the call. In the meantime, they staked out his villa.

The police immediately questioned his driver, Tony, who confessed that only a week before he arrived, he was hitchhiking along the freeway and Sir John picked him up and offered him a job. Tony figured he had it pretty good and was told to keep his mouth shut and play the role of driver/valet. The police kept him in the villa so that he'd have no contact with Sir John.

Sir John called me back several times during the evening, pumping me for more information. However, I was vague and told him the police were stonewalling me. I just wanted him to return safely so that I could collect on the $4,200 he owed me and get my belt buckles back. Needless to say, he wasn't enthused to make a return trip.

When I began to fret over the lost income, the police informed me about the Innkeepers Protection Law, which basically gives innkeepers the right to impound any possessions of a guest until the bill is settled. They carefully pointed out that everything in Sir John's villa belonged to me until I got paid. Did I mention that I love the law?

When I arrived at work around seven o'clock the next morning, one of the bellmen ran up to me and said, "One of the policemen is removing something from Sir John's villa." I rushed down there and found the detective who had spent the entire night in the villa, removing the aquarium. I called him over and said nothing could be removed until I was paid. The detective acted embarrassed and asked to speak with me privately.

"I don't know how to tell you this, Mr. Haber, but I own the pet store where Sir John purchased this aquarium," he said. "Only he didn't pay for it; we extended him credit." The detective went on to say that he also extended credit to Sir John for all the exotic fish in my pond, but had never been paid. He was taking back the aquarium to recoup some of his loss. He was totally embarrassed by the situation. What could I say? Sir John was so believable that he had duped the detective along with everyone else in town.

While moving Sir John's belongings to my safe, we discovered about twenty pairs of new shoes, approximately fifty new garments, oodles of fine jewelry, several velvet robes, and all sorts of oddities.

Sir John called me the next day for more information, and I didn't give him much. He also asked that I please take care of all of his possessions, to which I replied they were in "very safe keeping" (everything was in the hotel safe). But as the situation unfolded, I began slowly giving those things back—not to Sir John, but to their rightful owners.

Sir John's loyal secretary of twenty years, Irene, was the first to approach me. We talked in the restaurant, where Irene came clean and admitted that she had only worked for Sir John two weeks before he came to the Ingleside Inn. He had pulled his act on her and managed to finagle $20,000 in cash from her for an investment as well as all of her jewelry, which I now had in my possession. She told me it was the only assets she had left. She knew the $20,000 was history but asked me to please give back her jewelry because she was virtually penniless. With the police's blessing and a letter from Irene's lawyer, I allowed her to go through several jewelry cases and pick out four pieces that belonged to her.

The next phone call I received was from a local singer I knew. She said she had to talk to me, and I invited her over for a cup of coffee. Her singing act was modeled after Sophie Tucker, and she had spent her entire life savings to buy two velvet robes that belonged to the famous songbird. She had used the robes in her act—until Sir

John managed to con her into lending them to him. She understood I had the legal right to keep them in my possession until I was paid, but they were rightfully hers, and had a lot of sentimental as well as monetary value. Would I please be kind enough to return them to her? There was no way I could deny this impassioned plea, so I dug them out of the safe and gave them to her.

No one was off-limits to Sir John, who had even made the rounds to my staff. A little seventy-year-old cashier working in the kitchen came to me with tears in her eyes and explained that she had given Sir John three valuable diamond rings she owned to be appraised by him. Sir John was going to tell her the value of the diamonds, but never actually got around to returning them to her. She asked if I had noticed them among his belongings. When I told her I had, she begged me to give them back as they were all she had in the world. Needless to say, I returned the three rings to the little lady. While my conscience felt good, it didn't do much for my bank account.

My reputation as a soft touch must have been broadcast on local television because suddenly I started receiving phone calls from people all over town. There was one common refrain—they were all owed money by Sir John. At that point my generosity had reached its end, and I arranged with the Palm Springs police to field all of the calls.

Three days had passed since the police had come looking for Sir John, and there was not a peep from our visiting royalty. Early in the morning of the fourth day, I called one of the people who had driven to Beverly Hills with Sir John. As soon as the voice on the other end of the phone answered, I knew at once it was Sir John. I asked for Steve, pretending that I had not recognized Sir John's voice, but he immediately recognized mine. He tried to disguise his voice, but it didn't work. I knew it was him. I left a message to have Steve call me when he returned. He was polite and said he would relay the message as soon as Steve came home. I instantly rang the detective in charge of the case and told them where Sir John could be located. Lieutenant Frank Colombo would have been proud.

Two hours later, the word was all over town that Sir John had been whisked away by Palm Springs police, and that he had a long and distinguished criminal career. Alas, it turned out that Sir John was to royalty what Cap'n Crunch is to Her Majesty's Navy. The blustery con artist was a house painter from Detroit who had fifteen different aliases and an arrest record stretching back forty years. He was wanted in several states for grand larceny, forgery, and issuing worthless checks.

When Sir John was arrested, he suffered a mild heart attack and was taken to the local hospital. Practically half the town visited him in his room to pay their respects, even those people that he had ripped off for a considerable sum of money.

Two months later, a local attorney was hired on behalf of Sir John, or whatever his name was, to pay his $4,200 hotel bill and retrieve his possessions. I got paid in full, and then some; you see, the story of Sir John's visit garnered the Ingleside Inn a million dollars' worth of publicity as it made the major news wire services and several tabloids around the world.

Three decades after his stay, and despite the fact he did some despicable things, I must say in all sincerity that I and everyone else who came into contact with Sir John only have fond memories of him. It didn't really matter whether this man was genuine or not—he was the most colorful and flamboyant character I have or ever will meet in my life.

Call me crazy, but I'll take a hundred more guests just like him.

# CHAPTER 10

# All That Glitters

It wasn't long after Sir John's departure that real royalty, diplomats, presidents, ambassadors, and dignitaries became hip to the elegant new resort and restaurant in the desert. Word of the Ingleside Inn's white-glove treatment of VIP guests had spread across the globe.

The Inn became a magnet for countless celebrities and luminaries because they could let their hair down, secure in the unspoken house rule that every guest and patron was entitled to his/her privacy. They loved the little touches I gave the place, which included a complimentary continental breakfast, a basket of fruit with champagne to welcome them, matchbooks inscribed with their name, a refrigerator stocked with free snacks and fruit, a card inviting them to the lounge for complimentary cocktails, a steam bath in every room, and a fleet of Rolls Royces to drive them around town.

I had our waiters bring them after-dinner drinks with my card, making the patrons feel important because the owner just bought them a drink. Now, some might say I might have killed my drink sales, but that wasn't the case at all—customers usually bought another round. I also came up with the idea of taking a picture of guests for special occasions (a birthday or anniversary) and putting it in a folder made for Polaroid pictures that said, "A Moment to Remember at Melvyn's." Every little touch that I could think of to make our customers feel special, I incorporated in the operation. I even had strolling violinists at night.

I eventually discovered that celebrities beget celebrities, and they like to hang out together. For whatever reason, the Ingleside Inn and Melvyn's became a playground for the rich and famous.

Over the years, the Inn has become a second home for Hollywood's elite and countless celebrities in Palm Springs. That included Frank Sinatra, Bob Hope, Marlon Brando, Liberace, Arnold Schwarzenegger, Goldie Hawn, Sylvester Stallone, John Travolta, Donald Trump, Liza Minnelli, President Gerald Ford, and George Hamilton, not to mention hundreds of other celebrities.

Ed McMahon, Johnny Carson's famous sidekick and TV personality, loved the Ingleside Inn. One day in 1975, he checked in for a weekend stay. He made it a point to seek me out and complimented me on all the little personal touches. He was especially impressed by his name on the matchbooks. He told me that he had been around the world, and he had never seen it anywhere. I thanked him profusely for his kind words. Several hours later he called to compliment me once more.

"Mel, I gotta tell you—you really are a class act," Mr. McMahon told me. "You've really outdone yourself now. We just ordered room service, and I really can't believe it."

I had no idea what on earth he was talking about, but was determined to act as if I knew. I asked one of my staff to see if they could discreetly find out what lit Ed's fire.

It turned out that Ed ordered two cocktails, which the staff served on a napkin with a big "M" on the front. Ed thought the "M" on the napkin was for McMahon, and I didn't have the heart to tell him it was for Melvyn's. I immediately had all the "M" napkins removed from the restaurant and substituted plain napkins for the rest of his stay. I felt there was no need to break whatever grand illusions he had of me or my place.

Not surprisingly, the glitterati flocked to the Inn, as did the paparazzi and tabloid reporters who have jockeyed ever since to get a glimpse beyond the velvet rope.

The first bit of national media we received ran in the travel section of the *Los Angeles Times*, where the Ingleside Inn was featured on the upper fold of the front page. Much to my good fortune, the travel section was used to wrap the Sunday paper that week, and the first thing millions of readers saw was my picture. Other major articles followed in the *New York Times*, *Detroit News*, and *Business Week*, as well as the Associated Press wire service and in many other publications.

The *National Enquirer* started calling me weekly, asking me for innocuous tidbits. They made a deal with me that if I fed them the names of the celebrities and their comings and goings, they'd make sure to say they were spotted at the Ingleside Inn or Melvyn's. In addition to that, they'd throw in $100 per item. It was easy money, and sometimes I didn't have to say a thing.

Gossip columnist and Palm Springs resident Rhona Barrett came in to Melvyn's frequently to retrieve her tips firsthand and became one of our best customers ever. Our relationship was a match made in heaven, until one night she didn't get seated as quickly as she would have liked. She huffed out of the restaurant, and I never saw her again.

One day a tabloid reporter called and asked what I knew about a serious fight between Frank and Barbara Sinatra. I told them I knew nothing about it, nor had I heard such an incident took place. The next thing I knew, there were two reporters from the tabloid at the front desk of my hotel. They asked where I might find the Sinatras. With total authority, acting as if I knew, I happened to mention the name of another local restaurant where they went on occasion. As fate would have it, the Sinatras were having dinner at the very establishment I named, and the reporters were thrilled. It was purely a guess. The following week I received a check from the *National Enquirer* for $200 with the stub marked "Sinatra story."

I got even more for doing less where it concerned Elizabeth Taylor. The actress had checked into the Betty Ford Clinic for the first time and sure enough, a reporter from the *Enquirer* asked what I knew. I said I knew absolutely nothing about it. He didn't believe me and tried to cajole me into telling him what I really knew. I repeated that I had no idea what he was talking about and he finally hung up. The next week I received a check from the tabloid for $250 and the stub was marked "Elizabeth Taylor story." I couldn't imagine what I would have gotten if I had actually known something.

But I usually complied, offering up a tidbit, though I'd embellish it to the point where the stories were so outrageous that no one could get mad at me. For example, I told them that one day Clint Eastwood and former president Gerald Ford bumped into each other in the restaurant. I said that Clint pretended he pulled a fake gun with his index finger and thumb on Ford and said, "Go ahead, make my day." Or that John Travolta took a break from filming *Saturday Night Fever* and flew in on a private plane to Palm Springs to see his buddy, Mel Haber. I'd then send them a picture to give the story a little veracity. Of course, Travolta was a guest, not really my buddy, but that was beside the point—they had their story and a picture, and I got some nice publicity in return. I just used my experience in the automotive novelty business to "merchandise" the hottest saloon in the desert.

In time I developed relationships with some of the most important columnists throughout the country: Herb Caen in San Francisco, Earl Wilson in New York, and Irv Kupcinet in Chicago, Jerry Hulse in Los Angeles, March Schwartz in Beverly Hills, and Richard Selzer, a syndicated columnist for several newspapers. Selzer was also known as "Mr. Blackwell," a fashion critic who became well known for his annual Worst Dressed List. He became a very dear friend and partner in crime.

I first met Blackwell at the Beverly Wilshire Hotel at a launch party for Crown Ruisse vodka. The dress code was white tie and tails for the men and ball gowns for the women and many celebrities and VIPs showed up for the event. The liquor company spared no expense in throwing a Russian Ball. They had imitation snow falling, Cossack dancers, and booze flowing freely. I was invited to appear on Mr. Blackwell's radio show at noon the following day. The only thing I knew about him was his famous "Worst Dressed List," which made international news every year.

His show was broadcast from the lobby of the Arco Plaza; a major office building in downtown Los Angeles. Blackwell was very kind in his introduction of me on the air, and described in vivid detail the previous evening's elegant affair. Then he threw me a major curve ball.

"Melvyn, did you see that fat pig who never stopped shoveling food in her mouth?" Blackwell asked. I was stupefied. I had no idea who he was talking about and I didn't know how to answer him. There was nothing but dead air. Finally he spoke.

"I'm talking about Shelley Winters," Blackwell said. In hindsight, I guess you could say he was the first "shock jock."

One year Blackwell was invited by the Palm Springs International Film Festival as a celebrity guest. Knowing that the paparazzi would be out in full swing, he wanted to make a big splash. Blackwell told me about the invitation and asked to borrow one of my Rolls Royces. I not only offered him my luxury automobile, but I volunteered to be his chauffeur for the night. I even rented an official chauffeur's uniform and bought black boots, a black hat, and a white shirt. The night of the big event I drove Blackwell to the entrance of the Palm Springs Convention Center. When I stopped in front of the center, I jumped out to open the door for him. Flashbulbs went off, and Blackwell received thunderous applause from the hometown crowd and the paparazzi. That memory always produces a smile. Blackwell has become a friend and a big supporter of mine over the past thirty years.

I was glad to help someone get a little of the spotlight. Lord knows I was getting my share of the glare. A clerk at the front desk informed me that a lady from *60 Minutes* was in the lobby and wanted to meet me. She introduced herself as Susan St. Pierre and that she was a producer for Morley Safer. Palm Springs was very much in the national news because President Gerald Ford had just moved here. Ms. St. Pierre said they were doing a segment on Palm Springs and would like to interview me for the piece. I was overwhelmed by the idea that I was going to appear on the number one TV show in the country. I immediately called my best friend, Bo, in New York, and said, "I think I just discovered the cure for cancer." For all they knew, I could be going broke, but because I had the hot restaurant in town they were putting me on *60 Minutes*. I certainly wasn't going to look a gift horse in the mouth.

When the word got out, a customer of mine, Marlo Lewis, called and advised me not to do it. Marlo was a very prominent television producer and told me that *60 Minutes* would only look to "chop me up." I felt that the publicity could only help, not hurt. As it turned out, the only fastball Morley Safer threw at me was when he asked if I went to many important parties. I believe the purpose of the question was to put the local society down by showing that a nobody like me could become important in Palm Springs. However, I cut him off at the pass by answering, "No, because I don't get invited."

Mr. Safer asked mostly about my clientele, and I shot from the lip.

"Palm Springs gets the crème de la crème and because I have the hot restaurant, I get the crème de la crème of the crème de la crème," I said, knowing as soon as those words came out of my mouth that they were tantamount to gold. This prompted a rash of T-shirts, charms, and many souvenirs with that expression.

The *60 Minutes* segment turned out to be a great piece and a major shot in the arm for the Ingleside Inn and Melvyn's, and it was aired three times. You can't buy publicity like that (and thank goodness for that—because there was no way I could afford it).

And of course, our greatest booster was Palm Springs's own newspaper, the *Desert Sun*. Almost every week they had my picture plastered in the paper with a celebrity. It became a running joke that the *Desert Sun* never went to press without my picture. But in all honesty, the publicity was justified because we were the happening place. You didn't need a PR person to get your picture published with President Ford, Frank Sinatra, Lucille Ball, John Travolta, and so on.

Because I catered to the jet-setters and celebrities, the press were always around. One of the top reporters from one of the tabloid newspapers hung around in order to pick up little tidbits about the stars. He befriended my son, Lonny, who worked for me, and he called him every week to find out what was happening. My son received a check for $100 to $150 every time he sent an item to the reporter. On many occasions, the tabloid would exaggerate or embellish the story so that it seemed a lot more sensational than it really was. After my son no longer worked there, the reporter started calling me.

While the American media was terrific, I learned that our British cousins across the pond had a different definition of journalism. One day I received a phone call from a man with an English accent who introduced himself as a freelance writer for several European magazines. He said he wanted to write a feature story on the Inn and the restaurant. I told him I would be happy to work with him.

After he arrived and checked in, we made an appointment to talk the following morning. Over breakfast we spent about two hours chatting about my background and the history of the Inn. I also told him several celebrity anecdotes, which always added spice to any story. I mentioned a few cute incidents—more to drop the names of the famous than to tell anything really newsworthy. I mentioned that Donald Trump and his fiancée at the time, the lovely Marla Maples, celebrated her birthday at Melvyn's the week before. I had not been in that evening, but my staff had told me how nice they were and that they even took pictures with the maitre d' and some of the staff. They were staying at another local hotel while Marla was doing some TV work in Palm Springs.

The writer asked if I had any pictures with celebrities that he might use with his story. He added that Europeans were in love with American celebrities. I showed him my collection of celebrity pictures on the walls of the lounge and I could tell by his reaction that he was impressed. He asked if I would mind if he took them off the wall so he could photograph them to use with his story. When he finished, he checked out and thanked me for my time. He assured me that I would receive copies of the articles as soon as they were published.

About two months had passed when a friend called and asked what I thought about the story in one of the "rags." I asked him what he was referring to, and he informed me that a friend had just called him from Michigan and mentioned that there was a two-page story about me with eight pictures of me with various celebrities. I immediately sent one of my people to the local supermarket to pick up a copy of the tabloid. When I got my hands on a copy, I was absolutely flabbergasted. The headline read: "OWNER OF DESERT LOVE NEST SPILLS THE BEANS ON STARS RAUNCHY ROMPS!"

As I read the story, I felt absolute panic. The story allegedly quoted me telling stories about eight different major celebrities, and none were very flattering. The worst was that he quoted me as saying Donald Trump and Marla Maples hardly ever left their suite, implying they had made love all day. The truth was I had told him that they didn't stay at my hotel and that I had never met them personally. He had taken some harmless little anecdotes and twisted them and exaggerated them until they had a dirty, sensationalist twist to them.

I felt betrayed, deceived, embarrassed, mortified, conned, and furious all at the same time. I started getting calls from friends, customers, and various members of the press wanting to know my reaction to the story. I refused to discuss it, and simply said it was all lies. I pretended that if I ignored the situation, it would all go away. I actually felt that a story like that could ruin my reputation and my business. The first thing you learn in a business that caters to high-profile people is that you don't tell stories about them. The entire article was contrived in the writer's imagination, but there I was in all the pictures, smiling like I was their best buddy. I was absolutely shocked. The entire story was false, but my photos substantiated his story.

All of a sudden it dawned on me that the culprit was the very polite British gentleman who paid me a visit a few months prior. He was the only person I had allowed to take pictures of those photos. I explored the possibility of a lawsuit, but my attorney advised me that it would call even more attention to the article. His advice was to "let sleeping dogs lie."

So, rule number one: You don't have to be a celebrity to suffer at the hands of the "rags." Number two: You can bet I check credentials very carefully before giving interviews.

By now, we had worked out most of the kinks that plagued the Ingleside Inn and Melvyn's. After a year of operations, we started to come into our own. About a month after we opened, I hired a female manager from the Rocks Resort, a company owned by the Rockefellers. Her management style was comparable to that of a marine drill sergeant. She was very tough on the employees. Her style didn't mesh well with a quaint thirty-room inn. She hired as her secretary a little English lady named Babs Rosen, whom everyone called "Granny."

Granny was about sixty-five when she came aboard, and it only took her about a month before she put a knife in the manager's back so she could get her job—Granny made sure I got rid of the manager quickly.

Granny was a very proper English lady, a tiny gray-haired woman who loved tea and the Queen "Mum," and faithfully celebrated Boxing Day every Christmas season. If my former manager was a marine drill sergeant, then Granny was a tyrant. She ruled the Ingleside Inn with an iron fist and made Adolf Hitler look tame. If she loved you, there was nothing in the world she wouldn't do for you. If she didn't like you, you couldn't get into the Ingleside Inn if we had all thirty rooms vacant. The guests loved her, but were terrified of her at the same time.

Granny, who was raised in England under the caste system, had no use for cockneys. One of our guests, Malcolm Kingston, had been knighted by the Queen of England. He was now *Sir* Malcolm Kingston. But his title didn't fly with Granny, who still wouldn't give him a room because he was reared in the wrong part of England. I tried to give her a history lesson to put things in perspective.

"Granny, I am from Brooklyn, which is considered the bowels of America," I explained. "You have discriminated against a cockney who has been knighted by the Queen of England. You worship me, yet you treat this man like dirt. Brooklyn is worse than cockney." That made Granny laugh, and the line became a standard joke between us.

But it was no laughing matter when I witnessed the time Granny brought *The Terminator* to his knees.

Back in the early eighties, Arnold Schwarzenegger and Maria Shriver stayed at the Ingleside Inn often. One day I was walking through the lobby, and Arnold was standing at the check-in desk in the lobby with Maria by his side. His tone struck me as funny because it sounded as if he were begging and pleading.

"Please, Granny; can't we stay here next time?" Arnold asked, practically on bended knee.

I found out later that Arnold had neglected to cancel a prior reservation and didn't show up. The next time he did, Granny put him and Maria in a derelict property that I was planning to demolish five blocks away. She was punishing one of my highest-profile guests, and there was nothing I could do about it.

Granny also instilled the fear of God in other guests. Bonnie Strauss was a regular guest before she became a popular fashion designer. After Bonnie had a major spread in *People* magazine, I hadn't seen her in a long time. A few months after the article appeared, I was in New York and spotted her in front of FAO Schwarz, the famous toy store on 58th Street and Fifth Avenue. I went over to say hello for old time's sake.

"Hey, Bonnie, ever since you were written up in *People* magazine you're so big that you don't even come to the Ingleside Inn anymore," I joked. She looked at me deadly serious and replied, "What are you talking about, Mel? You were the one who became a big shot. I can't even get a reservation." Something wasn't right.

When I flew back to Palm Springs, I decided to do a little investigating. It turned out that the last time Bonnie stayed at the hotel, she accidentally ripped the wallpaper. One of the maids told Granny, who decided that she was banished forever because she "damaged" the Ingleside Inn.

Granny also frowned upon relationships outside of marriage. Mark Harlig was a good customer and owned a famous hotel called the Sportsman Lodge in Encino, California. Mark spent almost every Sunday and Monday at the Ingleside Inn to relax and recharge his batteries. He was successful and single. He usually stayed alone, but one weekend he had obviously gotten lucky and was lounging poolside with a lady, holding hands with the occasional kiss while tanning in the sun over drinks. When Granny caught sight of them, she decided to take matters into her own hands and rushed out to the pool to put a stop to it.

"Mr. Harlig, we don't allow that sort of thing at the Ingleside Inn," Granny said in a tone of disdain with her arms crossed. Mark picked up a phone in the pool area and called me immediately.

"Mel, are you running a hotel or church?" I didn't know what to tell him. I knew what I was running, but I wasn't sure what Granny was running. She was a trip.

Like I said before, Granny was loyal to the *nth* degree. For example, if someone had stayed at the Ingleside Inn, in Granny's book that's where they had to stay for every future visit. Lodging anywhere else was tantamount to treason. I had several guests call me to say they were coming to Palm Springs but were going to stay with friends or relatives. They were coming to dinner at Melvyn's, but made it a point to tell me not to tell Granny that they were in town for fear if they wanted to come back and stay at the hotel, she wouldn't let them back in.

At the end of every July, Granny threw herself a birthday party to drum up business at the Inn because it was dead in the summer. Invitees got a free dinner but had to pay for their rooms. But the invitation was in fact a summons, because if you were invited and didn't show up, God forbid. Several guests flew in from all around the country to subject themselves to the scorching summer heat because they didn't want to incur the wrath of Granny. Arnold Schwarzenegger and Maria Shriver, who were still wondering whether or not they were going to stay at the Ingleside Inn again, sent Granny a beautiful bouquet of flowers in hopes of getting back in her good graces.

When I first got married to Stephanie, she asked me "Who owns the Ingleside Inn? You or Granny Rosen?" When we were redecorating the rooms, Stephanie and I bought a beautiful painting and proudly hung it in one of the rooms. A day later it was replaced by one of Granny's little needlepoints. The next day Stephanie said, "Now I know who owns the place."

Granny worked at the Ingleside Inn for a good two decades until she was eighty-five and we practically had to force her to retire. She finally left kicking and screaming. I kept her on the payroll for a year because of my overwhelming guilt in forcing her to retire. She defied everything you've ever read about being a good leader—she belittled employees in front of guests, and ruled with terror. But she earned both employees' and guests' respect because of her dedication and devotion to making everything perfect for the guests.

When Granny did finally retire, I put an ad in the paper looking for a replacement. Somebody called and asked, "Where's Granny Rosen?" I replied that she had finally retired. The voice on the other line begged to differ.

"That old bitch will never retire. Let me know when that bitch is dead," said the caller, who slammed the phone down so hard it almost gave me a concussion.

Granny, who is approaching the century-mark, is in a nursing home several blocks from the Ingleside Inn. I visit her every once in a while. Many guests when they come to town pick up Granny and bring her to the Ingleside Inn for lunch. She loves it. Her mind goes in and out, but when it's in, she's as ornery as ever.

With Alan Mald running the restaurant and Granny taking over the reins of the hotel, I had more time to schmooze with the guests. Of course, that didn't always produce desirable results. Take the case of Twentieth Century Fox studio mogul Darryl F. Zanuck, whom I continually confused with Cecil B. DeMille. The cigar-chomping Zanuck dined at our establishment at least three times a week with his lovely wife Virginia. He entered the restaurant for dinner one night and I cheerfully sang out, "Good evening, Mr. DeMille, how do you feel today?" "He's been dead for ten years!" Zanuck grumbled stonily. Ultimately I became friendly with Mr. Zanuck, and he gave me his polo mallets, which I proudly hung above his favorite table. (The famous Polo Lounge at the Beverly Hills Hotel was named in honor of Darryl Zanuck because he went there after his polo matches.)

At least I recognized that Zanuck was somebody. Such wasn't the case with Norman Brokaw, who was the head of the William Morris Agency. Mr. Brokaw had been in Melvyn's several times and was apparently miffed that I had walked by him several times without acknowledging his presence.

"I am Norman Brokaw of the William Morris Agency, and I handle several important clients," he said. "How come you never say hello to me?" I apologized and explained I had no memory and that I was guilty of being stupid but not guilty of being rude.

Perhaps the most embarrassing story I can think of that sheds light on my bad memory is when I saw my customer, Helen Rose, who was a friend of my wife, Stephanie. Helen was an Academy Award winning dress designer and a very classy lady. She came into Melvyn's one night and asked how Stephanie was doing and for me to send her regards. I promised I would.

About an hour later on the way to the ladies' room, Helen said, "Mel, now don't forget to send my regards to your wife." I said I wouldn't forget. On the way back from the ladies' room, Helen's whole demeanor changed. She suddenly went from dignified lady to chief interrogator.

"Mel, what's my name?" Helen asked. I drew a blank and confessed I couldn't remember. As a result of that incident, I decided never to fake it again. I developed a line that has helped me through similar sorts of sticky situations. If somebody today confronts me about knowing their name, I tell them, "Forgive me. I know your face, but I can't remember your name."

Over the years many people have told me that they thought I was stuck up or arrogant because I didn't personally greet them. I have no memory for faces or names and I am basically a shy person. However, once you know me, it's hard to get me to shut up.

I certainly had no trouble recognizing movie icon Marlon Brando when he checked in. I prided myself on my collection of books autographed by guests of the hotel. It was quite an extensive collection, and as soon as Mr. Brando checked in, I asked the bellman to run across the street to the bookstore and purchase any book on Brando. Then I instructed him to bring the book to Brando's room and explain that I had this collection and ask whether he would be kind enough to autograph the book for me. Brando's room was right behind my office, and the next thing I heard was someone screaming loudly. There was no doubt that it was the voice of Marlon Brando. It turned out that the book my bellman bought was called *Brando for Breakfast*, a scathing tell-all that had been written by the actor's ex-wife, Anna Kafshi. Her memoir trashed Brando.

When Brando saw the book, he went ballistic and almost ripped it up. Needless to say, I didn't get my autographed book.

We had the honor of having the famed method actor with us for three days, although most of his time was spent outside in his camper talking on his CB radio in our back parking lot. Remember the CB craze of the seventies? Brando was right there in the thick of things, chatting away with strangers using the latest CB lingo.

Brando had put on a considerable amount of weight at this point in his life, and I dare say he teetered around 300 pounds. Brando walked into Melvyn's for dinner looking rather scruffy with blue jeans, dusty boots, and a sweat-stained ten-gallon cowboy hat. I caught him in a jolly mood, and he agreed to pose with me for a picture. However, he had one stipulation.

"As long as it's not for the press," he said.

"Absolutely not," I replied. "It's for my private collection." This picture would have made every wire service in the country, but I convinced the thespian that the photo would never see the light of day. Turned out he didn't have much to worry about. The camera, I learned the next day, much to my dismay, didn't have any film.

No autographed book, no photo, no Marlon Brando. My batting average was a big fat zero.

This brings to mind another story where I managed to put my foot in my mouth, struck out, and dropped a clutch pass. When I first opened the hotel, the front desk informed me that a man flew in from Seattle on his own private Lear jet and was staying at the Ingleside Inn. I was very impressed. When I entered the restaurant that night I introduced myself to the gentleman, and told him that we were very happy to have him as our guest. He in turn invited me to have a drink with him. He informed me that he had just bought the Seattle baseball team. His name was Walter Schoenfield, and along with actor Danny Kaye and a few other partners, he had just taken over ownership of the Seattle Mariners. I felt pretty important hanging out with someone of his stature.

The very next night the restaurant was very busy, and there was an unusually long wait for a table. I noticed two couples standing at the bar and could see they were obviously annoyed that they had a long wait ahead of them. Trying to make conversation, I asked them where they were from.

"Seattle," answered one of the gentlemen.

Eager to impress them, I told them that I just had drinks the night before with Walter Schoenfield the owner of the Seattle baseball team. One of the two men said he knew him very well.

"I own the Seattle Seahawks football team," he said. His name was Herman Sarkowsky. As I walked away, I told myself, *Mel, you can't drop names because you're in a different league now. You never know who you're talking to.*

A few weeks later, I walked out to the restaurant patio where I was introduced to three men from Seattle. Trying to impress them I said, "I had drinks with the guy who owns the baseball team and dropped his name to the guy who owns the football team."

"I know both of them very well," said one of the men. "I own the basketball team." His name was Sam Schulman, who owned the Seattle Supersonics at the time. I responded the only way I knew how—with humor.

"God, I hope you guys don't have a hockey team up there," I said, which provoked a round of laughs.

The Ingleside Inn and Melvyn's became the center of the Palm Springs social scene, thanks to several clever promotional opportunities. One of my regular customers was actress Lita Baron, a former screen siren who was known for her sexy turns in film and television. Even though she had retired from acting, she had a telephone book to die for. She had been married to actor Rory Calhoun and had long-standing ties to people in the entertainment industry.

Lita was seeing a man named Bill Milner, a radio announcer. The two approached me about doing an hour long celebrity radio show to be held Monday through Friday on the patio of my restaurant. I agreed to buy the air time for seventy-five dollars a week and provide lunch for the guests. Lita would conduct the interviews, and Bill sold the spots, produced, and announced the show. The show was called *Lunch with Lita*. It was mostly a lightweight affair. Lita interviewed four or five guests every day—somebody opening a flower shop or new store, or someone promoting a charity event that needed some publicity. But one out of every five guests was a bona fide celebrity. She landed Lucille Ball, Debbie Reynolds, Donald O'Connor, writer Allen Drury, gossip columnist Adele Rogers St. John's, Elliot Roosevelt (the son of President Franklin Delano Roosevelt), and even Mickey Cohen, the famous gangster.

The show turned out to be a surprise hit, and many celebrities who visited Palm Springs either for vacation or for a golf tournament called Lita to promote their latest movie, book, or charity. People wanted to see celebrities, and Lita never failed to deliver the goods. The added bonus for me was my picture with the celebrities, which usually appeared in the newspaper. Lita's show stayed on the air for several years and established the Ingleside Inn and Melvyn's as a place to see and dine with celebrities. As a result, many of the celebrities who appeared on the show became friends of mine. They include Patrick McNee, June Allyson, Bill Dana, and Howard Keel, to mention but a few.

But nothing packed them into our place like TV. The Inn's image as the ultimate romantic getaway was gilded when I arranged for it to be the grand-prize destination of winning couples on several TV shows such as *Jeopardy*, *Wheel of Fortune*, and the ever popular *The Dating Game*.

The winners of *The Dating Game* were given a free weekend at the Ingleside Inn and were always accompanied by a chaperone. One evening when I arrived to work, the maitre d' informed me that a couple from *The Dating Game* was seated at a certain table. As I walked by the table, it was obvious the lovebirds were getting on quite well; they necked passionately while the chaperone helplessly looked on. When I returned to the maitre d's stand, I commented on their passionate kiss. But the maitre d' laughed and said, "Mr. Haber, he's necking with the chaperone!"

My place had a romantic affect on many people. The Ingleside Inn has the most charming European courtyard. The greenest grass surrounds a statue of Cupid in the center of a small pond, perfect in which to float lighted candles. Subsequently many people have chosen it as the ideal romantic setting in which to get married. Most notably, June Allyson married Mr. David Ashrow in this courtyard in 1976. Their union made headlines around the world as did David Boreanaz's (star of the TV show *Angel*) nuptials to bride Jaime Bergman in November 2002.

It was a red-letter day not only for the son of Charlie Rich, the famous country and western singer, who also got married in the courtyard but to other guests of the hotel. After the wedding and during the reception, his father gave one of the best impromptu concerts ever at the Inn.

I remember one day I was chatting with a friend of mine at the bar when a man walked up to me and asked me for a favor. I said, "What can I do for you?"

"I'm sitting with a lady at the first table on the left in the dining room," he said. "And if you wouldn't mind, I'd really appreciate it if you proposed to her for me? I have a ring and you can present it to her for me."

It was a rather odd request but sounded like a fun thing to do. He told me that he was going to retrieve the ring from his car and would be right back. I looked at my friend and said, "Just another day at Melvyn's." A while passed and the guy came over and handed me the ring. He told me that he would be sitting in the restaurant at the first table on the left and that I should come by in a few minutes. I did as he asked, waited a few minutes, then walked over to his table and introduced myself to his lady.

"Excuse me. My name is Mel Haber. Would you like to get married?"

Without a moment's hesitation, she said "I hardly know you," completely taken aback by my request.

"No to me," I explained, "but the gentleman next to you." I then presented her the ring. She screamed and started to cry and joyfully hugged her man and said yes. I've often wondered what would have happened if she said no. Would I have been stuck for the check?

Believe it or not, I can top that story. One night we held a wedding in the lounge because another wedding was taking place in the dining room at the same time. After the two exchanged nuptials in the lounge, I walked up to congratulate the bride. She said she knew I liked positive stories about incidents that occurred at my place, and this one might be one for the record books.

"Mel, the man who just gave me away was my sixty-year-old ex-husband, who walked me down the aisle so that I could marry my forty-year-old new husband," she said. I just hope one day she doesn't meet a twenty-year-old!

But my favorite wedding story is the morning I was sitting in my office and the hotel manager said that two of our guests from Canada were getting married in the courtyard at 11 a.m. and would be honored if I would serve as the best man. I was dressed casually but was told my attire was fine. Having no reason to say no, I agreed and was relieved to see that at least they had a bridesmaid. The wedding consisted of the bride, the groom, the preacher, the bridesmaid, and me. It was a very brief ceremony, and I had done my good deed for the day. That evening I saw the bridesmaid at the end of the bar. I asked her how long she knew the bride and groom. She said "Mr. Haber, I am a guest at your hotel, I was simply sitting on the patio having coffee this morning when your manager asked if I had a white dress and if I would do her a favor? I don't even know their names!" *Only* at the Ingleside.

Some people, however, don't need to exchange wedding vows to catch a whiff of the Inn's romantic setting. I remember one night a famous Hollywood Lothario sneaked into one of the Inn's bungalows through a window to bed a prominent socialite while her husband and family waited patiently for her in the restaurant. This romantic fling became an instant spectator sport because several staff members were outside the window watching, cheering on their favorite star just like they did in the movie theater.

All the time the Inn seemed to be succeeding, I was concerned. I continually waited for the other shoe to drop. Throughout my life, I was conditioned to accept bad things, and considered good things as almost accidental. It's like walking home and finding a twenty dollar bill on the street, and you stare at it in disbelief and can't believe your good fortune. That was the attitude I had toward my success at the time. Because of that mentality, I was always working and trying to make the place better; there was never a question of sitting back and feeling as if I had "made it." In a way, I think that had something to do with my ultimate success. I think people were attracted to a sincere guy who did not act like a big shot but constantly worked hard to please the customers.

I could never put my finger on why I loved the business so much until I struck up a casual conversation with a lady who was acquainted with Huntington Hartford, the multimillionaire and heir to the Great Atlantic and Pacific Tea Company fortune. She told me that she had asked Mr. Hartford what kept him going, what kept him stimulated. He said, "After you buy all your toys, all your boats and planes, and everything you can buy with money, the only thing that can keep you stimulated is new and interesting people." I found that statement to be so profound, and I never forgot it.

Now interesting is a relative term. Everybody has a different concept of what's interesting. And I'd like to make an interesting point about interesting people. I happen to be an admirer of people of accomplishments, who have achieved something in life. Even though the Ingleside Inn and Melvyn's was drawing the most well-known people in the world as customers, the people I find interesting are usually not the faces you recognize. For me, it's the little guy who built a business from nothing and sold it for millions of dollars. I attracted very interesting people from all over the world. They included everybody from business tycoons like Donald Trump to famous writers like Allen Drury, who won a Pulitzer Prize for *Advise and Consent*. In chatting with these folks, I played a mental game and tried to figure out what special trait they possessed that made them so successful in their field of endeavor be it politics, entertainment, or business.

There were many times in the past three decades when I didn't have the energy to throw my jacket on and march over to the restaurant with a smile on my face. But down I went, feeling beat up and bored, and then I'd meet someone who totally stimulated me and got me excited about life again.

Many people are bored going to cocktail parties with the same people and listening to the same chatter and small talk night after night. But in my business, there are new people all the time, and I have the choice of whom I want to spend my time with.

The flip side to that was there were some people who I never wanted to meet but came to my saloon anyway.

# CHAPTER 11

# Strange Bedfellows, Drinking Companions, and Con Artists

**W**hile the Ingleside Inn and Melvyn's have attracted their fair share of the rich and famous over the years, we've also had guests who represented the other end of the spectrum. I've had dealings with mobsters and celebrity mooches, politicos and heads of state, con artists and grifters. As long as they paid their bills on time and didn't adversely affect my business, I really didn't care what they did for a living. However, trouble invited itself to my establishment every now and then.

Palm Springs has long been a haven for mobsters because of its reputation as the "Playground of the Stars." Many top mafia guys owned homes or lived in the desert because even they needed a little rest and relaxation every once in a while.

In February 1976, Harry Adelman, a friend from the automotive business who lived in Cleveland, called to book seven rooms for his buddies. They planned on attending the Bob Hope Desert Classic Golf Tournament and needed a place to stay. Because Harry was an old friend, I personally made the arrangements.

When his buddies checked into the Ingleside Inn, I thought I was hosting a casting call for the movie *Goodfellas*. Each guy stood about 5-foot-4, was as wide as they were tall, and all of them smoked these big, fat stogies. As soon as they checked them in, I called Harry in Cleveland.

"Are you crazy?" I screamed at Harry. "When I lived in Brooklyn, I didn't know guys like these. Now you're sending them here to my elegant hotel?" Things got progressively worse. It rained the entire week they were in Palm Springs, which meant these wise guys spent every day in the bar and made it their own little domain. Beautiful, buxom women sat on their laps while they puffed away on their foot-long cigars and drank cognac. They talked and acted just like gangsters, which drew a lot of negative attention. My other guests instinctively knew to steer clear of this bunch.

One member of the group called up Tommy Marson, a former New York plumbing contractor who had relocated to a sprawling mansion in Rancho Mirage. Tommy did business in San Diego and Las Vegas and owned property in Otay Mesa, and seemed to be a good friend of theirs. After having a few drinks with them, he asked me if I had a phone he could use. I showed him a phone in the corner of the lounge, and I couldn't help but overhear his conversation because of Tommy's loud tone and angry demeanor.

"Frank, I need you to play the Westchester Premiere Theater. Frank, I don't care what the hell you have to do, just be there," Tommy said rather forcefully and slammed down the phone. When Tommy hung up the phone, it occurred to me that he had been talking to Frank Sinatra. The Westchester Premiere Theater, which opened in 1976, was a mafia front from its inception. Several of the families went into the venture together and had the place built. They needed a big-named artist like Frank to give it a nice kick-start. The next thing I knew, a picture of Frank posing with mafia capos, underbosses, and soldiers was plastered in newspapers around the country, which included the likes of Paul Castellano, Carlo Gambino, Gregory DePalma, and Jimmy Fratianno. And right next to Frank was Tommy Marson, their arms around each other.

In 1980, Frank Sinatra appeared before the Nevada State Gaming Commission as part of the application process for a new gaming license. He wanted to become a part-owner in The Sands Hotel. Frank also hoped to put to rest allegations that he had Mob connections, allegations that, in part, led to his previous license having been pulled in 1963. In the course of the hearing, the Gaming Commission showed Frank the notorious picture taken at the Westchester Premiere Theater in 1976.

The Chairman of the Board was asked how he reconciled his earlier assertion that he knew no mobsters. Frank shrugged his shoulders and said, "Hey, I get my picture taken with a lot of guys." Frank didn't get his gaming license, and it all started with that one phone call placed inside of Melvyn's.

As for my buddies from Cleveland, I never did get a return visit. I had heard through the grapevine that a major gang war erupted back in Ohio right after they left Palm Springs and half of them were killed. One of them, however, did reappear in my life, but not directly. After turning government witness, Jimmy "The Weasel" Fratianno appeared on *60 Minutes* to plug his book, *The Last Mafioso*, which tells of his eleven murders for the mob and his association with Frank Sinatra. It sounded like an interesting read, and when I picked up a copy, I didn't realize how truly interesting it was. In one of the passages, Fratianno revealed that in February 1976, he and six of his companions stayed at the beautiful Ingleside Inn in Palm Springs, and he even tipped his hat to Melvyn's, which he told readers was his favorite dining spot. Fratianno was one of the seven men Harry Adelman sent to my hotel, and my heart skipped a beat when I read the passage in his book. When a local reporter mentioned Fratianno's book, I quipped, "I guess you can now say we appeal to millionaires and mafia, at the same time."

There was one guy, a wannabe who lived in town and strolled into my place always acting like a tough guy. Even worse, he was anti-Semitic. He harassed me by calling me a kike and often told me that he was going to turn my place into a garage. I had never said a cross word or had anything to do with him, and it was unsettling. When Tommy Marson walked in one day, I complained about what the guy said.

"Tommy, I don't know why he talks to me like that," I said. "I've never bothered the guy and I always make him feel welcome." Tommy lifted up his hand and said, "Mel, I'll handle it."

The very next day the guy walked into Melvyn's, practically on bended knee and said, "Mr. Haber, I'm terribly sorry about my past behavior and I will never get out of line again." The next time Tommy came in, he received a very warm handshake and an ice cold drink.

I liked Tommy because he was a straight shooter. Over a drink, I had to ask him a question that had been gnawing away at me. "Tommy, how come I've never been hustled here? In New York, if you're in the bar or restaurant business, everybody hustles you, and they are all looking to take a piece of your action. I've never been approached here. Why?" I'll never forget what he said to me.

"Mel, as long as we come here to vacation or live, there will never be any business in Palm Springs," he said. I guess there is something to that old adage about "location, location, location."

Another well-known mafioso who worked for the John Gotti family decided to make Melvyn's his home away from home. This dapper fellow dressed as impeccably as his boss, and held court in Melvyn's almost every Saturday night for about two years. "Joey" was a charming guy who dressed to the nines in his $2,000 suits, with manicured fingernails and perfectly coiffed hair. He was just as magnanimous as he was funny, and liked to flash his cash and tipped our staff very well. He told stories that entranced locals, who belly laughed (most likely out of fear) whenever he delivered the punch line. Joey could also deliver a punch, and wasn't afraid to unleash his fury when aggravated.

One night a local restaurateur got a taste of Joey's anger. As soon as he walked into Melvyn's, Joey started beating him with the telephone from the maitre d's stand. I managed to wrestle the phone away from Joey and then hustled the restaurateur out of the place. When I inquired to why he assaulted my customer, Joey told me that the guy had hit on his wife at the bank. Joey said all he was doing was hitting back.

But Joey also used finesse in certain situations. One night while a song he had requested was being performed in the lounge, a party of four sitting in front of him was conversing a little too loudly. Joey told them, not so gently I'm sure, to shut up. When one of the men in the group stood up, an argument ensued. Joey reached inside his wife's purse and pulled out a gun and stuck it right in the guy's face. The argument ended immediately.

Joey literally threw down the hammer another night when ordering drinks for two of my valets. The bartender, however, politely refused on the grounds that it was against company policy for any employee to have a drink while on duty, especially ones who had to drive cars all night. Joey reached into his wife's purse again, pulled out a framer's hammer (he must have had an arsenal in that purse), and placed it on the bar to intimidate the bartender. Fortunately, I was there and was able to put out the fire. For some reason, Joey treated me with respect because I think he mistakenly thought I was somehow "connected." But that never stopped him from attacking my customers.

It was a busy Saturday night, and my wife and I were having dinner at Melvyn's with a high-profile decorator and his spouse, whom we had just hired for our house. We were pulling out all the stops to impress this couple when Joey decided to turn enforcer at the table right next to us. A drunken customer said something to Joey, who then pulled out a blackjack and clubbed the guy on the head several times. Blood was squirting out of this poor guy's head onto the next table while he was trying to shield himself from a further beating. Several staff members came rushing over and broke up the fracas. The mafioso calmly went back to eating his dinner while the gentleman who took the beating was rushed to the hospital. Other wait staff members wiped the blood from the next table and replaced the tablecloths. Everyone was in shock except for the head waiter. Without a moment's hesitation he announced to the dining room, "And for dessert we have sumo wrestling." Talk about a quick recovery!

Joey's Palm Springs reign of terror ended when he moved to Las Vegas, where I'm sure, he continues to be larger than life.

Another wise guy, who was the owner of Cavalleros, a private club I had belonged to back in New York, decided to pay me a visit on a West Coast swing. "I just couldn't come to the West Coast without saying hello to my buddy, Mel Haber," he said. I smiled at his feeble compliment but inside I felt like telling him, "You bum! I was in your place every night and you never even said hello to me, never even nodded. All of a sudden, I'm your best friend?" Over a drink, he said that he was on his way to rescue his daughter from a commune that she had joined in San Francisco. He was a typical-looking New York wise guy: monogrammed shirt, perfectly combed hair, strong cologne, a cigarette dangling from the corner of his mouth, and a big star sapphire pinky ring. He said he had to stop by to show his respect for me.

The most interesting part of this story is that he came back to Melvyn's three weeks later wearing a toga and sandals. Not only did he not rescue his daughter, but he ended up joining the commune!

Melvyn's wasn't the only establishment I owned where gangsters like to whet their whistle. One night I was in my disco, Cecil's, when my maitre d', Arturo Petorini, asked me if I'd like to meet Tony Accardo from Chicago. I knew the name well from all the mafia books—Accardo was a veteran Chicago mob figure who was once Al Capone's bodyguard. Known as "Joe Batters" because of his skill with a baseball bat, Accardo was rumored to be involved with the St. Valentine's Day Massacre of 1929. As I peered past Arturo's shoulder, I spotted Accardo with about a dozen men all sitting at one table with about a dozen women at a separate table next to them. It was a scene right out of the movies—the men and women sat separately. Something spooked me about the whole setting, and I politely declined Arturo's invitation.

"No thanks, Arturo, I think I'll keep my distance," I said, sitting at the bar. Moments later, a waiter came back to the bar with a tray of unopened wine and soft drinks. I asked the waiter why he was bringing the items back. He said the gentlemen had insisted that the bottles be opened in front of them as a safety precaution—they were, after all, in a different type of business. After dinner, the twelve men lit their big cigars and drank their brandies while the women had coffee, tea, and dessert. Those guys were a piece of work, but some were even quite generous.

Henry Hill, the famous mobster from New York, strolled into Melvyn's one night looking to give me a very special gift. For those of you who don't know who Hill is, he was one of several people who stole millions of dollars in untraceable money on December 11, 1978, at the Lufthansa Air Cargo terminal in New York City. That crime, known as the "Lufthansa Heist," and his life as a mobster was detailed in the book *Wiseguy*, which Martin Scorcese adapted for his movie *Goodfellas*.

One of my waiters told me that Hill specifically came looking in Melvyn's to leave an autographed copy of his latest book, *A Goodfella's Guide to New York*. The content was certainly eye-popping: It listed mafia hangouts, restaurants, bars, and social clubs. He even had a special section in the book where certain wise guys got killed. Hill's sage East Coast advice included tips such as, "New York has four seasons and five crime families," and "The worst trip to New York is if you don't come back alive." It was a good thing I never met Mr. Hill.

While members of the mafia were fairly easy to spot, that certainly wasn't the case with con artists and grifters who were looking for easy prey in my establishment. And while Sir John was an exceptional con artist, he certainly wasn't the only one who smelled the sweet fragrance of money in the desert air.

A man by the name of John Compton Harvey, who called himself a doctor, often came into Melvyn's to eat with a group of people. Little did I know he was using Melvyn's as a place to conduct business. Unfortunately, he was taking a scalpel to victims' bank accounts. Harvey was an extraordinary thief masquerading as a doctor. Here's how the con worked: Harvey would answer newspaper classified ads offering jewelry or rare coins for sale. He usually met the victims twice. During the first meeting Harvey portrayed himself as a doctor, which in turn gained the confidence of the seller. The first visit Harvey checked out the merchandise to ascertain its value.

A second meeting with victims was on weekends or after banking hours so the sellers couldn't verify or cash the altered cashier's checks he presented to them. Sometimes he met the victims at Melvyn's to show that he had money and could be trusted. But Harvey went from trusted to busted when he showed up at Melvyn's one night with a beautiful woman, whom I happened to know, on his arm.

During the middle of the meal when Harvey's date excused herself to go to the restroom, Harvey was swooped up by a task force comprised of detectives from Palm Springs, Laguna Beach, and the U.S. Marshal's Service. That was in addition to a helicopter that hovered above and focused a light beam on my two-acre slice of paradise. Two officers entered in the side door while three others went through the front. All five had their guns pointed at Harvey's head and quickly whisked him away. He was taken out so fast that when his date emerged from the ladies room, she wondered what happened to her dinner companion.

Brian Ellis, my long-standing maitre d', who was notoriously frugal, complained to the lead detective that Harvey hadn't paid his $150 bill. Around midnight, the officer came back and proudly gave Brian $150 that he took out of Harvey's pocket. That, however, wasn't good enough for Brian.

"What about the tip?" Brian asked.

While we're on the subject of Brian, allow me to digress for a second. Whenever Brian went skiing, he used a condominium at Mammoth Ski Resort in Mammoth Lakes, California. The condo was graciously loaned to him by a Melvyn's customer. One day, another guest of ours said to Brian, "Why don't you use my plane and my pilot." Brian and Mark, one of my bartenders, took the customer up on the generous offer and went skiing. When they were ready to fly back to Palm Springs, the pilot told Brian he needed some money for gas. When the pilot told Brian how much he needed Brian asked "Can't we make it back on half a tank?"

Back to the Harvey case: The veteran criminal used five aliases, was charged with fraud, robbery, forgery, burglary, and grand theft. He was also held on $9 million bail pending his trial. Harvey was also wanted in connection with crimes in ten other California counties, plus Arizona and Utah.

While that story certainly made the rounds in Palm Springs, it didn't make the front page like the next criminal who showed up on our front doorstep. Joseph Eugene Schultz, a forty-three-year-old Vietnam veteran suffering from post-traumatic stress disorder, had just robbed the Great Western Bank across the street. He was carrying a briefcase full of money when officers cornered him near his getaway car. Unable to open the car door, Schultz hightailed it across the street to Melvyn's where police had approached him with drawn guns and ordered him to stop.

Schultz hesitated, then put the pistol to his head and fired a single shot. He fell facedown on top of the briefcase right in front of the Melvyn's marquee. The *Desert Sun* snapped a picture of the corpse with the Melvyn's name prominently visible in the background and put it on their front page. The editor called me the next day and said, "Mel, I can't believe what you would do to get some publicity."

I also found out that in some cases, celebrities, or those claiming to be celebrities, weren't immune to frauds and schemes. And for the life of me, I'll never figure out why they usually seem to cross my path.

Actor Peter Lawford, like many celebrities, used his face like a credit card. He thought that being a celebrity entitled him to a free meal. In the late 1970s, Lawford was at a low point in his career and his personal life. Just one look at him and it wasn't hard to tell he had hit rock bottom from years of alcohol and drug abuse.

At that time, I was living in one of the villas at the Ingleside Inn, about thirty feet from the restaurant. A friend called and said that Lawford was coming in for dinner that night, and would I like to meet him? I was in bed, reading a good book. I was very relaxed and didn't feel like getting dressed, so I turned him down. A few minutes later I had second thoughts and actually felt a little guilty. Was I such a big shot that I couldn't throw on a pair of slacks and a shirt, and walk thirty feet to meet someone famous?

I met Peter and his fourth wife, Patricia Seaton, and we chatted for a few minutes and then I left. The next day I got his restaurant bill, which was marked "comped" and Lawford's business card, which read "Thanks, Mel." I had not invited Lawford to be my guest for dinner; therefore, I certainly hadn't intended to comp him. I had instructed the waiter only to buy him and his wife an after-dinner drink. Because he was a celebrity, he must have felt like he was entitled to a free meal. Not only did he sign the check, but he signed a 25 percent tip for the waiter and 15 percent for the maitre d'—all, of course, with my money. Rightly miffed, I called my friend the next day and chewed him out. "Don't do me any more favors by sending me your famous celebrity friends," I said, and then hung up.

Now, a real celebrity to me was a business mogul or tycoon, and they didn't come any bigger than Nevada billionaire Kirk Kerkorian. He visited Melvyn's one afternoon along with George Beebe, the former mayor of Palm Springs and a personal friend of mine. Kerkorian is known as one of the important figures in shaping the city of Las Vegas and the "father of the mega resort." I was absolutely thrilled George called me over to meet the famous entrepreneur. Kerkorian was the major stockholder of Metro-Goldwyn-Mayer Corporation as well as president/CEO of Tracinda Corporation, his private holding company based in Beverly Hills. I had begun accumulating a collection of books about or by people whom I had met over the years. As fate would have it, I had just finished reading a biography titled, *Kerkorian: An American Success* by Dial Torgerson. After our brief introduction, I made a mad dash home, which was about twelve blocks away, to grab the book for him to sign before they finished lunch. When I came back and presented the book for him to sign, he looked at me quite surprised. He hesitated and finally asked what I wanted inscribed in the book. I said, "To my friend, Mel and just sign your name." He seemed rather unsettled about the whole situation but signed the book nonetheless.

About a month later Mr. K was back at Melvyn's for dinner, this time with his famed LA attorney Greg Bautzer in tow. It was a very busy Saturday night—you could hardly walk through the restaurant—when my manager made his way over to me and said that Mr. Kerkorian wanted to see me. My heart skipped a beat because the manager said it seemed to be a matter of importance.

Nervous that the food or the service had been unsatisfactory, I fought my way through the jammed lounge to the front where Mr. Kerkorian was waiting by the exit. I politely inquired if everything had been to his liking. He responded, "Mel, the last time I was in here, you embarrassed me." I was totally taken aback and shocked. I searched my mind frantically for what had transpired the previous time he had been in, and could think of nothing significant. Very humbly I inquired what I had done.

"Don't you remember?" Mr. K asked. "You embarrassed me by asking for my autograph." I was sure he was putting me on. As I looked into his face, much to my shock, I realized he was dead serious. Suddenly feeling relieved that this was the extent of the damage I had done, I said, "Mr. Kerkorian, do you have any idea who you are?" Then it dawned on me in that very second that he really felt as if he was not worthy of somebody asking him for his autograph. Talk about humility.

I wish I could say the same thing for his son.

Over the next few months, Mr. K stayed in the hotel several times, and we exchanged greetings whenever possible. One day the front desk clerk informed me that MGM Studios had called to make a reservation for Kirk Kirkorian's son, who was planning on coming in the following weekend. I was extremely flattered that the Kerkorian family was making the Ingleside Inn their home-away-from-home.

As the young man checked in at the front desk, I went over and introduced myself. I inquired to his father's well-being and he told me "Dad" was in London working on a big business deal. He had been told by Kirk Sr. that if he went to Palm Springs, the only place to stay was the Ingleside Inn. That kind of endorsement was music to my ears and made me feel great. I asked the young man what he was doing in town and he told me that he was checking on the Canyon Hotel as a potential business deal for his father. The hotel, which was located about twenty-five blocks away on East Palm Canyon Drive, was a large property and had been closed for a year. I told him to feel free to contact me and if there was anything I could do to help him, I'd be more than happy to do so. That Saturday evening, several of my customers in the restaurant told me that they had met Kirk Kerkorian's son, and that he was very friendly and charming. He socialized with everyone at the bar and won them over with his affable personality. In addition he was quite a sport, buying everybody drinks.

The next day, while driving down Palm Canyon Drive with my wife, I stopped at a traffic light. Lo and behold, in the car next to me was George Beebe, the man who had originally brought Kirk Kerkorian into my restaurant. I leaned over and quite proudly yelled to George that Kirk Kirkorian's son was staying at my place, and that it was the beginning of a beautiful friendship. George leaned over and yelled back, "That's great, Mel. Kirk Kerkorian has no son!" I immediately drove to the Inn to see if he was still there only to find out that he had already checked out. He had signed the hotel bill for $1,250 and left specific instructions to bill MGM Studios. I didn't have to wait until Monday morning to find out that I had been had again. I found out later that I wasn't the only person in Palm Springs the young con man had fooled. It turned out that he had purchased a vast amount of jewelry from several shops in town and was able to secure the merchandise based on the Kerkorian name. Guess that's just the price you pay for doing business with the rich and infamous.

In the early eighties, there was a big Canadian presence in Palm Springs because the Canadian dollar was doing very well against the American dollar. A gentleman by the name of Colin Thatcher strolled into Melvyn's one day and someone told me he was very important in Canada. I eventually found out that Colin was the son of Wilbert Ross Thatcher, the Saskatchewan premier from 1964 to 1971. After his father's 1971 death, Colin rose in the political ranks and was elected to the Saskatchewan Legislative Assembly for a third time in 1982. He was appointed minister of energy and mines, a position that fascinated me very much because I had this fantasy that some day he would give me a tip on a penny stock that might turn it into two cents.

I treated Mr. Thatcher like a king and even introduced him to a couple of different ladies, including Lynn Dally, whose father owned a hotel down the block from the Ingleside Inn. One day Mr. Thatcher came into Melvyn's grousing about the fact that Canadian prime minister Pierre Trudeau was accusing him of murdering his ex-wife. Taken aback, I didn't know what else to say other than to ask him if he actually did.

"Why would I murder my *ex*-wife?" he responded. I sort of knew where he was coming from. If you're going to murder someone, why would it be your ex-wife if the divorce papers have already been signed, sealed, and delivered?

What I didn't know at the time was that he and his ex-wife, JoAnn, his wife of seventeen years, had been embroiled in a nasty and very public custody battle for their children three years after their divorce was granted.

In January of 1983, JoAnn was beaten and shot in the head at her home. On the day he did it, Thatcher called Lynn Dally and confessed, "Well, I finally did it. I just blew away my wife." It was her testimony that convinced a jury to charge Colin Thatcher with first-degree murder almost sixteen months after the incident. He was sentenced to life in prison with no chance of parole for twenty-five years.

There have since been no fewer than five books on the murder and a TV miniseries based on Thatcher's life. My association with Thatcher was referenced in a couple of books, most notably *Deny, Deny, Deny: The Rise and Fall of Colin Thatcher* by Garret Wilson and Lesley Wilson.

Thatcher made headlines again in May 2006 when he was released on parole to a halfway home. He now lives quietly in Moose Jaw, Canada.

But far and away the biggest thing to hit Palm Springs in the eighties was the arrival of Jim and Tammy Faye Baker, the couple who headed up the Praise the Lord ministry empire. Of course, PTL had a couple of different meanings in the desert—"Pass the Loot" or "Pay for Tammy's Lashes." Take your pick.

The couple significantly raised the profile of the Palm Springs area, with reporters and television crews constantly hounding the couple as their empire crumbled around them. Forget Bob Hope, Frank Sinatra, Dinah Shore, or Liberace, the Bakers ruled the headlines because of their flashy and opulent lifestyle and eye-popping spending sprees. They reportedly owned six mansions, including a $600,000 home on Greenbriar Lane. They later upgraded to a more secure place in the Las Palmas area of Palm Springs as the dough kept rolling in to the tune of $500,000 a day. Court records show the couple eventually burned through $158 million of their ministry's money, which included $60,000 for gold-plated bathroom fixtures, matching gold dog collars for their pets, and an air-conditioned doghouse. The Bakers even spent $100 in cinnamon rolls just to imbue their hotel suite with the smell. Interestingly enough, Tammy spent a lot of her time in the aisles of a local Thrifty Drug Store looking for discount cosmetics and makeup. Eventually the couple found their way to Melvyn's and the Bakers became regulars for lunch. Tammy bought a lot of costume jewelry from a jewelry store located inside the Ingleside Inn, which almost dragged me into a North Carolina court.

You see, in 1989 Jim Baker was indicted on federal charges of fraud, tax evasion, and racketeering. The prosecutor in the case subpoenaed me to testify against him. I called the prosecutor when I received the subpoena and said, "I really have nothing to offer you. It doesn't pay for the government to fly me to North Carolina. They had lunch at my place a few times and Tammy bought some inexpensive costume jewelry. That's it." The prosecutor took me at my word and didn't push the issue. However, he didn't need me to convict the defrocked evangelist. His own lawyer pretty much did him in with his closing remark: "If a man raises over $150 million for a business that competed with Disney and the major networks and kept $3 million for himself, he may be guilty of mismanagement, naiveté, even stupidity, but should it be a crime? Do you think (Jerry) Falwell lives in a five-room house?" The defense failed and Baker was charged with twenty-four counts of fraud, sentenced to forty-five years in prison, and ordered to repay $500,000 in restitution. Later his sentence was voided as was the half-million-dollar fine.

After the trial, Tammy remained in Palm Springs and divorced Jim in 1992. A year later she got remarried to Moe Ressner, a former

Heritage USA (the giant PTL theme park) contractor who was very devoted to her. I had always liked Tammy and got to know her even better as she participated in one of my charity events by volunteering to sing. Underneath it all, she was a very nice and sweet lady. Sadly, Tammy Faye passed away in 2007, God rest her soul.

Even though the Bakers epitomized the excesses of the eighties, life in Palm Springs just hasn't been the same, or as much fun.

# CHAPTER 12

# I Take This Man...
# For Everything He's Got

By the spring of 1976, my relationship with Barbra Khan began to unravel. We had been drifting apart for some time. I thought by throwing myself into my work, our problems would magically disappear.

While ours was a case of opposites attract in the beginning of our relationship, the bottom line was that we had radically different values, and we weren't really compatible as a couple. Despite my success, it was obvious that nothing short of living with the King and Queen of England would satisfy her. While I liked the high standards Barbra set for a lot of things, she carried them to an extreme, even when she couldn't really live up to the image she created.

To cope, she began drinking heavily, and her behavior turned self-destructive. In the beginning, she came to Melvyn's with me all the time, but that became less frequent over time. I constantly called the condominium to make sure everything was all right.

When she was at the bar or restaurant drinking, there was no telling what would come out of her mouth. David Ladd (son of actor Alan Ladd) who at the time was married to *Charlie's Angels* costar Cheryl Ladd, and was a very good customer, tried to get Barbra's attention one night. He spent a good deal of the evening fighting the overflow crowd to get to her. Finally he got to Barbra at the bar where I was sitting next to her.

"Barbra, I've been trying to say hello to you all night," he said in an exasperated tone. She was pretty well lit and shot him a disdainful look.

"Big deal," she said. That was fairly typical of hundreds of similar, minor incidents.

Another time, we hosted a charity event and the bar was jammed. I noticed that Barbra was getting loaded, and so I ordered the bartenders not to give her any more alcohol. About twenty minutes later, I saw her lurching around drinking again. I was so incensed at the bartender that I was going to fire him for disobeying me. He told me that he hadn't served her, that she'd been getting other people to buy her drinks, and they were sneaking them to Barbra on the side. It was a pretty hopeless situation.

More and more, we'd end up having conversations about the probability that our three-year relationship had run its course. We'd even discussed how we'd be able to handle splitting up. It was obvious that it was just a question of time.

Barbra never talked about what she would do if we broke up, although I had no doubt that she'd end up on her feet. She had kept her little black book of contacts, and she had places to go and people to lean on. I felt that I'd be the one who'd have a much harder time after we split up. In her own little way, she'd let me know that I was the one who was dating up and that she could do much better than me. I always lived with the understanding that Barbra felt she was destined to go on to bigger and better things.

By this time, there wasn't much left to our relationship, and so Barbra took on another tack. Whereas she had always put down everything and everyone around me, Barbra started to level her attacks at me directly. I was very passive about the whole thing, and I thought I would just ride it out. I tried many times to discuss the situation but gave up when I realized I was wasting my breath. All I could do was wait for the straw that would break the camel's back. Or in this particular case, wait for Barbra to literally break my back.

One evening we had a dinner date with another couple who happened to be two of my favorite people. The couple hadn't seen each other for a while; she was a local lady and he was from out of town. I felt it was an honor to be asked to join them on their first night back together. Barbra could not have cared less and was not particularly thrilled.

Because we were very close friends, they knew Barbra could be very difficult, so they were tolerant of her for my sake. I was not deluded about how people reacted to Barbra, but I hoped they saw her good qualities as I did. I always hoped that they had enough respect for me to realize that there had to be more to Barbra than what they saw.

During our dinner, Barbra proceeded to get drunker by the minute. Eventually, she started to berate me in front of my friends and the atmosphere at the table was very tense. She became totally obnoxious and descended into name-calling. I put a cap on the evening, mumbling something to the other couple and told Barbra it was time to go home. She reluctantly agreed, because at this point she was actually enjoying herself.

Out in the parking lot I walked her to her car. She was going to drive her car home and I was going to follow in mine. As I walked in front of her vehicle to get to my car, she started her engine and then tried to hit me. I jumped out of the way and screamed, "Barbra, are you crazy?"

When I tried to walk to my car again, she made another attempt to run me down. Once again, I jumped out of the way, and she finally drove off. We went to sleep that night without speaking.

The following morning I got up around seven, and went to the Inn. A few hours later, Barbra called and asked, "Sweetheart, why did we leave in such a hurry last night?" I told her I'd be right home.

When I got to the condo, I told her that she tried to kill me using a 3,000-pound assault weapon. She didn't believe me. As usual, Barbra didn't remember a thing.

After we spent an emotionally filled hour discussing the fact that we had to break up, Barbra packed her things, got into her car, and drove off. I had no idea where she was going.

When I got back to the Inn about an hour later, I sat down on the veranda trying to shake off the cobwebs, playing back in my mind what had just happened. I felt very lonely, lost, and empty. As I was sitting there thinking about my newfound single status, a beautiful woman with chestnut hair and brown eyes walked up to me and said hello. As we chatted, I realized that I'd met her several months before at the hotel and even played a few games of back-gammon with her. Her name was Deann, and she was visiting from Newport Beach.

When I had originally met Deann, I thought that if Barbra and I ever broke up, she was the kind of woman I would like to go out with. As I stood there in my dazed and confused condition listening to her talk, all the memories came flooding back. I asked her to have dinner with me that evening.

I explained to Deann that I had just broken up with Barbra, and she accepted my invitation. It was a nice evening, and it helped me to forget about my problems for a while.

The next day Deann left and went back to Newport Beach. Larry Perino, a local restaurateur/friend of mine, called to say that he had two guests at his establishment. He said they were looking for a place to stay for a few nights. One was the actress Susan George and the other was her secretary. He asked if I had a room to accommodate them. I told him to send them over. I made arrangements at the front desk to make sure they were given VIP treatment.

After the two ladies checked in, I called their room to ensure everything was to their liking. Ms. George answered the phone and was lovely. Feeling a little lonely, I took the bold step of asking Susan and her secretary to join me for dinner as my guests. Turned out, Susan had just broken up with singer Jack Jones, whom she had been living with for the past several years. She was as emotionally distraught as I was and gladly accepted my invitation.

After I greeted the two ladies in Melvyn's, I led them to a table and sat down with them. I was paying a lot of attention to the lady who was sitting closest to me, thinking it was Susan George. Predictably, I spent a lot of time romancing the wrong person. When I called her "Susan" one too many times, the blond movie star said in exasperation, "Mel, I'm Susan George."

Susan quickly forgave me and I became her escort for the next couple of days. I showed her around Palm Springs, and we ate at great restaurants and drank and danced at all the hot spots. We had a very nice time together. One night we ventured to the famous disco, Pal Joey's, and soon word got around town that we were an item. I must say I enjoyed the attention.

About a week after Barbra left, I received a phone call from her, asking what the hell I was doing. I asked her what she meant, and she told me that she'd heard through the grapevine that I was dating someone else.

"Why shouldn't I date someone else?" I asked in all sincerity.

Barbra told me that she was at a health farm, and she was not aware that we had actually broken up. It was just another flim-flam game with my emotions where she completely ignored reality. The fact that I had broken up with Barbra threw her for a loop. I finally got her to remember the conversation where we had both agreed we should break up. I assured her that I was still her friend and that if she were ever in trouble, I would be there for her and help in any way I could. In spite of the fact that I was hurting for money, I told her that she could keep the $10,000 Mercedes sports car that she had driven away in and that I would give her $5,000 cash to help set her up in an apartment.

When we hung up, I felt everything had been ironed out and that there should not be any misunderstandings of any sort between us. During the call, Barbra asked about picking up the rest of her personal belongings. I told her to call and let me know when she wanted to come. I wanted to make sure I was out of town so that we'd avoid any hassles.

The day Barbra came to Palm Springs I did go out of town, but arranged for my son Lonny, who was now working for me, to help her. As far as I was concerned, she was free to take whatever she wanted out of the condominium. As it turned out, when she arrived in town, she went straight to Melvyn's to pick up a bottle of Dom Perignon and proceeded to drink it all while she emptied the apartment.

Toward the end of the summer, I received a credit card bill in the mail, and it was for approximately $3,500. I looked at the list of charges and saw a number of strange entries: a round-trip ticket to Las Vegas, as well as purchases at shoe and clothing stores in Beverly Hills and a few restaurants thrown in for good measure. I wrote back to the company asking them to send me copies of the slips on the statement. They sent me back a bunch of charge slips signed by "Barbra Haber." I couldn't believe her nerve. I had given her the car and $5,000, and she still felt I should pay all of her bills.

A few months after we split, Barbra moved in with a guy who lived in a large mansion in Holmby Hills, an affluent suburb of Los Angeles. She regaled me with stories about her exciting social life, the elegant functions she attended, and the life of leisure she was leading.

Theoretically, Barbra should have been very happy living in such splendor. The gentleman she was living with could buy and sell me several times over, and had introduced her to a very exclusive social circle. It sounded as if she had everything she ever wanted. Yet I couldn't help but notice she seemed unhappy when she called, and was obviously still drinking more than was good for her.

Often she hinted about the possibility of us getting together again and would list all the changes I would need to make in my life. I'd end up pointing out all the reasons why it was impossible for us to get back together. It was a conversation that followed the same route every time. Inevitably, Barbra would get annoyed and began dicing me up verbally, and it would just revive all my bad memories of her.

Back to the credit card—when I brought up the $3,500 in charges, she sort of giggled, as if it didn't mean anything. She was right. The next bill she would present to me would have many more zeros behind them.

Some time right at the beginning of 1977, I remember walking into Melvyn's and hearing a couple of customers discussing a recent lawsuit involving actor Lee Marvin and his former girlfriend Michelle Triola. Triola claimed that Marvin, who was still married at the time they began living together, had promised to support her for the rest of her life. The California Supreme Court handed down what became known as the Lee Marvin Decision, the case which set legal precedence for unmarried cohabitants to sue for support and other property rights with the same equal force of law as married partners.

I stood there and listened for a few minutes while one of the men outlined the details of the case. I remember being totally amazed, although it had nothing to do with my life. I laughed and slapped my friend on the back and told him not to waste much time worrying about it.

"We're just regular guys—you've got to be rich and famous to attract that kind of attention from an ex-girlfriend," I said. "It might just be some kind of publicity stunt."

"Marvin doesn't need it," replied my friend.

"Well, maybe the girl wants publicity," I replied. "Who knows what kind of craziness might be going on? I don't think they can make laws like that and make it stick in court. There wouldn't be any dating anymore, nobody would stand for it."

Several days later, I was in my bar when a lawyer, who often came to Melvyn's, pulled me aside. He told me that Barbra was shopping around Los Angeles for a lawyer. My immediate thought was that she'd gotten herself into some sort of trouble, and I wondered whether I should call her. My friend was staring hard at me and said, "You don't understand, do you? Barbra wants to sue you; she's going to take a shot at you."

I still didn't fully comprehend what he was talking about, so he spelled it out for me: "She's going to sue you along the same lines that Michelle Triola is suing Lee Marvin."

I couldn't understand on what basis Barbra would be suing me. We'd been broken up for a good six months and she was now living with a very wealthy man. I was also still paying her car and medical insurance. Why would she sue the one person she could always count on? It was ludicrous.

The conversation ended with the lawyer saying: "To be fore-warned is to be forearmed." The statement struck me as rather dramatic, and I told him that I would call Barbra to find out what was going on. A couple of days later, I called her on some unrelated pretext. During the conversation, there was no hint that she intended to sue me. I let it drop because I was convinced my lawyer friend must have gotten his wires crossed. Turned out, his wires were working just fine and mine had short-circuited.

A month later I was sitting by my pool doing some paperwork when I received a call from a *Desert Sun* reporter. He was calling from the Indio Courthouse, and informed me that a lawsuit had just been filed against me by a lawyer representing Barbra. He wanted a comment from me about the case, but all he got was dead silence as I reeled back in my chair with shock and disbelief.

Seven days later, I had the papers in my hands, after being formally served. I went momentarily comatose, to the point where my mouth would open but no sound would come out. Barbra was suing me for $400,000, and I had no idea why or how she could do it.

When I thought about it, I could not think of anything Barbra had done that was of financial benefit to me. All I could think of was that I'd paid for everything when we lived together. If anything, she had been a drain on my finances, though I bore no grudge as to the vast amount of money I'd spent on her. She certainly didn't give up a career for me, nor was there a promise to financially compensate her for not working. Furthermore, when she had divorced her husband and was entitled to some money, she didn't take two cents from him. This was all about "hell hath no fury like a woman scorned."

My first reaction was that my children were in danger of losing whatever money I had managed to accumulate. I'd never stopped to consider what a $400,000 loss could do to my entire financial structure, but when confronted with Barbra's claim, I realized that such a loss would totally wipe me out. It was an incredible sum of money at the time, hardly what I could pass off as spare change.

I spent several frustrating hours pacing my house before I decided to call Barbra and find out what she was thinking and feeling.

Mostly, I called to find out why she had initiated legal proceedings.

She told me that she worked for a large real estate firm in Beverly Hills and just made a large sale with a big commission. Barbra added that she didn't need my money. I asked her then why was she suing me? I'll never forget the words that came out of her mouth.

"The only reason I'm doing this is because I want to make sure I'm the first thing you think about when you get up in the morning and the last thing you think about before you go to bed at night," Barbra said. Then the phone clicked dead, and I was left holding onto a silent telephone receiver. I was even more frustrated and shaken up than I had been before I had placed the call.

Barbra's pot shot was more than just a setback, it had the potential to completely devastate my little world, shattering the life I had created for myself and my family over a twenty-five-year period.

What was really mind-boggling was that I was still married to Pat, although legally separated (eventually leading to divorce a few years later). So how could I possibly be obligated to two women at the same time? I was actually served with the lawsuit at Melvyn's one evening. Coincidentally, the famous attorney Greg Bautzer was dining at the time and I asked him if he would be kind enough to look at the papers for me. After reading them he said "meretricious—there is no case—she can't be paid for sex." He then called a very famous Beverly Hills divorce attorney and made an appointment for me for the next day. I anxiously drove to Beverly Hills early the next morning. The lawyer explained that we would have to take a deposition from everybody who knew Barbra and me. After he told me his hourly charge I realized that if I paid Barbra the $400,000, I would save a lot of money over what he would cost me. After a lot of networking I finally picked an attorney to defend me.

Just at that time *Los Angeles Magazine* was doing an article on the very same subject. Because I was the first person to be sued (Lee Marvin had not been served yet), the writer called me up and interviewed me. In the course of the interview, the reporter asked, "If you're married and the money you have to pay your wife is alimony, what is it called if you're not married?"

"Palimony," I said without thinking. Immediately recognizing the fact that I had just created "gold," I attempted to register the word with the Screen Writers Guild only to be told I needed a title. I sent them a title, only to be told I needed an outline, only to be told I needed something else. In total frustration, I simply sent myself a registered letter stating that on that day I invented the word "palimony." To this day that envelope is in my safety deposit box. Why? I don't know. It's never earned me a dime. Turned out it didn't do me much good anyway. Attorney Marvin Mitchelson, who represented Michelle Triola, is often (and wrongly) credited for creating the word that I had originally coined.

As a result of my lawsuit, I was invited to appear on several talk shows. I figured I would use the publicity to promote the Ingleside Inn and Melvyn's and salvage some good out of the situation. In other words, I was going to try and make lemonade out of lemons.

Knowing that the upcoming Lee Marvin trial would generate headlines, I decided that I could make some money if I wrote a book on palimony. I figured the book would have to be on the shelves by the time his trial rolled around, so I rolled up my sleeves and got to work.

Loaded with boundless energy, I got up every day at four o' clock in the morning, dictated several pages, dropped them off at a secretarial service, and picked them up at the end of the day to edit. I had a great title all picked out, *I Take This Man…For Everything He's Got: The Case Against Palimony*. My creative juices were really flowing, and I even took a picture with my current girlfriend for what I thought would be a very provocative cover: a man and woman in a passionate embrace. However, while the woman's arms are around him, she is slipping his wallet out of his back pocket.

The message of the book was that you didn't have to be a movie or rock star to get sued for palimony. It was not the great American novel, but it discussed the issue in a serious vein and at the same time poked fun at the problem. I wasn't going to win a Pulitzer, but I must say it was a good read on a very timely subject. The content really didn't matter because the Lee Marvin trial would sell the book. I knew that simply based on all the requests for interviews I was receiving.

I was going to New York on family business, so I contacted a literary agent and asked him if he could set up an appointment with some publishers. He was able to get me in to three major publishing houses. I explained that I didn't write for a living but was just trying to capitalize on my unfortunate situation. I explained that the headlines from the Lee Marvin trial would sell the book. If necessary I was willing to pay for the production, but I needed them for the distribution. I said I would do as many radio, print, or TV interviews as they wanted. All three companies turned me down, and the only reasons I could come up with were that I talk too fast and you can't sell yourself. You really need an agent to do that for you.

The Marvin trial made national headlines for approximately a month and there is no doubt in my mind that any book on the subject would have been hugely successful. I know this because in addition to being bombarded by reporters, I was invited to make several TV appearances, including the *Steve Edwards Show*, the *David Suskind Show*, and the *Phil Donahue Show*.

The morning of the *Phil Donahue Show*, which was taped in Chicago at that time, they had a long elegant limousine and driver waiting for me in front of the hotel with coffee and pastries. I realized I could get used to this sort of treatment very quickly.

I debated attorney Marvin Mitchelson on the show, and after we verbally jousted for almost an hour, I was ready to head back to Palm Springs. When we finished I asked the producer where I would find the limousine. She said, "He left. Would you like me to call you a cab?" I felt like saying, "No problem, I'll just walk the twenty miles to the airport." At least I was a big shot one-way!

Much to my surprise, I was quite articulate and eloquent on the subject. As a matter of fact, when the show started, it was explained that I had left a wife and three children, then lived with a woman for three years and broke up with her, and she was now suing me for support. I was actually booed by the conservative, Midwestern audience. I said that I was being penalized because I had been monogamous after a long marriage. If I had been promiscuous and slept around, I wouldn't be having this problem. My argument was simply that marriage is basically a legal contract, and people know exactly what their obligations are when they enter into matrimony. People who choose not to get married are voluntarily and consciously avoiding those legal obligations.

It seemed as if the government was suggesting that if a man pays a woman's way during a relationship, he must keep on paying her way when their relationship is over.

The reality would seem to be that there is no freedom of choice anymore. It doesn't matter that two people choose to live together and not get married. The courts can put them in the position of being married anyway. At the end of the show I got a standing ovation.

A *60 Minutes* producer thought I was so articulate on the *Phil Donahue Show* that she called and wanted me to do their show on palimony. It seemed that the Lee Marvin case had broken the dam, and several people across the country were getting sued, including rockers Rod Stewart and Alice Cooper and Paramount movie executive Freddie Fields.

The producer asked me not to appear on any other national television shows until I did *60 Minutes* first. I was all set to appear on *The Cathy Crosby Show*, which was nationally syndicated, but I canceled as per the request of the *60 Minutes* producer.

Two days before the *60 Minutes* crew was to show up at my house to tape me, I got a call from Marvin Mitchelson. He told me that he'd gotten into a hassle with Mike Wallace and ended up telling Wallace to take a hike.

What Mitchelson really wanted was for me to call up *60 Minutes* and tell them that I could talk him into doing the show. He was too embarrassed or too egotistical (probably the latter) to call them back and ask to get back on the show himself, so he was asking me to do it for him so he could save face. I know it sounds strange, but we had become friendly because of the many television appearances we made together despite the fact that we held opposite positions. We became unofficially known as "The Melvyn and Marvin Show." The two of us made a good pairing for television and we both knew it.

Having me do Mitchelson's bidding was a way for him to protect his interests in the issue.

So I called Mike Wallace and asked if he was having a problem with Mitchelson. He said he was pretty angry with my counterpart. I asked him that if I could smooth things out, would he reconsider putting Mitchelson back in the show. Wallace said yes, and we were back in business.

The day before my segment was to be taped, Wallace's producer, Marion Goldin, called me to tell me that they couldn't use me. She told me the segment was already filled and they wouldn't be out to tape me after all. I took what she said at face value and figured they must have found another man to present the argument against palimony. But I was still a little uneasy and frustrated and wondered whether there was any relationship between my getting Mitchelson back on the show and my own part being canceled. To say I was disappointed is a major understatement.

The real frustration came on the day the show was actually aired. During the entire segment they chose to present only the woman's side of the case. It was a rerun of so many other shows I had seen where Mitchelson and a variety of his celebrity clients—all of them women—made their pitch for palimony.

Of all the comments Mitchelson made on that show, I objected most to his comment that the Lee Marvin decision was a way of providing protection for women. It's degrading to insinuate that women are incapable of looking out for themselves, that women should be considered almost the same as minors and need the courts to look after their personal lives. It's also very strange that the courts did not consider the problem when these women made the decision to enter into relationships where there were no obligations and responsibilities. Nobody saw any reason to protect them then, probably because the protection was already there by way of marriage if they wanted it.

Wallace said in the segment that they had tried to find a man to represent the other side of the issue, but could find no one willing to speak up. I had steam coming out of my ears.

To add insult to injury, during my meeting with the producers of *60 Minutes*, I told them about the book I was in the process of writing (*I Take This Man…For Everything He's Got*). If you guessed that was the title of the segment *60 Minutes* used for their piece, you get a prize. Unfortunately I got the booby prize—I still had to go to court and fight this case.

Our case finally wound its way through the system, and we faced off in the Indio Courthouse for seven days. While waiting for the judge's decision, I hid out at a friend's house in Beverly Hills. I was so nervous I couldn't function. The judge's last name was "Slaughter," which I took as a bad omen. Fortunately for me, he ruled that the case had no merit and found in my favor. Oddly enough, I found out about the verdict from a *Los Angeles Times* reporter. Somehow, he tracked me down and was the first to call, even before my own lawyer. I cannot describe the feeling of relief when he told me the verdict.

A few years later, the California Supreme Court ruled that Michelle Triola had not proven the existence of a contract between herself and Marvin that gave her an interest in his property. Thus, the common law rule applied to the situation without alteration, and she took away from the relationship and the household what she brought to it—nothing.

But neither case stopped the flow of palimony suits. In 1982, pianist and Palm Springs resident Liberace was sued for $113 million in palimony by his live-in boyfriend Scott Thorson. Most of Thorson's claim was dismissed, but he did receive a settlement of $95,000.

Three years later, following the death of Rock Hudson, his live-in lover Marc Christian filed a palimony lawsuit against his estate in 1985 and won.

And even as late as 2004, comedian and TV host Bill Maher was sued for $9 million by his ex-girlfriend, Nancy Johnson, a.k.a. "Coco Johnsen," for palimony. In May of 2005, a superior court judge dismissed the lawsuit.

At the end of the relationship, I wrote a beautiful line to sum up my feelings for Barbra: "The days may come when I stop loving you, but I will never stop loving the days I loved you." Fortunately I did not have to change it to "The days may come when I stop loving you, but I will never stop *paying* for the days I loved you."

I was lucky that the law sided with me in my palimony case: I was able to keep my money, my kids kept their inheritance, and the Ingleside Inn and Melvyn's got a new cousin called Cecil's.

# CHAPTER 13

# When Disco Was King: The Story of Cecil's

When rubbing elbows with some of the biggest names in show business, politics, and high society, a fellow can't help achieving his own level of fame, no matter how minuscule. As a result of my palimony case and as the owner of the Ingleside Inn and Melvyn's, I became "half a celebrity."

For example, one evening I was having drinks with a buddy in Melvyn's after I had just completed a two-month period of television appearances as well as giving several interviews to the print media. I had appeared on *60 Minutes* (a segment on Palm Springs, not palimony), on the *David Suskind Show*, and on the *Phil Donahue Show*, which were all very popular national shows at the time. My buddy asked if I had seen any benefit to my business as a result of all my media exposure. I told him I really wasn't sure, but many people recognized me on the street and in various places. Just then, a restaurant customer was passing by on the way to the men's room. He stopped dead in his tracks, looked at me, and said, "Hey, I know you—I just saw you on the *Phil Donahue Show*." With that, I turned to my friend at the bar and shot him a smug look as if to say, I told you so. The customer then said, "Yeah, I thought you were very good on the show. By the way, what do you do?"

While I had my ego indulged many times, this fame business took a little getting used to. I received personal regards from people who had never spoken to me before, and customers would drop names of relatives I never knew existed in hopes of either impressing me or to cut down their wait time for a table. Once a woman called me over to her table to show me her charm bracelet—it had my picture on one of the charms along with various members of her family. I had even been asked for my autograph on several occasions.

For a while it seemed as if I went to school with every New Yorker and that everybody in the Big Apple seemed to know who I was. One day a customer called me from New York City in a very excited tone and said she had to tell me what just happened. She had been shopping and hailed a taxicab (there are probably some 25,000 in New York City) to return to her hotel. On the way, the driver inquired where she was from. She told him Palm Springs, California. Without missing a beat, the cabbie asked, "Do you know Mel Haber?"

When you're big, you're big!

It also paid to be half a celebrity. One of the more interesting things that happened to me during that period occurred one Saturday night when Melvyn's was jammed. A customer I had never met before practically fought his way through the crowd to meet me.

"I understand you're the owner?" he said.

"Yes, I'm Mel Haber," I said rather formally.

"You've got a really nice place here," he said. "Really super place." He then shook my hand and pressed my palm with some cash—something that had never happened to me before. Hey, I don't care who you are or how much money you have; a little more disposable income is always a good thing. As the guy left, I looked in my hand excitedly and discovered he left me a single dollar bill!

I also learned that instant fame was not only intoxicating but potentially fatal. When I first came to town, I discovered that one of Palm Springs's old guard was a retired doctor, Norman Haber. His wife was a lovely lady, whose name was Minette. Her car's personalized license plate was "M. Haber." Frequently people around town mentioned seeing me at various places because they had seen the vanity plate, M. Haber, and assumed it was me.

One day Minette was driving on the street behind the Ingleside Inn when her car backfired rather loudly and stalled in the middle of the road. There wasn't much she could do, so she left the vehicle in the middle of the street and came into the restaurant to call for a tow truck. One of the neighbors heard the loud backfire, looked out the window and saw the license plate. The neighbor naturally assumed that it was my vehicle and determined that the loud noise had been a gunshot. She called the police and reported that Mel Haber had just been shot.

Minette and I were sitting in Melvyn's, having a cup of coffee, waiting for her tow truck to arrive. Two cops rushed into the restaurant and informed the maitre d' that Mel Haber had just been shot. I almost had the chance to read my own obituary.

I could have died and gone to heaven when Joe DiMaggio stayed at the Ingleside Inn for a week. The famed New York Yankee slugger was a very low-key person but possessed a lot of class. I was thrilled and honored to meet him.

A friend of mine had just returned from a celebrity golf tournament in Las Vegas and said that when he told his celebrity golf partner he was from Palm Springs, Joe DiMaggio replied, "I have a good friend there. Do you know Mel Haber?" Even though I grew up rooting for the Brooklyn Dodgers, Joe almost converted me into a lifetime Yankees fan with that one statement.

But nothing illustrates better my newfound fame than the time when football icon Sid Luckman planted a big smooch on my cheek in broad daylight. I was having breakfast in Las Vegas in the Dunes Hotel coffee shop with my maitre d' and friend, Arturo Petorini. All of a sudden, a large man walked up out of nowhere, took my head in his hands, gave me a big fat kiss, and said, "Arturo says you're the greatest."

"Who are you?" I said, a little taken aback.

"It doesn't matter," he replied. "If Arturo says you're the greatest, then you're the greatest." He then gave me another kiss. "If you ever come to Chicago, just give me a call."

Moments later, football coach George Allen walked up to my demonstrative new friend and said, "Come on, Sid, let's go." Like a bell that went off in my head, it hit me—Sid Luckman, the Hall of Fame quarterback for the Chicago Bears and fellow Erasmus High School alumni just treated me, Mel Haber, like a prom date.

When Luckman later came to Palm Springs, he got in touch again, but spared me the kiss. He called me at the hotel and said, "How can I come to Palm Springs without calling my good buddy, Mel Haber?"

Life was good, and I thought I could do no wrong. I decided to parlay my success with the Ingleside Inn and Melvyn's and take a chance on another venture because I recognized a big void in the marketplace for two products—an elegant discotheque and some really great Chinese food.

I will concede it was a peculiar entertainment concept, but I knew the town, I knew the clientele, and I knew their tastes. I was on a roll, and I knew it would work.

In the mid-to-late seventies, when disco music was in full bloom, Palm Springs had only two discos—Zelda's, which catered to the younger crowd, and Pal Joey's, which was jam-packed every night. Unless you knew somebody at Pal Joey's, you weren't getting in.

In early 1978, I thought about opening my own private club/disco in the back of Melvyn's where everyone would have to pay for a membership. I was going to call it "Shhhhhh." I even went so far as to have a logo made up of a woman's finger over her lips.

I was going to knock out six hotel rooms in the back of Melvyn's and build a very private and exclusive club. It was going to be a nice, posh setting with couches and tables, a bartender, and its own dance floor. But just then one of my customers came to me and said he knew of a large restaurant that just closed and the space could be leased at a very reasonable rent.

I went over and looked at the building, which was located in the Smoke Tree Shopping Center at the corner of Sunrise and Palm Canyon, approximately twelve blocks from the Ingleside Inn and Melvyn's. The site was the former location of Ethel's Hideaway, a famous restaurant that closed down because the owners were retiring.

The place had several things going for it—all the kitchen equipment was available, and the center offered lots of parking because all of the other tenants were closed at night. But best of all was that I would get a year's concession on the rent. I negotiated to take over the 9,000-square-foot building in September 1978.

When I lived in New York, I belonged to a semiprivate club called Cavalleros, which had a very unique concept. The front area consisted of a bar and lounge that was open to the public. This was a great observation point from which to see everybody coming and going into the exclusive private club in the back. The club consisted of a backgammon room and a beautiful dining room with a dance floor in the center. Members of the club would stroll nonchalantly through the front public area to the receptionist of the club to make sure everyone knew they were VIPs. After spending a few minutes inside, single members would come back out to the public area and choose a lady to invite to go back with them into the club. Make no mistake, every woman there was dying to get back into the private club. I loved this concept.

I was really excited about building a first-class discotheque and gourmet Chinese restaurant. I wanted to open a place where a man could take a date for a night of dinner and dancing or, if he were single, could meet a nice lady, and vice versa. I wanted to bring back the grand elegance and glamour of nightclubs like the Copacabana, the Stork Club, and the Trocadero, which served sumptuous food with superb service for a memorable night on the town. It would be a place that you would want to get dressed up for; a place where you were sure the members of the opposite sex were of the highest caliber.

After I signed the lease, I headed to Las Vegas to look at several discos; including one owned by singer Paul Anka called Jubilation. In my opinion, there was something wrong with every one of them. I noticed the same problems at every club: if you did not dance, it was obvious that you were a wallflower, and the music was so loud that patrons could barely talk to each other and were practically screaming in each other's ears. I wanted my club to rectify both of those problems.

I also spent many weekends in Los Angeles, where the club scene was off the charts. I went to all of the "in" clubs at the time—the Daisy, the Candy Store, Pips, and the Sports Page. They catered to the beautiful people and had the customers that I wanted.

One of the clubs I visited in Beverly Hills was Chamois, a club located behind the Beverly Wilshire Hotel. It was tastefully decorated, and it had an elegant, comfortable ambiance. I decided to seek out the designer of that club.

I found the club manager and inquired who the decorator was. It turned out to be a French Canadian gentleman named Gilbert Konqui. I contacted Mr. Konqui in Canada and explained that I wanted to put together a very elegant nightclub in Palm Springs and asked him if he'd be interested in helping me. Coincidentally, he had also been the decorator of Zelda's and had gotten into a disagreement with the owners; giving him a personal motivation for designing and decorating a competitive club. He flew down, we met, and I was very impressed. I found him to be very creative, and he said that he was extremely motivated to do a great job.

"I helped decorate Zelda's (the rival disco in town), and the owners never paid me in full," Gilbert said. "I'm going to make your club drop-dead gorgeous. That's how I will get even with him." You can bet that I was going to make sure that Mr. Konqui got paid on time.

I explained to Gilbert my vision, which was to divide the clubs into two halves—one would be a full-blown, state-of-the-art discotheque, and the other would be a gourmet Chinese restaurant with a dance floor in the middle of the room for slow dancing after the dinner hour. The idea was that if a gentleman met a lady in the disco and wanted to talk, steal her away from the competition, or dance cheek-to-cheek with her, he could simply bring her into the restaurant side for a more romantic setting. The restaurant would also cater to the older crowd who didn't like disco music. But what was essential to the club's success was the long bar at the entry where patrons could watch all the beautiful people who went into the disco. The disco was not only going to be fun, but it was going to be a great people-watching event.

I wanted the disco to be a theater-in-the-round, with the people on the dance floor as the show. It was going to be the most talked about nightclub since Studio 54. It took several months of planning, blazing new methods for sound systems, exploring new eras for lighting, and so on.

I wanted it to be more than just a disco. It was my fantasy, my dream. I was going to implement every idea I ever had for an elegant club. It was a place where you would always find fun and friends. I didn't want a room with music blaring and flashing lights. I wanted a place where people could sit and watch the dancers, or just chat in normal tones. Everywhere I turned, the experts told me I couldn't have all the things that I had wanted. But I was very clear in my vision, and I was intent on finding a solution.

I visited several theaters-in-the-round and saw how the audience could surround the stage, feel a part of it, yet still be separate. I decided that the dancers should be the stars of the show, and patrons could either take part or simply kick back and watch. Gilbert described what he was going to do, painting a visual picture that was even better than what I ever imagined. We started work in December 1978.

I pored over many architectural drawings until I found the right one. Once the customer seating—tables, booths, and comfortable chairs—was placed in staggered elevations, the dance floor got the Haber touch. It was made out of brass and steel, which had a mirrored column in the center that was set under a huge glass umbrella, which was fifteen feet in diameter. A galaxy of star-lights, a halo of strobes, was set to flash their light to the beat of the music, and fog portholes at the base of the twelve-foot high DJ booth emitted dry ice smoke to swirl out around the dancer's feet. The walls had approximately fifty niches with lighted artifacts. When activated, the niches pulsed to the tempo of the music. There were also fifty different lighting effects in the room generated by the computer in the disco booth.

Of course, the biggest challenge was the sound system. Everyone told me there was no way a disco could provide all that energy on the dance floor, and yet be soft enough to permit conversation for the other patrons. But I was determined. It took months of visualizing, thousands of dollars, and many experts to make it work, but I finally did it. We arched a halo of speakers aimed at only the dance floor and not toward the booths, tables, and bar area. It worked beautifully.

While the disco was in good hands, there was the restaurant portion of the puzzle still to solve. Gourmet Oriental cuisine in an elegant setting was the theme I was shooting for. Being from the East Coast, I had always found Chinese food on the West Coast mediocre at best. Pips, a private club in Los Angeles to which I had belonged, served pretty good Chinese food. I wanted something similar in Palm Springs, which at the time had only two Chinese restaurants, both of which were inexpensive buffet style. I wanted something upscale and gourmet.

I had no idea how to get a Chinese restaurant off the ground, so in February 1979 I advertised in a San Francisco newspaper that catered to the Chinese community. I was contacted by a Chinese man named Eddie Chin who said he could set up anything I wanted.

Mr. Chin was a restaurant consultant by profession and knew all the heavy hitters in the business. We met in Palm Springs at the new location, and I described what I had in mind. He said he would get back to me in one week. Exactly a week later he showed up with a contract. His fee was $30,000, and he said he would deliver the entire thirty-member staff of the Imperial Palace restaurant, a world-famous five-star eatery in the Chinatown section of San Francisco—the head chef, Ben Cheung; cooks; bartenders; the maitre d'; and the wait staff. He said he would get them to relocate to Palm Springs a month before I opened.

Mr. Chin's fees also included the development of the menu, specifying the special kitchen equipment, training the employees, and overseeing everything the first month we were in business. I figured it would take six months to remodel the place and I planned for a September grand opening.

Now I had to focus on what to call the place.

I met with a local advertising firm and we kicked around several ideas. A friend of mine in New York had recently opened a club called Cecil's. For some reason, the name intrigued me because it sounded classy and erudite (I personally had never met a Cecil). The picture I conjured up in my mind was that of a sophisticated English gentleman on a hunting expedition wearing a safari hat and a monocle. Some say I have a vivid imagination. I wanted to work around the name Cecil's even though my friend's club had opened and closed in a very brief amount of time. I explained my idea to the advertising rep who said, "Let me work with it."

He eventually came back with a picture of an old rugged but wise Asian man with fabulous character in his face. To top it off, he added a Fu Manchu mustache, a safari hat, and a monocle. He nailed him on the first try, and that character was Cecil to me.

Everything was pretty much in place. We now had the restaurant concept nailed down, thanks to Eddie. Meanwhile, Gilbert was spinning his magic on the disco and working with Eddie on designing the Oriental restaurant side. It was then I got the bright idea that if we bought everything for the restaurant—chairs, silverware, dishes, artifacts, decor—in Hong Kong, we might be able to save some serious money. So in March I took Gilbert and my girlfriend to Hong Kong for a week. The express purpose of the trip was to save a few bucks on the furnishings and artifacts for the club and restaurant.

After flying for almost eighteen hours we arrived in Hong Kong, and after three days of shopping and purchasing, my girlfriend and I flew back to the States and left Gilbert to finish the ordering. I was stressed to the max, working eighteen hours a day while still running the Ingleside Inn and Melvyn's. And yet I was so excited and turned on I couldn't sleep. I had so many great ideas spilling out of me—how the club would operate, what sorts of functions we'd be holding, who our clientele would be, and on and on. I was full of dreams. However, one day the city of Palm Springs stopped me cold in my tracks.

A planner from the building department stopped by during a routine inspection. He casually informed me during the middle of construction that I couldn't have a restaurant with dancing in this particular location. I wasn't sure I had heard him correctly. I had had my plans approved by the city, had paid for all the appropriate permits, had been working on the remodeling for four months, and had already spent a lot of money. He explained that this particular location had a conditional use permit (C.U.P.) that allowed it to function as a restaurant with dancing. However, the C.U.P. had a stipulation that if during a twelve-month period the restaurant was not open for a period of ninety consecutive days the permit would expire. The permit was going to expire in ten days.

At this time, there was no roof on the building and no equipment in the kitchen. Desperate times call for desperate action, and I finally figured out an angle. If I could function for one meal, it would extend the C.U.P. for another year. I cleared a small area among all the rubble and construction workers, and set up a table for two people. I brought over a complete meal from Melvyn's along with a waiter and took pictures of two of my friends dining and dancing. In both pictures I had an enlarged copy of the front page of the *Desert Sun* to establish the date. I then submitted the pictures to the city council to prove that my establishment functioned as a restaurant and dance club and my C.U.P. was extended, or in this case, runneth over.

I was very relieved I had cleared that hurdle, but then the bills started pouring into my office and hit me like a tidal wave.

I had originally figured I could put the place together for $400,000, but knowing how construction projects work, I had allowed for up to $600,000 for overruns. I was now up to $800,000 and not quite finished.

I had moved the entire Chinese crew down too early because the September opening was delayed by almost a month. I bankrolled a rental house for the entire staff as well as paying for beds, furniture, television sets, and rented cars so they could get around. It was like supporting thirty children.

The cost to put everything together was astronomical and required a lot of up-front cash. I was starting to run out of money and panicked. I complained to my manager, Alan Mald, who suggested that I call the president of City National Bank, which was known at the time as the bank to the stars. Being a shy person and having only done business with only the local branch, I was reluctant to call such an important man. Alan said, "Mel, I guarantee you the head of City National Bank knows who you are, and if you called him, you'll get whatever you want." So I made a call to Bram Goldsmith, the president of City National Bank. Mr. Goldsmith invited me to have lunch with him at the Hillcrest Country Club in Beverly Hills, where unbeknownst to me, he was the president of the club.

To say that Goldsmith held clout was a major understatement. While we were dining, Milton Berle, George Burns, and Jack Carter all came by the table to pay tribute to Mr. Goldsmith. We chatted for about an hour and went back to his office where he cut me a check for $1.2 million, using the Ingleside Inn and Melvyn's as collateral on the loan. My hands were shaking as he handed over the check. It was as if I were starting all over again. If this venture failed, I was going to lose everything. But, it was an exciting time and I was an adrenaline junkie. For me, at this point in my life, there was no greater natural high than living every day to the fullest with everything on the line.

With my cash pile stocked once again, I started spending like crazy. I wanted everything to be first class, and so I had the inside of the building remodeled from scratch with silver doors, glass engravings, brass rails, silver cutlery, huge mirrored Casablanca fans, a special balcony dining area designed for private parties and functions, and an area for backgammon, which became my unofficial hangout.

For celebrities and VIPs, I had a separate entrance constructed in the back where they could ring a buzzer and a doorman would escort them through a private entrance into the restaurant or discotheque without the hassle of dealing with the public.

I even hired a maitre d' to the stars—Arturo Petorini from Chicago. Arturo was a legend in the business and today has a restaurant named after him in the Windy City. Arturo had worked at the famous Pump Room for fifteen years and he knew everybody. He looked like Cary Grant and lent an air of sophistication to Cecil's. Plus, he knew all the movers and shakers in the jet-set crowd and he knew how to cater to the rich and famous.

For all the headaches, cost overruns, and inordinate amount of preparation I put into Cecil's, the end result was worth the effort—the place was sensational. The dining room had a white tile floor, bamboo furniture, hunter green upholstery, suede booths against the wall, and a beautiful bar at the entrance. I couldn't get over how gorgeous it was.

And the food was to die for. Today P. F. Chang's is considered a happening place and usually has a waiting list, but the food there doesn't hold a candle to Cecil's. We offered world-class Chinese cuisine, and the menu boasted items such as thousand year-old eggs, sweet and sour seabird, and Peking duck.

As with the Ingleside Inn and Melvyn's, I looked for every personal touch to make Cecil's unique. I bought a big gong, and every time we sold a Peking duck we hit the gong. Everybody in the place would wonder, "What is that?" I'd tell them, "It means I just made another fifty dollars." I even wrote individual messages to put in the fortune cookies. For example, if I knew a customer was coming in with a beautiful lady, I'd write, "Joe, what a pretty date!" The best one I ever came up with was when President Gerald Ford was being challenged by California governor Jerry Brown for president. I put in President Ford's fortune cookie, "Jerry who???" and had a photographer on hand to snap a picture at the moment of truth. The picture was so good that it even made the UPI wire services.

We opened Cecil's on October 1, 1979, and it was a smash. Business was gangbusters from the start, and we had a line out the door every night. The crowds poured in, often waiting in line two, three, even four hours, just to get inside those double, polished brass doors. It was wall-to-wall on both sides of the building. It's hard to imagine today, but in the late seventies and early eighties, before AIDS and Mothers Against Drunk Driving (MADD) people were partying almost seven days a week. It was a real happening.

Cecil's was to the West Coast what Studio 54 was to the East Coast. I've always believed Cecil's was much classier than Studio 54, but because they were in the media capital of the world, they got a lot of ink. But we were the playground for the movers and shakers of the world and got our fair share of media coverage in both national and local publications. Besides, the discotheque was the most beautiful that anybody had ever seen.

I posted a sign above the disco that read: "Through these doors walk the most beautiful women in the world." I wasn't exaggerating.

We attracted many celebrities and the place was star-studded from day one. Frank Sinatra, Kirk Douglas, Evel Knievel, Reggie Jackson, Smokey Robinson, and George Hamilton all boogied there, and John Travolta was often spotted performing his *Saturday Night Fever* dance moves. The man who showed Travolta those patented moves, Deny Terrio, also visited Cecil's on a regular basis. One night, former president Gerry Ford toe-tapped with his First Lady Betty while Jack Paar took Mary Martin for a spin on the dance floor. Every celebrity in the world came to Cecil's. We created a Wall of Fame at the entrance with pictures of over one hundred celebrities that came to party at Cecil's.

Some celebrities complained that I didn't pay much attention to them. *Hills Street Blues* star Ed Marinaro once griped to the manager, "How come Mel never comes over to say hello?"

Another time comedian/actor Lyle Waggoner came in with a group of friends, one of whom was Carol Connors, an Academy Award–winning songwriter. She was miffed that I was too busy to take a picture with her and walked out in a snit. I was always the one trying to get my mug in a picture with a celeb, and now they wanted a picture with me. In those days I was going every which way at once and everybody wanted a piece of me. (Today, I am very good friends with Carol, and we have taken many pictures together since then.)

Celebrities liked my place because it was the perfect setting, complemented with a professional staff, from the doormen in elegant tuxedos to the young and beautiful waitresses in sexy form-fitting gowns, split high at the thigh.

The disco business at that time was absolutely amazing. Everybody had the mind-set that a disco was the place to have a good time. Patrons were either drunk or stoned; they were either with a woman or sure they would find one. There was no such thing as a hot scotch, cold scotch, undercooked scotch, or overcooked scotch. Even better was the fact that the club scene was only four hours a night from 10 p.m. to 2 a.m. It was far different than running a restaurant where everybody was a food critic.

In the restaurant business, if a guest doesn't like something about his dining experience, he would make sure to tell everyone who would listen about it. For example, one evening a customer at Melvyn's sought me out to complain that the string beans were cold. I apologized and asked him how he liked the soup, the salad, the dessert, the potato, and the entree. He said everything was great but the string beans were cold. He said the service was good, the ambiance was charming, but the string beans were cold. This went on for ten minutes. I felt like saying, "If everything was free I couldn't make more than twenty-five dollars, how much grief do you want to give me?"

Keep in mind that this same customer would go to my disco and pay ten dollars at the door just to walk in. He would buy a drink for eight dollars that he knows cost only two. The first person that walks by accidentally knocks it out of his hand, and he thinks it's the funniest thing to happen. This is the same person who spent ten minutes complaining about my cold string beans. I have come to the conclusion that dining is serious business, but when you go to a disco you have a mind-set that you are going to have fun.

And speaking of which, I never had so much fun in all my life. Cecil's was a high-energy place that attracted a clientele that was rich, sophisticated, and beautiful, all of whom liked to have a lot of fun. The record was forty-two Rolls Royces in the parking lot one night. I doubt there is a dealership in the world that has forty-two Rolls Royces on their lot. And that's not to mention the limousines, Excaliburs, Mercedes, and Clinets that lined the front of Cecil's and dumped out movie stars, heads of state, and business moguls with their gorgeous women, who all came to dance the night away.

I'd wake up every morning at six o' clock and go to the Ingleside Inn and spend the day there, making sure everything was going smoothly. I couldn't wait to get to Cecil's at night, and I spent every evening greeting customers making sure they were having a good time. The night's partying didn't become official until I climbed the ladder of the DJ booth, spun Donna Summer's "Bad Girls," and blew a whistle at the now-famous "beep beep" segment in the middle of the song. People went nuts and screamed. I became famous for blowing the whistle at exactly the right time to different songs. When I walked down the streets of Palm Springs during the day, people would walk up to me and hand me whistles. That led to a unique marketing idea: I had a load of whistles made up with the Cecil's name on the side and passed them out to the crowd, who blew to their heart's content.

Because of who I was, women flocked to me. Many females wanted to get involved with me but I spurned all offers because I was having way too much fun. I was even being sought out by the rich and famous.

One of the highlights of my time at Cecil's was when I had the pleasure of meeting and dancing with the beautiful actress Joan Collins. The next day I found an envelope with her photograph personally autographed with a lovely thank-you card on my desk at the Ingleside Inn. That sort of thing tends to go to a guy's head, but there were also moments that brought me crashing back down to earth.

I recall at the time a lovely lady in the disco kept staring at me for the longest time.

"Oh my God," she exclaimed. "You're absolutely perfect!"

All excited, I said, "Thank you," smiling from ear to ear. "For you?"

"No, for my mother," she said, while wiping the smile right off my face at the same time.

I was becoming somewhat of a big deal then, and many people asked to have their picture taken with me. A gorgeous woman walked up to me one night and asked, "Would you take a picture?"

"I'd be honored," I smiled, hoping that this might be the start of a beautiful relationship.

She handed me the camera and said, "Wait here until I find my boyfriend."

Men sought out my company as well, but it's not what you think. After I'd climb down from the DJ booth, I'd have a line of guys waiting to play me in backgammon. I wasn't particularly interested in playing for money, but I played because I loved the game. Eventually, I acquired a reputation as a good player. Everybody wanted to take on the "boss" and play me for big stakes. I didn't think it would be good for business, and I certainly didn't want to take my customers' money or lose a lot of my own. It is a very addictive game, and we'd often play until after closing. My own bartenders would end up throwing me out of my own place. I was literally a backgammon junkie and played everyone from Lucille Ball to Gaby Horowitz, who was a professional backgammon player and wrote books on the game. There was never a shortage of competitors. The manager at Cecil's would call me at Melvyn's early in the evening to tell me that there was a list of people waiting to play me. Some even called me at home to schedule a game for that night. It was great.

Everything I touched was turning to gold. I had the Midas Touch, and Cecil's made me the toast of the town once again. I raised a glass and toasted back in grand fashion. The only problem was that I didn't know when to put the glass down.

# CHAPTER 14

# Peaks and Valleys

Trying not to drink when you own one of the world's greatest discos is like trying to stay celibate when you live in a brothel.

The energy level inside of Cecil's was unbelievable, and it was nearly impossible to be in that environment without imbibing. Every evening, as soon as I walked in, the bartenders would place a glass of Beefeaters gin at five different locations so that I didn't have to go far to wet my whistle. When I settled down to play backgammon at the end of each night, the drinks kept coming. Between the excitement, the energy, and the adrenaline rush, I was able to consume an extraordinary amount of alcohol and still function. I came to discover some of my customers could also sock away the booze.

One customer, a pretty big boozer, walked into Melvyn's on a Saturday afternoon and told me the most amazing story. He said that he got so drunk the previous night at Cecil's and was ready to drive home to the other end of the valley—until, that is, a police checkpoint ahead stopped him cold in his tracks. He said that he made a U-turn and headed toward the Palm Springs Airport, where he owned a small plane. He said with a straight face that he was too drunk to drive, so he flew home instead, thus avoiding the checkpoint. (There is a small private airport at the east end of the valley.)

Business was booming, and the money was rolling in. The Chinese food was excellent and receiving rave reviews, and the disco was jammed every night. We were open about three weeks when my manager, Alan Mald, informed me that one of the Chinese bartenders was stealing from me. We set up a trap and caught him red-handed. I told Alan to fire him, but that was easier said than done. When Alan informed Ben Cheung, the head of the oriental crew, Ben replied, "If he goes, we all go." I was feeling pretty secure and cocky because of all the whiskey we were pouring and told Alan that nobody was going to tell me that I had to live with an employee who stole. I didn't want to lose the whole crew, and the huge investment I had in them, but Ben left me no choice. I told Alan that if that was my only option, to let them all go.

I really thought Ben was bluffing, but low and behold, he and his entire crew of thirty pulled up stakes and left within twenty-four hours. It was bad enough that I blew all the money I had invested with the consultant, the décor, and keeping the crew happy, but more importantly, I had created a gourmet Chinese restaurant with no competition. Within forty-eight hours I realized I had made a huge mistake. (To this day I wonder if I could have saved the crew somehow.) In hindsight, it was the biggest mistake of my entire business career.

Since I had to move fast, I asked the chef from Melvyn's to take over the kitchen at Cecil's. I realized that there was no restaurant in the desert at the time that specialized in steaks, so I decided to convert the restaurant to a steak house. I called it "A Place for Steak." Within seventy-two hours we had an entirely new kitchen crew and were back in business. The steak house concept did only fair business, and over the next year I tried seafood, continental, Polynesian, and even went back to Chinese on two separate occasions, but the food was just mediocre. (I was about ten years ahead of my time—because a decade later, steak houses became the biggest rage in the food business.) I was never able to recapture the special uniqueness that I had under Ben Cheung. The disco, the dancing, the whiskey sales, and the newly implemented door charge provided plenty of cash and were able to carry the restaurant operations. The food was good, but the restaurant really only did business mainly because people wanted to make sure they would be in the building before we had to close the doors. The disco was packed—we were constantly at the maximum occupancy.

The fire department would come in almost every night and count the crowd. One night I was given a ticket for overcrowding, and as that was the third violation, I was given thirty days in jail, suspended sentence, and sixty days probation. I ended up having to hire somebody whose sole job was to count the customers and at capacity close the doors. There were nights when the manager of Cecil's would call me at Melvyn's and tell me not to come over because we were full and several friends and good customers were waiting out front for me to get them in. I wasn't going to jail for anybody, so I was forced to stay at Melvyn's like a caged tiger. On certain nights I would arrange for the manager to open the back door of the kitchen so I could sneak in. It was unbelievable.

So many people were trying to get in that one day, my maitre d' Arturo Petorini suggested that we should add a cover charge on weekends. There had never been a cover charge anyplace in the desert, and I was skeptical. Charging at the door could be a financial bonanza, but it raised more questions than answers. Who should we charge, who should we not charge, and how would we make that determination? Would we charge VIPs? Do we charge locals? What about customers of the Ingleside Inn and Melvyn's? Or what about my relatives or people who had become personal friends? What if someone slipped the doorman ten dollars to get in? Was that considered a tip, or did that go to the house? I knew most clubs in the major cities had a cover charge, so why shouldn't we? Arturo assuaged my doubts and concerns.

"Mr. Haber, I know who the locals are, and I can pick out the tourists. I know who to charge and who not to charge," Arturo said. "I'll charge them five dollars on weekends and we'll see how it goes." I agreed to try it for a few weeks. I warned him, however, not to antagonize the locals with the cover charge.

When we first started charging at the door, I fielded hundreds of phone calls asking me to explain the door charge policy. Some were outraged. I remember standing next to Arturo when a customer berated him when he asked for the cover charge.

"If Mel Haber knew that you charged me, he'd be outraged," the customer said as he stood right next to me. "Do you know what a good friend I am of his?"

I realized that I couldn't put a judge in a black robe sitting at the front door to make those decisions. I decided that I would start charging from 10 p.m. to 1 a.m. on Fridays, Saturdays, and holidays. I finally decided that Arturo would have to be my sole judge and jury. I agreed to give it a trial run and told Arturo that I would give him 10 percent of whatever he collected. It turned out to be a very sweet deal. Every Friday and Saturday at the end of the night Arturo would hand me $500 to $600. Business was so good that within a few months I was able to raise the charge to $10 a head.

However, several people, including my own son Lonny, told me that Arturo was robbing me blind. We had an employee named Harry who stood with Arturo at the door as his "bodyguard." When Arturo used the restroom or tended to some other business, Harry would collect the money in his stead. After Arturo handed me one night's take, I decided to bluff him and take a shot in the dark.

"Harry's been ripping us off," I said. "I had somebody in the parking lot count the people who were charged and we're short about $200." Arturo looked worried and upset, but didn't say anything. When I got to the Ingleside Inn the next morning at 7 a.m., he was there waiting for me. That in itself was suspicious because Arturo was a night owl and rarely got up before noon.

"Mr. Haber, I feel so stupid," Arturo said. "When I got home I discovered the missing $200 in my jacket pocket." That was all I needed to hear to realize my trap worked. I had to let Arturo go. Oddly enough, Arturo and I remained friends over the years. I felt I owed him a debt of gratitude because his idea of a cover charge made me a lot of money over the next few years.

But the tragedy of losing the original Chinese restaurant and Arturo was nothing compared to what happened next.

My son Lonny had been living with me since 1976. When he turned sixteen, I made him a parking lot attendant at Melvyn's. He was a good-looking and charismatic young man who didn't fight the stigma of trying to live in his old man's shadow. In fact, he embraced it. Lonny had business cards printed up that simply read: "Lonny, son of Melvyn."

Lonny was a natural born schmoozer and members of the opposite sex were crazy about him. He wasn't intimidated by anyone's social status and befriended just about everyone. Lonny had major chutzpah.

I recall one time when movie producer Bob Evans and his brother Charlie were dining at Melvyn's and hanging out with Lonny. The three of them looked like old pals, chewing the fat and having a ball. I have to admit, I was somewhat envious. This was my place, my turf, and I was the one who should schmooze with the celebrity clients. When Bob and Charlie left, I asked Lonny, "What do you have to do with the Evanses?"

Lonny said that Bob asked him if he knew the beautiful lady at table 50. Bob said that he was going to Manhattan to set up a movie he was doing called *The Cotton Club*. He wanted to know if Lonny could get that lady to join him in New York. Lonny told him, "Sure, I can take care of it." I asked Lonny who the lady was and he said, "I have no idea." Totally confused I said, "Lonny, how can you promise Bob Evans to send the girl to him in New York when you don't even know who she is?"

Lonny looked condescendingly at me and said, "Dad, cool it. Bob won't remember that particular lady, so I'll find a pretty blonde who wants to go to New York and he won't know the difference." Sure enough, that's exactly what Lonny did, and he and Bob became even closer friends.

After Arturo left Cecil's, Lonny was the man to know. Unless you knew him, there would be quite a wait to get in the place. And it didn't matter if you were famous or not. Lonny wasn't going to let you in if he didn't like you. For example, Lonny didn't really care much for baseball slugger Reggie Jackson, who was at the peak of his Hall of Fame career. Reggie was cocky, arrogant, and had an enormous sense of entitlement. Lonny made sure Reggie paid the full ten dollar cover every time he came to Cecil's. The fact that Lonny let in Jackson's teammate Rod Carew for free really frosted "Mr. October."

I was sitting at the bar one night when Reggie came running up to me with Lonny in hot pursuit. It was a sight I'll never forget.

"Melvyn, Lonny always charges me ten dollars to get in this place and I don't think I should have to pay it," Reggie said.

From behind him Lonny yelled, "I never saw a baseball game for free!" It was one of the few times in his life Reggie Jackson was speechless.

Reggie gave as good as he got. When I asked him to take a picture with me for our Wall of Fame, he said he'd be glad to—for twenty bucks.

Lonny was tough and didn't take any lip off anyone, which probably played a role in his untimely death. On March 21, 1981, Lonny got off work around 2:30 a.m. and drove home to his apartment complex, six blocks from the Ingleside Inn. As he approached his front door, he was summoned to the pool area by a stranger. A few hours later, he was found floating in the pool. He was only twenty-one.

The Palm Springs Police Department investigated his death and found that Lonny had exchanged heated words with a local drug dealer. I don't know if Lonny wouldn't let the guy in the club or if it was over another matter, but that information led nowhere.

To this day, the case remains unsolved. The death of a child is simply something a parent never gets over or makes peace with. It's a pain that never dulls or goes away.

Mentally, I was a mess and couldn't seem to figure out what to do next. I spent a lot of time at Newport Beach just hanging out with my best friend Bo Eisner, who flew out from New York to keep me company. After a month, I decided I needed to get back to work.

After Lonny's death, I couldn't bring myself to go into Cecil's.

I entered into escrow to sell the place to a group of customers. Six weeks into escrow, I began experiencing what is known as "seller's remorse," and I really wasn't sure I wanted to sell Cecil's after all. It was a Friday afternoon, the liquor license had just transferred to the group of buyers, and we were in the lawyer's office for the closing. The buyers' group was unaware that I was having second thoughts and that I had decided that I really didn't want to sell Cecil's. They thought they could squeeze another $50,000 out of the deal for new carpet. I said that I would not give them $1 off the deal. They thought I was bluffing and threatened to cancel the deal. I said that was okay with me. I met them back at the liquor authority office to transfer the license back to my name, and I refunded them their money. It was 4 p.m. on a Friday afternoon. That night when I walked into Cecil's everybody in the room—guests and employees—stood up and applauded. I looked around to see what celebrity walked in when it dawned on me that the word got around that I was keeping Cecil's. The applause was all for me and almost brought me to tears. I was home again.

I threw myself back into my work with a vengeance. It was around that time I was approached by a prominent landlord in town who, to paraphrase a famous movie line from *The Godfather*, made me an offer I couldn't refuse.

The landlord owned several properties on Palm Canyon Drive and approached me about taking over a 3,500-square-foot space he had leased to a restaurant that recently went belly up. He told me that the building was going to be torn down in the next year to make way for a large shopping center and hotel that was going to be built by entrepreneur Eddie DeBartolo, who owned many shopping centers and the San Francisco 49ers. The landlord didn't want the space to sit vacant until they started construction and offered me a smoking deal. He said I didn't have to pay him any rent, just give him 5 percent of the gross to take over the space and run it anyway I saw fit. The place was fully equipped, and all I had to do was staff it, and buy the food and liquor. I was instantly in business. It was a pretty good deal.

The building was used brick inside and out and reminded me of T.G.I.Friday's, a restaurant I had enjoyed many times when I lived in New York. I developed a hamburger and chicken menu similar to Friday's. I decided to call it Saturday's. It was a lot more casual than Melvyn's or Cecil's. It was a place where you could go dressed in a T-shirt and shorts and get a burger and fries in the heart of downtown Palm Springs. I also put in a dance floor and sound system for late night business. I discovered that many of the young people didn't want to go home at 2 a.m. on Friday and Saturday nights when the local discos closed. Then I had another brainstorm—an after-hours club with no liquor. I would charge customers five dollars at the door and let them dance until 4 a.m.

For this business venture, I enlisted the help of Vito Russo, an Italian butcher from New Jersey.

After 2 a.m. we served food, soft drinks, and coffee. The ironic thing was, not only was I charging ten dollars to get into Cecil's earlier in the evening, but when Cecil's closed, half of my customers trotted on over to Saturdays to pay me five bucks more at 2 a.m. I got them coming and going. I was beginning to think I knew what I was doing.

Because of my newfound celebrity, I was approached by Bob Osterberg, the owner of a local radio station, who had a business proposition for me. Bob was known in the desert as "The Red Baron" because he broadcast many of his shows from his private plane while flying over the desert. Bob suggested I host a call-in radio show. He said I'd be a natural and it would be a great way to promote my businesses. It sounded like fun, so every Saturday morning from 11 a.m. until 12:30 p.m. I'd broadcast a ninety-minute show from Melvyn's and take phone calls. I called myself "The Professor of Love."

Ever since I had opened Cecil's, I had developed a special insight into the dating scene. I spent many hours listening to men and women complain about the opposite sex. Many of them often asked me for advice. Men didn't complain as much about the women. The women seemed to always complain about the men. Most guys were looking for fun and games while women were looking for a permanent relationship with Mr. Right. It was frustrating because the women were complaining there was no one available as I watched them turning down dances with guys right and left. I'd tell them, "You're looking for a 10 when right now you have nothing. Isn't it nice just to have a male friend to go out with even if he is only a 6? Nobody says you have to jump in bed if you don't want to, but go out with the 6 until you find a 7. Keep trading up. You might be surprised to find out what you thought was a 7 turned out to be a 10 when you gave him a chance."

My show was an instant hit, and I really enjoyed myself. Listeners loved my glib answers and witty repartee, and there was no shortage of callers. One caller who stands out in my memory is a lady who asked how I would answer when a woman says she doesn't want to become a one-night stand. I replied as best as I knew how—with humor and logic.

I said I always ask, "How many nights would you like? Two? Four? Eight? I don't know how to get to the second night without the first. Nobody wants a one-night stand. Everybody would like for the experience to be so good that they want many more."

I rarely had guests on the show, but I was approached by a representative of *Cosmopolitan* magazine who was promoting a sex survey editor Helen Gurley Brown just completed. It seemed to be a perfect segment for "The Professor of Love." The significance of this survey was that they had 100,000 respondents whereas the famous Kinsey Report had only 5,000. Being a bottom line kind of guy, I asked her what was the most significant thing she learned from this landmark survey. Without a moment's hesitation, she said, "That the readers of *Redbook* magazine have more anal sex than the readers of *Cosmopolitan*." I wasn't sure if I had heard her correctly, but fortunately, the engineer did and immediately cut to a commercial break.

All that talking got "The Professor of Love" to thinking that it was time to step out of the classroom and find my own "10."

The lady who is now my wife over twenty-five years loves to tell the story of the first time she came to Cecil's with her girlfriend. She saw me up in the disco booth, poked her friend in the arm, pointed to me, and said, "Isn't that guy a little old to be a disc jockey?" I was forty-four years old and in the prime of my life. Is that what they mean by love at first sight?

Stephanie Martone was a beautiful, dark-haired Italian who taught high school in Newport Beach. She came to Palm Springs almost every weekend with her girlfriend just to dance at Cecil's. Stephanie was a textbook disco queen and a great dancer. She never came with a date and never left with anyone, but she always had a steady stream of men that lined up to dance with her. She was not only stunningly gorgeous and wholesome but a class act. I had been introduced to Stephanie on several occasions by different people but it didn't go much beyond a simple greeting and a few minutes of conversation about the club. However, I couldn't get her out of my mind. Every time I saw Stephanie I found myself thinking more and more about her. I was busy running the club and at that time was dating a lovely, redheaded Irish lady named Shawn Shelton. Shawn was sweet, kind, and never had a cross word to say about anyone. Unfortunately, the chemistry wasn't there and deep down I knew our relationship was not going anywhere. I think she did, too. Shawn took our parting like she reacted to everything else—with class and dignity.

It was a Saturday night, and I couldn't take my eyes off Stephanie, who was dancing with a friend. With every drink it seemed my desire for her increased. I asked a mutual friend of ours, Jim Davis, if he could possibly get Stephanie to meet me at my house at 2 a.m. after Cecil's closed. I told him if he could pull it off I would owe him big-time.

I had just gotten home around 1:30 a.m. when Jim called. He said that Stephanie had agreed to meet me at the house later. At the time, I lived in a big house high on a hill overlooking the city of Palm Springs. I had already had a lot to drink at the club, but was so excited and nervous that I grabbed a bottle of Beefeater Gin and went out to the backyard to fantasize and gaze at the beautiful view of the city. I began taking huge gulps from the bottle to calm my nerves. I paced back and forth talking to myself, "Sure, this beauti-

Sneaking a shot with Frank Sinatra, which is my prized possession.

That's me with baseball great and New York Yankee, Joe DiMaggio. He was one of my idols and one of the most elegant and refined men I have ever met.

Showdown with *60 Minutes* correspondent Mike Wallace, who sandbagged me on a segment they aired on palimony.

Mr. Blackwell is a pussycat and a good friend. His annual Top 10 Worst Dressed List never fails to make headlines.

Actress Joan Collins sent me this signed 8 x 10 after a night of drinks and dancing at Cecil's. She was a picture of beauty and class.

Television personality Jack Paar and Broadway star Mary Martin twisting the night away at Cecil's. This 1978 photo made the AP newswire and appeared in newspapers all across the country.

I was introduced to John Forsythe when he was filming *Dynasty*. He helped organize a fund-raiser for the Angel View Crippled Children's Foundation.

With former president Gerald Ford and first lady Betty Ford. The Fords were a delightful couple and frequent guests of Melvyn's and Cecil's.

My invitation to the Playboy mansion in the early '90s meant that I had truly arrived as a member of the male species.

There wasn't a hotter star on the planet or a nicer guy than John Travolta, who visited the Ingleside Inn frequently in the late '70s and early '80s.

Comedian/author Steve Allen possibly paid me the greatest compliment of my life. He told a spellbound audience he couldn't follow me after I gave a speech to promote my *Bedtime Stories*.

The two Mels. I can't open a movie, but he can't open a restaurant.

One day when I heard a Barry Manilow song, I wished aloud to my wife Stephanie that I could meet him. She promptly took me into my office and showed me this picture.

Actor David Hasselhoff spent the weekend at the Ingleside Inn with wife Pamela. I always admired David's taste in reading. Here he is posing with a copy of my *Bedtime Stories*.

Larry King, another Brooklyn boy makes good.

Arnold Schwarzenegger and Maria Shriver were frequent guests in the late '80s and early '90s. As governor, he stopped by to show his staff his favorite place in 2007.

Me, Jimmy Randall, Sonny Bono and Susie Coelho. Sonny Bono and I were buddies and drinking partners. We later became parents at the same time. I've always contended he was good for Palm Springs in his tenure as mayor.

Actor Patrick Macnee was every bit as debonair as his character in *The Avengers*. He's a super guy and a good friend.

Actress Rita Hayworth visited the Ingleside Inn in 1976 directly after her stay at a sanitarium. Here she looks as radiant as ever.

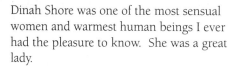

Dinah Shore was one of the most sensual women and warmest human beings I ever had the pleasure to know. She was a great lady.

Comedian/actor Richard Pryor and I became unlikely buddies in the late '70s. He invited me to the Oscars one year.

Me, best-selling author Danielle Steele and actor George Hamilton, whose taste in books is as refined as his taste in wine and women.

Comedian and Palm Springs most prominent citizen Bob Hope during a night of fine dining at Melvyn's.

Actress Debbie Reynolds (right), along with her mother (left), celebrated her 50th birthday at Melvyn's.

Actress Lucille Ball was one of the grandest ladies I ever had the pleasure to know. She made me feel ten feet tall when greeting me by my first name.

My jaw dropped when singer Liza Minnelli asked me if she could sing at Melvyn's.

Jerry Lewis dined at Melvyn's immediately following his Labor Day Telethon.

Superstar Cher spent a week at the Ingleside Inn in the late '70s.

Pianist and Palm Springs resident Liberace always had a smile on his face when he came into Melvyn's. Here he is with friend Tido Minor.

ful girl is just going to come up to your house and jump into bed."
I took another gulp. "What are you, sixteen years old you moron?"
A few more gulps and I was getting pretty woozy. Finally I had to
lie down on the bed. On the remote possibility that this beautiful
woman might show up, I turned up the TV as loud as possible to
prevent me from passing out and falling asleep. The next thing I
knew the phone rang at 8 a.m., and it was Jim Davis. He sounded
very upset.

"I can't believe you, Mel," Jim said. Instantly I got a sinking feeling in the pit of my stomach.

"Don't tell me she showed up last night?" I said.

"Yes, she showed up. You don't know what I had to go through
to get Stephanie to go to your house. I told her that you just wanted
to meet her for coffee, and it was tough for you to talk to her at the
club. I had to vouch that you were a legitimate guy. I even said that
I would probably join her there. It took me a half hour to talk her
into doing it, and on top of that, she said you had a party going on
and wouldn't even open the door," Jim said disgustedly.

Shaking off the cobwebs, I explained that the truth of the matter
was that I got so nervous that I drank myself into oblivion. I begged
Jim for forgiveness. Jim told me I needed Stephanie's forgiveness—I
needed to call and apologize to her. He then gave me the phone number of her parents' house where she was staying in Palm Springs.

I drove to the Ingleside Inn, downed five Irish coffees, bit the bul-
let, and called Stephanie. I told her exactly what I told Jim—that I got
so nervous about her coming to the house that I drank myself into
oblivion. I mentioned that the party she thought was going on was
actually the TV, turned up to maximum volume to keep me awake.
There was a dead silence for a moment, then she finally spoke.

"Well, nobody could make up a story like that," she said, laughing on the other end. I laughed too, somewhat relieved she wasn't
going to hold it against me.

"Let me make it up to you and buy you lunch," I said. She said
she was on the way back to Newport Beach but would stop by Melvyn's on the way out of town. She came by and we chatted.

I didn't know much about her, but I was smitten. Stephanie was beautiful, intelligent, and handled herself well, and was a great conversationalist. She was also a very nice person, which was very important to me. She seemed to be everything I was looking for in a woman, and I definitely was interested in seeing a lot more of this lady.

Pretty soon our romance flourished, and we were dating almost every weekend. Her parents lived in Palm Springs, and she'd visit them while seeing me. I'd also drive to Newport Beach during the week, check into a hotel, and take her out at night.

After a year of dating her exclusively, Stephanie got a job at the high school in nearby Indio so that we could be closer. Stephanie was the old-fashioned type who didn't believe in living together before marriage, so she rented a condo eight blocks away from my house. The funny thing was, Stephanie would never sleep over at my house. I would often come home from Cecil's around 1:30 a.m., tiptoe into her apartment, and go to sleep. She had to get up at 6 a.m. to teach school. I'd get up with her, walk out shoes in hand, and drive eight blocks to my house so I could shower and shave and go to work. For the life of me, I could never get her to stay the night at my place. I eventually discovered Stephanie wouldn't sleep over because she was worried that her parents might call her at night, and she wouldn't be at home. It didn't matter that Stephanie was thirty-one, a grown adult who had been previously married for five years. Being the good daughter that she was, Stephanie didn't want to upset her parents. What a breath of fresh air in this day and age!

When she finally told me the reason, I said, "Why didn't you tell me, dummy? I'll extend the phone from your house to mine, and when they call you'll answer it here and they'll be none the wiser." I had a red phone installed and instructed my kids when they came to visit never to answer that phone. Ironically, the Martones constantly asked if she was still seeing me because every time they called, Stephanie was at home.

After we dated for a while, her mother actually asked me what my intentions were. I was thirteen years older than Stephanie, and Momma Martone had heard that I was a playboy, so she wanted an answer. I expected Papa Martone to come out with a shotgun. After very little contemplation, I told them my intention was to make Stephanie an honest woman—again.

We decided to have a small wedding at the Hotel Del Coronado in San Diego. I knew the owner of the hotel, Larry Lawrence, who was a regular customer of Melvyn's. One night Larry came into Cecil's with three of his affluent friends. He told the manager that he wanted to see me. Larry asked me why he had to pay forty dollars at the door just to get in.

"Because I think eighty is too much," I said and we all shared a good laugh. It was my standard answer to anyone who asked.

I sat with Larry and his friends for almost an hour. He proceeded to tell me how rich he was, and how many corporations he owned and controlled, but he continually bitched about the forty dollar door charge. I thought about refunding him his money, but fortunately came to my senses. When we decided to get married at the Del Coronado Hotel, I called Larry just to make sure that Stephanie got the VIP treatment. After Larry made sure everything would be taken care of, he asked what he could do for me personally.

I said, "Larry, if I had given you back your forty dollars at Cecil's, I would be asking you for a comp, but I didn't, so I can't ask for anything." Talk about outsmarting yourself.

We had been married for about six years when I came home one night and Stephanie said, "Mel, the water turned blue." I told her that I don't know anything about plumbing, but she should call a plumber in the morning. Problem solved. Stephanie shook me and said, "Sweetheart, you don't understand. I took a pregnancy test and we are going to have a baby." For the life of me I still couldn't figure out how blue water got my wife pregnant.

I'll admit, I was somewhat taken aback and knew that my life was about to change drastically. When it finally sunk in, I said "I'm not sure I want a baby. It has taken me thirty years to be independent enough to go and do anything I wanted, whenever I wanted." Stephanie said, "But you never go anywhere or do anything other than work." I replied, "That's because I can. When I won't be able to, I'll want to do everything." But actually, I was really thrilled with the idea of another child.

People in town reacted as if Stephanie's pregnancy was like the coming of the Messiah. There were numerous baby showers held all over town, and I must admit I was very excited. Somebody told us that we could find out the sex of the baby by placing a few drops of Stephanie's urine on Drano crystals. If they turned brown, it's a girl. If it turns green, it's a boy. The unofficial test results showed that we were having a girl. The doctor suggested Stephanie take an amnio-centesis test because she was in her late thirties at the time. When we went for the test they asked if we wanted to know the sex of the child. I told them I already knew from the "sophisticated Drano test." When they called to give us the test results, they confirmed we were having a girl.

I've bragged about Stephanie's physical and inner beauty, and it's all true. She's a dead ringer for actress Lynda Carter of *Wonder Woman* fame. Prior to our marriage, she occasionally worked for Ron Smith's Celebrity Look-Alike Agency wearing the Wonder Woman costume at parties, gala events, and other various modeling assignments. I was with her several times when people asked for her autograph, thinking she was Lynda Carter.

Because of my restaurant and disco, Stephanie could pretty much meet any celebrity she wanted, but the only one she had a picture of in our house was Rachel McLish. Stephanie was into body-building at the time, and Rachel McLish was her hero. Ra-chel was the inaugural Ms. Olympia in 1980 and again in 1982. She was also featured in the movie *Pumping Iron II* and starred in a handful of films once her weightlifting days were over. One day as I was working out at the local Gold's Gym, I recognized Ms. McLish working out with a guy on the next machine. I walked over to in-troduce myself.

"Ms. McLish, you don't know me, but my wife is a big fan of yours," I started out. "I have a restaurant in town and you would do me a great favor if you and your friend would join my wife and me for dinner."

She looked at me as if I was crazy, but she went up to the front desk to ask about me. The owner of the gym confirmed that I owned a very popular restaurant in town and that I was a legitimate guy. She agreed to have dinner with us at 7 p.m.

Excited, I called Stephanie and told her to meet me at Melvyn's around 7 p.m. because I had a surprise for her. Stephanie was Christmas shopping and said she was going to be a little late, but that she'd be there.

Rachel and her fiancé, movie producer Ron Samuels, arrived at 7 p.m. sharp. We chatted for a few moments, and then Stephanie walked in. I looked over at Ron, who turned white as a sheet and looked as if he were going to keel over with a heart attack.

"Ron, can I get you some water or something?" I asked, but he couldn't answer me. When Stephanie walked up and introduced herself as my wife, Ron calmed down. I came to find out Ron had been married to Lynda Carter for five years until she left him for Washington, DC–based attorney Robert Altman.

At the time, Lynda Carter was also pregnant and from across the restaurant, poor Ron thought his ex-wife was approaching the table. After Ron regained his composure, we all had a good laugh about the situation. Ron and Rachel are now married, and we run into them from time to time.

But there is an interesting footnote to this story: On January 14, 1988, at 12:21 a.m., Stephanie gave birth to our first daughter, seven-pound Autumn Nicole Haber at Desert Hospital. On exactly the same day, January 14, 1988, eleven minutes later at 12:32 a.m., Lynda Carter gave birth to her first child, a seven-pound boy named James Clifford Altman, in a Washington, DC, area hospital. *Variety* columnist Army Archerd wrote a story about the two births, remarking, "Talk about doing a good job as a double!"

My wife is also a very formidable person. Stephanie always wanted to visit New York during the Christmas season. We decided in December 2005 that we were going to go to see the department store windows, Rockefeller Center, the Christmas tree, and so on. As it turned out, it was our daughter's first year in college. The holiday break would be the only time since high school graduation when Autumn could see her friends who had gone off to different colleges. So we planned to go January 3 right after the holiday season.

Stephanie called Rockefeller Center and found out that the Christmas tree would be up until January 10. She then called the local Saks Fifth Avenue to inquire about their Christmas windows display in New York. After a handful of calls, she discovered that nobody on the West Coast had a clue, so she finally called New York and asked for the head of the window trimming department. She found out that the decorations were coming down January 4, the day after our arrival. Stephanie expressed her disappointment but said she would get up very early on the fourth, and hopefully she and Autumn could get a glimpse of them before they were taken down. Two days later the Saks representative called her back to say, "I have never had anyone tell me that they were coming 3,000 miles just to see my windows, so for you, I will keep them up an extra four days until January 8."

Feeling as if she were on a roll, Stephanie then called Macy's to tell them what Saks was doing for her. Would they do the same? Macy's didn't care what Saks was doing—they were taking theirs down on the appointed day. I don't care if you're Ted Williams or Mickey Mantle—batting .500 ain't bad.

Stephanie not only proved to be a wonderful partner in marriage, but also a wonderful mother to our beautiful daughter Autumn. She was a great acquisition and the smartest move I've made. Many years later, she's still paying big dividends.

# CHAPTER 15

# King Kong of the Desert

With the opening of Doubles in October of 1983, I had scored another "ace" with my fifth successful business establishment.

At this point, I was pretty much working seven days and six nights a week. Running another restaurant was not on my radar screen, but when opportunity knocked, I was never one who could shut the door.

Santa Monica real estate developer Ray Watt had built approximately 80,000 homes in twenty-two states and developed eight million square feet of commercial property in his career. In 1983, he purchased The Tennis Club, which was a legendary property in Palm Springs. It was three blocks from the Ingleside Inn and Melvyn's. Not long thereafter, Mr. Watt had his secretary call me to set up a meeting. I was flattered that he wanted to meet with me and was curious as to what was on his mind. We met at the club, and he got right down to business: Watt wanted me to operate the club's restaurant, the Bougainvillea Room, which I had always felt was one of the world's most beautiful spots.

Nestled against the majestic San Jacinto Mountains, the place was once the private domain of kings, stars, and captains of industry, as the elite members of The Tennis Club of Palm Springs. The second-floor site had the most fabulous views of the desert with walls of glass overlooking the city of Palm Springs. The back of the building was literally built into the mountain and there were waterfalls cascading down the mountainsides, a crackling fireplace, and an outside terrace for dining under the sun or stars. It was just breathtaking.

Despite the glitzy location and its storied history, The Tennis Club restaurant never quite made a go of it. Though flattered by the offer, I had to decline.

"Mr. Watt, my plate is very full right now," I said. "It's a wonderful offer but now is just not a very good time for me." Undaunted, Watt upped the ante.

"Mel, I'll tell you what I'll do for you," he started off. "I won't charge you any rent, and the first year I'll pay you $1,000 a month to run and promote the restaurant. After the first year, the rent will be a straight five percent of volume with no guarantee." It was a smoking deal.

So when Mr. Watts made me an incredible offer it got my creative juices going once again. As with Cecil's, I went a little overboard in the spending department to give the place the "wow" factor.

To run the restaurant, I once again enlisted Vito Russo. Vito successfully managed Saturday's for me, and I felt he could easily run both places.

"Vito, I'm going to make you a deal you can't refuse," I started off. "I'm going to lay out the money to fix up this restaurant, and you will run the place. When I get my investment back, you will own 25 percent." It was a helluva deal because I was already paying Vito a salary at Saturday's and was going to pay him a small salary to run The Tennis Club, and he would get a piece of the action once I was in the black.

I hired Gilbert Konqui once again to decorate the place, and he did a marvelous job. He came up with a color scheme of blue and white, accented by mirrors and multicolored lights on the mountain.

I built a new bar, reactivated the waterfalls that cascaded down the mountain, enlarged the dance floor, and renamed the main dining room "Doubles"—it was absolutely drop dead gorgeous. I named the small private dining room the "Stephanie Room" in honor of my bride. It took three months and approximately $450,000 in renovations to achieve the elegant look and feel I desired.

We served lunch and dinner daily as well as an unrivaled Sunday Champagne Brunch, which started 9 a.m. and ended at 3 p.m.

I also updated service at the Court Bar by the tennis courts and the Barefoot Bar, adjoining one of the pools. I installed a new sound system in the restaurant with music of the forties and fifties and some disco music for nightly dancing.

I did everything to ensure Doubles's success; including extending an open invitation to the public through a small ad in a local newspaper to attend the restaurant's grand opening. More than 3,000 people showed, including celebrities John Forsythe, Dick Van Patten, and Donna Mills. The libations flowed freely, and bartenders served almost 10,000 shots of free whiskey. Guests also feasted on rib roast, Gulf shrimp, canapés, and caviar. My food and liquor came to about $15,000, but it was money well spent. The local paper raved about the success of the grand opening, touting me as the "man with the Midas touch."

With the opening of Doubles, I found myself the second largest employer in Palm Springs (the local hospital was the largest) with approximately 200 people on my payroll. I had to meet $250,000 a month in payroll expenses for the four restaurants and my small hotel. I was definitely King Kong of the desert. I nearly had a heart attack when I first walked into my new accounting office across the street from Melvyn's where six bookkeepers and one controller oversaw all of my operations. Realizing that I was paying for all of these people on the accounting staff, I broke out into a cold sweat. I rarely stepped foot inside that office again.

It was around that time that I made another key hire. I had placed an ad in the local paper for a public relations person to promote my five establishments. A few days later I received a phone call from a woman who said she wanted to apply for the job. I told her I would gladly meet with her the very next day. She said that was a problem because she lived in San Francisco. However, she said she wanted to return to the desert where she formerly lived but couldn't get to Palm Springs for a few days.

"The only person I want to work for is you," she said, which raised my eyebrows. I'd never heard that one before. I probed further and asked her how much money she was looking for.

"Well, last year I made $100,000," she said, and then added, "but for me, it's not about the money. I understand you can't pay anywhere near that, but promise me you won't give away the job until you talk to me." I was now very intrigued by this mystery woman and promised her I'd wait until the end of the week to meet her.

On a Friday afternoon, the mystery lady walked into my office, and introduced herself as Marilyn Baker. She was very impressive and had impeccable credentials. I hired her immediately.

A week after Marilyn came on board, she left an old copy of *TV Guide* on my desk. It had her picture on the cover. Ms. Baker, I learned, was an investigative reporter from San Francisco who broke the Patty Hearst kidnapping story in 1974. As a result of her coverage, Marilyn won a Peabody Award. She was very well known in media circles. Best of all, she agreed to work for $1,500 a month.

Marilyn ended up writing a column for the *Desert Sun* and the *Desert Weekly* called "Palm Springs People." The column focused on the great social happenings in Palm Springs, grand openings, celebrities visiting town, charity events, and golf tournaments. Being the great writer she was, Marilyn subtly dropped the names of all the celebrities who visited my establishments. It was money well spent.

While I made a great deal with Marilyn, I found out that my partner Vito Russo was no bargain. Every month Vito handed me $3,000 (profits from Saturdays), and I was loving life. But like all good things, it came to an abrupt end. I discovered that Vito was shaking down one of my employees for all his tips.

I had employed a nice kid at Doubles named David Sonnegrath, and he worked his rear end off for me and Vito. He did absolutely everything from managing the place to seating patrons to scrubbing the toilets. There was nothing David wouldn't do. When Vito took over as manager, he demanded a whole lot more from David. In time, David had hit his limit. He called me a few months after we opened, sounding very frustrated.

"Boss, do I really have to give all of my tips to Vito?" David asked me. Flabbergasted, I asked him to repeat what he had just said. David told me that Vito had been taking all his tips and that he had turned over approximately $2,220 so far. I immediately called Vito and told him that I wanted to meet with him. When he showed up, I got right down to brass tacks.

"I understand you took about two grand in tips from David," I said. "First off, that's not right. Second, even if it doesn't rightly belong to David, then the money should go to me. Our deal was that I am supposed to recoup my investment in Doubles and then we're partners." An argument ensued and then Vito ran out of the room. He came back and promptly handed me $1,100. I guess he already assumed we were fifty-fifty partners. That was it and I told him that we're through.

I had to part ways with Vito because I could no longer trust him. Rather than hash it out in court, I let him have Saturday's while I took over the operations of Doubles. Looking back, I should have let Vito take Doubles, because after opening night, the restaurant gave me some major headaches. Doubles had a seating capacity for about 300 people. Friday and Saturday nights weren't a problem filling up the place but come Sunday through Thursday, it was like a ghost town. Even a crowd of fifty made the large room look virtually empty. I remember one summer night when I walked into the dining room and counted only twenty-two people in the restaurant. A buddy of mine walked up to me, slapped me on the back, and sarcastically said, "Mel, I see you're jammed tonight." It was like a dagger through the heart.

The other problem Doubles presented was that on weekends I might need twenty waiters and waitresses, but I'd only need five on weekdays. How do you hold on to staff that are willing to work those sorts of shifts? When I compared labor and food costs for Doubles, it was the least profitable of all of my businesses.

I thought I'd found the answer to all of my problems when I'd met the husband and wife team of Bill and Mary Lane. Bill was an LA-based businessman who owned a very successful seafood restaurant in the Valley. I didn't know it at the time, but Bill had made his fortune as a bookmaker and still had a very large operation in Los Angeles. Bill was a native New Yorker, who was a hard worker and a real hands-on kind of guy. I made a deal with him, and he came to work for me. Every night he stood on the cooking line and watched every dish that was served.

Bill was a character. Whenever he traveled, it was usually in a long, white stretch limousine, chauffer and all. When he flew, it was always first class. At restaurants, he was known as a very big tipper. Bill also befriended some interesting people—it seemed as if every wise guy in Palm Springs eventually made his way into Doubles under Bill's watch. A group of ten to fifteen guys would usually show up near closing time every Saturday night and order tons of food, champagne, and caviar. They'd spend thousands of dollars, and it was all because Bill was the main attraction.

Doubles was doing fine for about a year with Bill and Mary in charge—that is, until Bill made the unfortunate mistake of hiring a hostess more gorgeous than his wife. He seemed to be taking a more than professional interest in this young lady's career. I was having food problems at Cecil's, so I asked Bill to spend some time there to straighten it out. He said he would only do it if he could bring the hostess with him. That should have sent up a red flag, but I didn't care about the particular arrangements, only that business was tended to. Bill told me that his wife Mary could very easily run Doubles by herself while he oversaw Cecil's.

About three weeks into this new arrangement, Bill disappeared with the beautiful hostess. One day the two didn't show up for work, and it turned out they had skipped town together. Bill left his wife Mary at Doubles, and she stayed on for a few more months. Business slumped at Doubles after Bill left, and I eventually turned the place over to my chef, David Church, who made an unsuccessful attempt at running the restaurant. Then I decided it was time to cut my losses and sell the place.

I tried for two years to recoup my initial $450,000 investment, but to no avail. It was the first time I had to admit defeat in Palm Springs.

I eventually sold Doubles in 1985 to an investor for about $100,000. Over the years, Doubles changed hands several times until businessman and philanthropist Harold Matzner bought the restaurant in 2002. Matzner had pioneered the marketing concept known as "shared mail," which has become a billion-dollar industry and he has very deep pockets. He called the restaurant Spencer's, after his dog, and it became his personal pet project. It's still not a money-making proposition for Matzner, but he has restored Spencer's to the former glory of The Tennis Club and has made the restaurant a Palm Springs landmark once again. I've got to say, I admire his style.

Losing Saturday's and Doubles was nothing compared to the heartache of watching Cecil's die a slow and painful death. With the eighties came the death of disco, but in the desert, it was still very much alive and kicking. In fact, I had my best year ever in 1983. I was even going to open another Cecil's—this time in Newport Beach, California. I met a lot of people from that area who drove down almost every weekend just to dance at Cecil's. They were well dressed and young, and they appeared to be affluent.

I discovered that there wasn't a great club in the Newport Beach area and with the following that I had developed, it would be the perfect place to open a second Cecil's. I spent a couple of weeks scouting the scene and finally found the perfect location—a restaurant for sale on MacArthur Boulevard, a main thoroughfare in the heart of the area. I negotiated a lease and was very excited at the prospect of expanding.

During this time, an out-of-town group was building a new nightclub in Palm Springs about ten blocks away from Cecil's. It was called Last Nights of Pompeii. I was concerned about the effect it was going to have on my disco. The final papers to close the Newport deal arrived on my desk December 14, 1983. Pompeii's grand opening was the next night, so I decided to wait a few days before I signed them. All the people flocked to the new place in town, and in twenty-four hours, Cecil's was dead in the water. Thinking it was a passing fancy, I figured I would just wait it out. For two years I waited for my customers to come back. They never did.

The nightclub business is very trendy, and either you change with the times or the times will change (and date) you very quickly. I was never one for gimmicks, and the club scene tends to get stale after a while. Owners need a fresh atmosphere after a while to continue bringing in the crowds. Cecil's was still the most gorgeous club on the West Coast, but it didn't seem to matter to the younger crowd. They wanted a new playground, and Pompeii's was the desert's newest hot spot. From the day they opened their doors Pompeii practically put me out of business.

The diminishing returns were the handwriting on the wall, and I was always one who was faithful to the numbers. They never lie. I didn't have the heart or the energy to try and change Cecil's look and concept, because I didn't want to cheapen such a great product. Everything is relative, and it was tough to accept Cecil's not being jammed every night. My ego was crushed.

I gracefully bowed out of the nightclub business and started looking for a new buyer. As it turned out, I didn't have to look very far.

Gil Levy, a customer of mine who was in the used furniture business, and his partner, Barney Spizman, a neighbor and a very wealthy entrepreneur, thought it might be fun to get into the nightclub business. They bought Cecil's from me for $600,000 in the summer of 1985. The two men eventually learned the hard way that the times were indeed a-changin'. Barney eventually bought out Gil, and Cecil's became Jacqueline's in honor of his wife. After a few years, Barney ended up selling Jacqueline's to a new owner, who as it turned out, owned Zelda's. He ran it for a few years, and then sold it to another owner, who turned it into a gay nightclub. After that club had run its course, the space was subdivided into several different retail stores in the Smoke Tree Village Shopping Center, which is what it remains today. But if those walls could talk, what a story they could tell about the celebrities who put on their boogie shoes and lived life to the fullest during those crazy disco nights.

When Saturday's, Doubles, and Cecil's fell by the wayside, my life wasn't as hectic as it had once been. As a result, I began taking a more active role in the Angel View Crippled Children's Foundation, a nonprofit organization that has been helping physically challenged young people since the fifties.

I had first become aware of Angel View a few years earlier when Cecil's was still the hottest club in town. Like most nightclub owners, I had looked for ways to create daytime business because the doors didn't open until 6 p.m. Believe me, I tried everything. I even had my own radio show on Sunday afternoons, broadcast from Cecil's in hopes of drawing a crowd. I held dances for teenagers at the club on Saturday afternoons because I had heard from many parents that there weren't many activities for kids in Palm Springs. I'd charge five dollars at the door while my son Lonny spun records for the kids. After a while, the dances drew the wrong element, and I had to close it down.

I decided that since I couldn't make any money with it, maybe I could do some good with the site. I asked my publicist Marilyn Baker for ideas, and she suggested that I offer the space to a charity. At first, the idea didn't make much sense to me. What charity could use a discotheque during the day? I was told to contact the Angel View Crippled Children's Foundation, which was based in nearby Desert Hot Springs.

I learned that the foundation was originally created by a small group of people from the Coachella Valley who felt the area's natural hot springs found in Desert Hot Springs would be useful in the rehabilitation of children with polio. The dry desert climate, along with the local mineral waters, seemed to help the condition of these children. As a result, these visionaries created a charitable facility on donated land and initiated a free Sister Kenney Polio Clinic for children in the area. With the advent of the Salk vaccine, polio no longer posed the threat it once did to children, therefore, the focus of Angel View's original mission broadened to include those children afflicted with a wide range of physical challenges.

When I first contacted Marty Gittleman, Angel View's director at the time, I felt I was doing a pretty good deed. I was simply giving back to the community that had been so good to me, and didn't think the extent of my generosity would go much beyond that.

"Do you think you might be able to use the club?" I asked Marty. Without a moment's hesitation, he said, "Absolutely."

Marty and I picked a date for the kids' first field trip to Cecil's, and it was a life-changing event for me. About fifty kids, all in wheelchairs, made their way out of the special bus and into my club. It was heartbreaking and as a father of three children, I could barely handle it.

Once they were situated, we turned on the music and the kids started having a ball. Stephanie, whom I was dating at the time, walked up to a small boy in a wheelchair, pulled him out by the hands and swung him around. He was squealing, and I must admit, I got a little nervous. Little did I know he was squealing with delight.

"They're not eggs, Mel," Stephanie said with an all-knowing smile. "They're not going to break." The kids laughed, screamed, and actually danced to the music in their wheelchairs. The outing was such a success that we made it a monthly ritual the first Saturday of every month. Before long, I started raising money on the foundation's behalf.

One day actor John Forsythe popped into Doubles on a Saturday, and we chatted amiably for a while. John's career was red hot again thanks to *Dynasty*, which was the No. 1 rated show on TV. After we started talking, I asked him if he had anything pressing that day. He said he was down for the weekend, just hanging out. I asked John to take a car ride with me, which he gladly did.

I took John to Cecil's, where we were hosting the monthly dance for the Angel View kids. John took one look at the children having a blast, and a big smile plastered his face.

"Mel, I'd like to sponsor a tennis tournament on behalf of these kids," John suddenly said. Who was I to try and stop him?

True to his word, John Forsythe hosted a benefit tournament at The Tennis Club on behalf of the Angel View Foundation, and raised several thousand dollars for the nonprofit. John was very gracious and a true gentleman. I guess Marty Gittleman was impressed by the company I kept and began seeing all sorts of possibilities. He asked if I would consider serving on Angel View's board of directors. I was taken aback and honored, because I had never served on any board or committee. I must admit, it was a daunting proposition. I've always been the kind of guy who was able to do what I wanted whenever I wanted. I liked shooting from the hip. I never had to consult with other people to get their permission to make a decision. I was very scared of getting involved with a charity because I knew it carried a very big responsibility. However, I was very thankful and grateful for the luck and success I had in the desert. The timing was right to start giving back.

I asked Marty what was involved in being a board member, and he explained that the main responsibility was to attend a monthly board meeting. Whatever extra work I wanted to do or perform was strictly up to me. I felt nervous about making the commitment, and I asked him if I couldn't make a meeting for some reason, could I send a representative in my place. That's how responsible I felt to the obligation of being on a board. Marty looked at me like it was a silly question and said that it would not be a problem. After that, there was really no reason for me to say no. The funny thing is, I've been on the board now for over twenty-five years (fifteen as president), and I think I've only missed one meeting in a quarter century.

I'm not a religious man by any stretch of the imagination, but I have seen many amazing things at Angel View. One of my favorite couples, who owned a small grocery store in Desert Hot Springs, lunched at Melvyn's about three times a week. They told me about the time in the fifties when former First Lady Mamie Eisenhower pulled up into their tiny store with a motorcade of four Secret Service cars. Mrs. Eisenhower, who was a big booster of the organization, popped out of her black Lincoln Town Car to personally thank this couple for providing food to the children of Angel View.

In 1988, an Angel View administrator came into Melvyn's with a Hasidic Jew named Nuchem Friedman, who hailed from New York.

Mr. Friedman represented several orthodox Jewish families who had many children in need of our services. He said he researched the entire country and came to the conclusion that Angel View was the best facility for physically challenged youth. Mr. Friedman asked whether, if he raised the money to build a house (approximately $250,000), could we build one for six Jewish children? The only provision was they needed two kitchens in order to observe the kosher laws.

I told Mr. Friedman that I didn't know if it was legal or not to specifically build a house for only Jews, Mexicans, African Americans, and so on. However, I told him that I would approach the board with his request. The board did not have a problem with the proposition and approved. Mr. Friedman raised the funds, and we built the place and named it "Joel's House" in honor of Nuchem Friedman's eight-year-old son, who was brain damaged at birth. Sadly, Joel passed away before the home was finished.

When Joel Friedman died the administrator called to inform me that an Arab child from Kuwait was put in the empty bed.

"You put an Arab child in the Jewish house?" I said. "This I have to hear."

He explained to the Arab family that the only opening we had was in the home for Jewish children. The child's father said, "No problem." I called Nuchem Friedman in New York, and he said, "No problem." He said the house should accept the child. His belief stemmed from the basic tenets of Judaism, which teaches that helping the helpless defines the dignity of our own existence. That certainly defined Angel View's outlook as well.

In 2,000 years, the Jews and the Arabs could barely talk to each other, but when it came to their children's welfare, it was no problem.

Presently, Angel View oversees seventeen homes located in residential neighborhoods throughout the Coachella Valley. Each six-bedroom house is built with wide doorways, low countertops, and sinks, and roll-in showers to facilitate wheelchairs. In addition, Angel View offers an assortment of beneficial services such as physical therapy, occupational therapy, speech therapy, twenty-four hour nursing and attended care, and psychological services. These homes provide round-the-clock care in a family-like atmosphere and give clients more privacy and a sense of belonging. The facilities are very popular and have no problem filling up. Angel View also offers a unique summer program at its own Camp Forrest, located in the high desert on seventeen acres in Joshua Tree, California. The camp was named after Forrest Shacklee from Shacklee Corporation, who made a large donation to Angel View.

With donor support, the organization has built six cabins that house a total of thirty-six campers at each weekly session throughout the summer months. Activities include swimming, basketball, archery, arts and crafts, campfire gatherings, and field trips.

The purpose of the summer camp is to create an enjoyable environment for both disabled and nondisabled Coachella Valley children. The idea is to send underprivileged children from the various Boys and Girls Clubs throughout the Coachella Valley to the camp to partner them with disabled youth. It gives healthy youth a better understanding of disabled children, which they might not have had before. For example, there is a basketball court at the camp. At one end the hoop is fitted at the ten-foot regulation height while at the other end of the court the hoop is at wheelchair height so the two sides can play against each other.

One anecdote that never fails to put a smile on my face is the time a lady who ran a Boys and Girls Club for underprivileged youths called me at Melvyn's. She told me that when she brought her kids to the camp on the first day, they didn't want to stay. Her kids hadn't been around disabled kids before, and they felt uneasy. However, she said at the end of the seven-day session, they didn't want to leave.

"I think it's an experience they will carry with them for the rest of their lives," she said, which almost brought me to tears.

My proudest moment involving Angel View took place November 14, 2002. That's when the foundation opened our seventeenth home and named it the Melvyn Haber House. It's certainly one of the highest honors ever bestowed upon me.

About two years after the opening of Joel's House, Nuchem Friedman contacted me from New York and asked if we would build another house for Jewish children if he raised the money. We did, and when the second house was ready, Nuchem said they wanted to honor me at the dedication because I was the person they initially contacted. Six different rabbis flew in from New York for the ceremony, and one of them was a Rabbi who was the right hand of Rabbi Schneerson, the most important rabbi of that particular sect. (He was their equivalent of Jesus on earth.)

The ceremony was scheduled on a Sunday, and my wife and daughter planned to attend. When we arrived, everybody was busy setting up an elaborate feast while the Rabbis were busy putting up mezuzahs on all of the doors. Nuchem brought me over to meet Rabbi Schneerson's assistant and we shook hands.

"What a great honor to meet you, Rabbi," I said. "I would like to present my wife, Stephanie." Stephanie, who is Catholic, extended her hand, but the rabbi looked at it with disdain and walked away. Stephanie stood there in total shock with her hand outstretched and her mouth wide open. I was not aware that according to the Hasidic religion a man is not allowed to touch another woman other than his wife.

After all the preparations were finished, the men sat down at the tables in the living room while the women huddled in the hallway to listen to the dedications. Stephanie took one look at this arrangement, came over to me, and said, "Mel, I will not put up with this. I'll go to McDonald's and wait for you outside." As she walked across the dining room I yelled, "Stephanie, does this mean you will not convert?"

A good friend, Larry Delrose, recently told me that he believes my work with Angel View will be my lasting legacy, not as the proprietor of the Ingleside Inn, Melvyn's, or the several restaurants that I have owned and operated. It would be an honor if that is my lasting legacy. I'm very proud of my association with Angel View and would highly recommend charity work to anyone who feels they have something to offer. The rewards are astronomical, and I've learned through Angel View that giving back is what life is all about.

And it might even carry some weight a little later on: I know that my work at Angel View won't get me upstairs, but hopefully it will slow my descent from going downstairs.

# CHAPTER 16

# Peter's Principle and Mel's Self-Realization

**M**y work with the Angel View Crippled Children's Foundation gave me a chance to become a productive citizen and good corporate neighbor.

One day I received a call from a representative at a local television station informing me that I had been chosen to receive the prestigious Jefferson Award. I had never heard of the award, but the representative informed me that the program was started in the early sixties by First Lady Jacqueline Kennedy to honor outstanding citizens for their contributions to their communities. This was going to be the launching of the program in the Palm Springs desert area, and I was selected along with four other prominent people to be in the first class of inductees. The awards were going to be presented by former president Gerald Ford at a public ceremony. I was thrilled and couldn't wait to tell my wife.

Stephanie congratulated me and told me how proud she was. However, after checking our calendar, she said, "Oh, we can't make it on that date." I wasn't sure I heard her correctly and asked her to repeat herself. She said the date conflicted with our daughter's high school volleyball game and that we'd have to cancel or reschedule the award ceremony. Knowing Stephanie the way I did, I knew she wasn't kidding. Totally frustrated, I gave Stephanie the name and phone number of the lady at the TV station and told her to handle the situation. Stephanie called the station and explained the situation, and the lady told her she would see what she could do.

Lo and behold, we got a call the next day from the representative at the TV station, who told us they'd move the date back a week. It was totally unbelievable—Stephanie got the former president of the United States and four prominent Palm Springs residents to shuffle their schedules to accommodate Autumn's volleyball game. The kicker, however, was that the day before the ceremony, President Ford suffered heat stroke on the golf course and was admitted to the hospital. U.S. Representative Mary Bono, Sonny's widow, made the presentations in Ford's stead. It was still a great honor.

While I received lots of accolades for being a decent citizen, it was the birth of my daughter, Autumn, who finally allowed me to become a decent father.

Unfortunately, I was too focused on my career with my first go-round with fatherhood, and quite frankly, I wasn't around much to help pitch in with the parental duties. Like so many fathers of that generation, I mistakenly thought that bringing home the bacon was my only real obligation. As a result, my first wife Pat raised our three kids with an absentee father footing the bills and showing up for dinner every once in a while.

When Autumn was born, all of my ill-conceived notions on parenting went out the window. But some old habits were hard to break.

I really couldn't relate to Autumn when she was an infant. As a result, Stephanie spent a lot of time rearing her while I tended to business as usual. As Autumn got older and began to speak, my attitude toward her totally shifted.

Because my older children were grown, there was no longer pressure on me to support another family, so I had the time and the energy to devote to Autumn. I attended every school function, was on top of her academic progress, and took the time to get to know her friends. I drove her to school every morning, and we often had lunch together. We spent a lot of quality time together. As Autumn grew older, we never missed any of her volleyball games.

Autumn is every parent's dream—an all-honors student, a great athlete, and popular with her classmates. She even got involved in the Angel View Crippled Children's Foundation and started a teen chapter, which made group visits to the homes.

Most recently, she graduated high school with a 4.4 grade-point average and is now enrolled in a Southern California university, where she is studying business. If you can't tell, I was and continue to be extremely proud of her and the young woman she has become today. Autumn is everything wonderful and good about having a child.

As a result of my relationship with Autumn, my bond with my other children blossomed as well. My daughter Shani, who lives in New York, visits about three times a year with her husband and two children, while my son Gary relocated to Los Angeles. He's married and has two children. We see each other about a dozen times a year. It's to their credit that they've never held a grudge toward me for not being around when they were growing up. Obviously, it was me who was the one who missed out but I'm so grateful they're in my life today.

An added bonus to becoming a father again was that I developed a burgeoning friendship with Sonny Bono. I had known Sonny for a few years, as he was a big patron of Cecil's. When he opened his restaurant, Bono's, in Los Angeles in February 1983, I sent him a bouquet of flowers with a card that read: "Dear Sonny, if you stay out of the restaurant business, I promise not to sing." Not only did he not stay out of the restaurant business, he brought Bono's restaurant to Palm Springs three years later. It was during a dispute with city zoning officials over a sign permit he needed for his Palm Springs restaurant that Sonny became interested in politics. He set out to become mayor of Palm Springs so that he could help to change the bureaucracy. He won the election and served as mayor from 1988 to 1992.

Sonny married his third and last wife, Mary Whitaker, in 1985, and our wives became pregnant around the same time. Sonny and I were also born the same year and we joked that when our daughters turned eighteen, they'd be pushing us around in wheelchairs down Palm Canyon Drive. Unfortunately, Sonny never got to see that day. He died on January 5, 1998, in a freak skiing accident at age sixty-two. His widow Mary ended up taking his seat in the U.S. Congress and has done a wonderful job in his absence.

Sonny got mixed reviews during his tenure as mayor, but I believe that he was quite good for the city. He gave Palm Springs a much higher profile because of his fame and came into office with a lot of fresh and innovative ideas. He cracked down on hell-raising high school and college students who visited during spring break, asked merchants to clean up their act when it came to selling obscene and offensive merchandise, and made the municipality more business-friendly. He also addressed the area's deteriorating neighborhoods, high retail vacancy, crime, and homelessness. Perhaps Sonny's greatest legacy was establishing the Palm Springs International Film Festival in 1990, which enjoys continued success and infuses the city with millions in revenue each year. Even though Sonny was in Palm Springs a relatively short time, he left a lasting legacy in the desert.

Speaking of mayors, I'd be remiss if I didn't mention my long-standing friendship with Frank Bogert, who is arguably the most famous mayor the town has ever produced. A resident since 1927 (when the population was 200 people), Frank served as mayor from 1958 to 1966 and again from 1982 to 1988. Frank, a former horse wrangler, hotel manager, and magazine publisher, helped shape events that led to the town's evolution from main street village to cosmopolitan desert resort. Frank was very outspoken and is famous for saying what's on his mind. I remember watching him on *Good Morning America* when I first came to town. The interviewer asked Frank if there were any minorities in Palm Springs. His answer nearly knocked me out of my chair.

"Sure we have minorities in Palm Springs," he replied. "Go into the kitchen of any restaurant, and they're the dishwashers."

Frank wasn't crazy about Sonny Bono's bid for mayor because Sonny had compared himself to Clint Eastwood when he was the mayor of Carmel, California. For some reason Sonny's comparison galled Frank, who wasn't shy about his feelings to a local reporter.

"Comparing Sonny to Clint," snorted Frank, "is like comparing chicken shit to chicken salad."

Even though Frank might not have been the most politically correct diplomat, he knew a thing or two about power. He once told me a story about the time the city council tried to block him from greeting President John F. Kennedy during his visit to Palm Springs in the early sixties. Frank had already greeted two previous presidents, and they were tired of him getting all the glory. He was told by his fellow council members that somebody else was going to greet Kennedy when he stepped off the plane. The feisty cowboy didn't like receiving marching orders from anybody, much less politicians who were looking to grab some cheap glory.

Turned out that JFK himself heard the story and invited Frank to jump aboard Air Force One in Los Angeles. When it touched down in Palm Springs, he and Kennedy were smiling from ear to ear as they walked down the steps of the plane together. That was Frank in a nutshell.

Today, at almost the century mark, Frank is still as spry and outspoken as ever. An authentic cowboy, he continues to ride his horse daily. He is considered one of Palm Springs's true treasures and was immortalized with a bronze statue outside the steps of city hall. Frank recently wrote in the second edition of his excellent book *Palm Springs's First Hundred Years* that I did more for the city than any other resident or politician because of all the publicity I garnered over the years. That's quite a compliment coming from Frank. I'm just very happy that I've managed to stay on his good side for all these years.

By the time Autumn reached five, I was able to enjoy life without going 100 m.p.h. The Ingleside Inn and Melvyn's were as popular as ever, and I had a well-trained staff running things when I wasn't around. Most of my days were spent raising my daughter and indulging in two of my biggest passions—working out and reading. I was very satisfied with my new domesticity, but the disco beat was calling me back for one more dance.

For years I had been hearing from friends and former customers that ever since Cecil's closed its doors in the mid-eighties, they really had nowhere to go. I tried my hand at the disco business again when a friend built a new hotel in 1987 in the middle of Palm Springs. The hotel was called the Marquis.

Because of a $20 million overrun, my buddy opened in bankruptcy. He had a lounge on the second floor with live entertainment, but it was losing $20,000 a month. He asked me if I could do something to stem the losses. He offered to turn it over to me for 5 percent of the gross, but said he could not give me a lease because he was in bankruptcy. He explained that I should not invest any serious money because the bank could remove me at any time. But not giving it my all isn't in my nature.

I flew Gilbert Konqui in from Canada and with a $35,000 budget, we got busy. After four days of working around the clock, we opened Club Marquis, a small and intimate disco.

It seemed as if Palm Springs had been awaiting my return. From the first day, we were gangbusters. Even better, it was an easy operation. No food, limited hours, and a small staff. The drive was just five blocks from Melvyn's, and every night after the dinner hour I'd pop into the club to see what was shaking. It was a lot of fun and I banked about $5,000 a month after expenses. But the good times came to an abrupt stop. After six months, the bank took possession of the hotel. The bank's manager felt that he could run the disco and there was no reason to keep Mel Haber. Six weeks after I left, the Club Marquis closed.

By the nineties, society in general had become more casual and jeans and T-shirts had become regular attire in clubs. Palm Springs's old guard still missed getting dressed up to dine, dance, and find romance.

"Mel, where can we go dancing after dinner?" was a constant question that was put to me. The answer was that no such place existed.

Most of the discos that had put Cecil's out of business had run their course, and people started looking elsewhere. Grunge, hip-hop, and industrial music began dominating the club scene all around the country. The only place to go dancing in Palm Springs at the time was inside a large corporate hotel. It was cold and sterile, and to be frank, it was really a kid's disco.

The demographics in the desert were changing as well. Palm Springs was no longer the center of the action and more and more people began moving to the east end of the Coachella Valley such as Rancho Mirage, Palm Desert, and La Quinta.

Even though I was domesticated, I still had more business worlds to conquer. I was bored and had a couple of bucks in my pocket. So in 1993, I decided to build a new bar, nightclub, and restaurant from the ground up.

I signed a very favorable lease in a former Moroccan restaurant called Dar Mahgreb, which was located in Rancho Mirage on Bob Hope Drive and Highway 111. Gilbert Konqui, who had tastefully decorated Cecil's, Doubles, and Club Marquis had passed away. I turned to Gail Bradley, who had done some work for me at the Ingleside Inn, to design my new club. She didn't let me down.

In picking a name for the club, I sought something elegant and French-sounding. My wife Stephanie suggested, "Touché." Stephanie went above the call of duty by designing the logo, which was two stemmed champagne glasses with a starry clink. Perfect.

As usual, I did my homework by traveling to Los Angeles to catch up on the club scene in order to incorporate a few ideas. I visited places such as The Gate and the Trocadero, a club tucked inside the Beverly Hilton Hotel, which was owned by Merv Griffin. I wanted Touché to top Cecil's elegant look and feel. I must say, in all humility, I managed to top myself.

I pretty much had my hands in every detail from the table linens to the wallpaper to the dinner menu. Once again, my adrenaline was pumping, and I'd get up at three o' clock each morning to start the day. Not only was I excited, but the whole desert was buzzing that Mel Haber was building another nightclub.

With its Moroccan architecture, intimate atmosphere, and dim ceiling lights, Touché resembled an exotic desert getaway. The dance club was furnished with soft-cushioned sofas and chairs featuring two bars, two backgammon tables, and an Italian marble dance floor that held approximately 200 people.

The separate piano lounge had soft, sleek black-and-gold striped sofas and a small dance floor for intimate dancing, just like Cecil's.

The adjacent dinner club served steak, chicken, seafood, duck, and other culinary treasures, as well as an extensive selection of wines. A fountain sprouting Egyptian lilies around a statue of the Greek goddess Athena was placed in the middle of the room as a focal point, and celebrity portraits adorned the walls.

Cocktail waitresses sashayed about in full-length, black velour spaghetti-strapped dresses while bartenders wore all black as well. Touché pulsated with class and was even more opulent and beautiful than Cecil's.

Of course, class and opulence comes with a price tag. I spent $1.3 million on construction and decoration costs to get Touché ready. Thanks to the Americans with Disabilities Act, which went into effect in January of 1992, I had to spend an extra $100,000 to make my club wheelchair accessible. Six months after I opened, finally, a man in a wheelchair came into the club—he was the first. Once I spotted him, I said, "Sir, I've been looking for you for a very long time." I personally took him around the club, running him up and down every ramp the government required me to build, including a special lift that granted access to the dance floor. At first, he thought I was crazy. Then he realized the amount of money I had to spend to accommodate the disabled, and knew where I was coming from. He then started laughing his head off, and we ended up having a ball.

It was the local fire department, however, that gave me the biggest headache of all. Before we were allowed to open our doors, they had to test the smoke detectors, water sprinklers, alarms, and entrances and exits. The testing took several days, and until they gave us the green light, we couldn't announce a grand opening date. Finally, at 4 p.m. on a Friday, we opened our doors.

There's an interesting aside to this story. Back east I had befriended businessman Tommy Quinn, a multimillionaire who owned a big home in Connecticut and a villa in the south of France. He was so powerful that he walked with God. Tommy knew everybody. However, he always treated everybody with the utmost respect. As I was excitedly getting dressed for the opening of Touché the switchboard called to say a Mr. Quinn was on the line. Tommy said he just called to wish me luck with the opening. I hadn't heard from Tommy in eight years.

"What did you just say?" I asked Tommy, not quite believing I heard him right.

"I called to wish you good luck with your grand opening," he said once again.

"Where are you calling from, Tommy?" I asked. He told me he was in France. I asked how he knew that information since I only found out two hours before.

"Good luck, Mel," he said with a touch of mystery, then hung up.

To this day, I still don't know how he got his information. Like I said, Tommy walked with God.

Touché's grand opening was in January 1994, and it appeared as if the New Year was going to bring lots of prosperity. More than 500 people showed up on opening night, and a line formed around the block with people wanting to get inside. Celebrities and the jet-set crowd frequented my place and fancy cars filled my parking lot. People like Andy Williams, George Hamilton, Connie Stevens, Jack Jones, Englebert Humperdinck, and Jackie Mason partied at Touché, enhancing the club's image. Of course, the infamous sometimes tag along with the famous. I remember one night, Ivan Nagy, Heidi Fleiss's Hungarian boyfriend, came to the club and made a point of walking up and introducing himself. He was a nice enough guy, and I didn't mind him coming to the club just as long as he didn't use Touché as a proving ground.

Speaking of which, it was around this time that my longtime friend and actor Marc Lawrence asked me if I had ever been to the Playboy Mansion in Los Angeles. Marc, a pock-faced character actor, had appeared in hundreds of movies as a heavy since the 1930s and was a regular at Melvyn's. I told him I had not but like any guy would love to go. Marc mentioned that he was friendly with Hugh Hefner and was a regular guest at the mansion. He said that next week he was going to the mansion to watch a major prize fight on

TV. He said he would check with Hefner to see if it was okay for me to go with him. About two days later Marc called to say Hefner said I was welcome. I was very excited and told everybody who would listen about my upcoming adventure. I especially couldn't wait to tell my wife. That evening, I told her that I had finally "arrived" as I was invited to the Playboy mansion. Somehow I didn't detect the same enthusiasm from her. Around 2 a.m., she nudged me from my sleep and said, "You know, I am really bothered about your going to the Playboy mansion without me," Stephanie said.

"Stephanie, the only reason I am going is to say I've been to the Playboy mansion," I said. "Bragging rights is all." The ironic part was that Stephanie had been there years before with her girlfriends. Perhaps that was the problem.

I mulled it over and decided that if going to the mansion would only aggravate my wife, I wouldn't go. It wasn't worth it. I explained this to Marc, who said he completely understood. A day later he called with some unbelievably good news.

"Mel, this is unheard of, but Hugh Hefner says you can bring your wife," Marc said. "There's no guy that comes to the Playboy mansion with their wife, but you can bring yours if you want." Naturally, this produced an ear-to-ear grin from me. I couldn't wait to tell Stephanie the great news.

"I don't want to go," Stephanie replied. "But you go ahead if you really want to." That was it—I was going without her.

On the night of the planned outing, we took the hotel limousine, and Marc and I arrived at the Playboy mansion in grand style. The mansion was magnificent, the food and liquor were plentiful, and Mr. Hefner was a most congenial host. Of course, all of the parties at the Playboy mansion are well attended by celebrities and the flavor of the month. It just so happened that the flavor of the month when I visited was John Wayne Bobbit, the unfortunate ex-marine who had his penis lopped off by his temperamental, knife-wielding wife, Lorena. I would think that having Mr. Bobbit at an adults-only party is the alcoholic equivalent of a buzz kill, but people were fascinated by him. I wish I could say the same. The truth of the matter was, for a Friday night the Playboy mansion was not nearly as swinging as Touché. After I had my picture taken with Hef, I told Marc "Let's go back to Palm Springs." The fight hadn't even started yet, and Marc thought I was crazy. But we had come in my limousine and that's what I wanted to do, so we headed back to Palm Springs.

Touché was an immediate hit, and once again I was the toast of the town. *Lifestyles of the Rich and Famous* had a successor show called *Run Away with the Rich and Famous* that brought a celebrity to the location featured in the show. I was told by producers that not only would they promote the Ingleside Inn and Melvyn's, but they'd promote Touché as well. I was picturing some gigantic star, and when I asked what celebrity was being featured, they told me Fyvush Finkell. I had no clue who they were talking about. Actually, I thought they were kidding because I had never heard the name. It turned out that he was an old Jewish actor who was hot again due to his role in *Picket Fences*, which was a very popular show on CBS.

Mr. Finkell was an octogenarian who had the energy of a teenager. He had a five-course meal at Melvyn's, danced the night away at Touché with his lovely wife, and returned to the lounge at Melvyn's and sang with the piano player until 2 a.m., all in front of the camera. He turned out to be a delightful man.

Despite the great plug from *Runaway with the Rich and Famous*, a curious pattern started to emerge at Touché: I had no midweek business whatsoever. On Fridays and Saturdays, I had to turn people away at the door, but come Sunday night, Touché was as quiet as a public library.

While I was in Los Angeles doing my homework, I hadn't noticed most nightclubs were only open four nights a week. However, I failed to ask the million-dollar question: Why? The answer eventually came to me—people weren't partying as hard as they did in the late seventies and early eighties. AIDS and Mothers against Drunk Drivers had severely affected people's work and play habits. There was also more enlightenment about alcohol and substance abuse through the media, which I believe also played a role in curtailing attitudes about drinking responsibly, and the fact that club owners were successfully being sued in court for overserving custom-ers who didn't have the willpower to call it quits. The burden now rested on the nightclub owner's shoulders, which I've always felt was terribly unfair.

I tried everything under the sun to generate business during the week: theme nights, live musical acts, promotional giveaways, VIP packages, private parties, and so on. None of those ideas seemed to boost business on weeknights.

There were other problems as well—chiefly, finding good help. I noticed the values of the workforce began to radically change, es-pecially in younger people. Rather than working their way up the ladder, the attitude was, "What can you do for me?"

One night I had a piano player walk out on a busy Saturday night for no apparent reason. Luckily another piano player filled in for him and saved the day, but that sort of unprofessional behavior had never happened to me before.

There were also temperamental chefs and waitstaff who seemed to constantly be at odds with each other. No one worked in har-mony, and often it was the customers who had to suffer.

I even had problems with my manager, who felt it was his job to flirt and schmooze with the ladies rather than oversee the operation. He only paid attention to the big tippers and spenders, and ignored the rest of our patrons. That wasn't good, either.

I remember one night a local restaurateur walked through the door. I asked my manager to seat him and his party right away as a show of respect to my colleague. My manager shot back, "Why don't you seat him?" I couldn't believe my ears. Of course, with an attitude like that, he didn't last very long.

It was a hard adjustment for me to make, and one I wasn't will-ing to put up with as I got older. The place needed more of my en-ergy and time, but it wasn't something I was willing to do now that I was married and had a child.

Besides, I had no great financial need at this point. Nonetheless, I decided to make one last-ditch attempt at making some serious money at Touché. I wanted to start a chain of upscale nightclubs. I got the idea after I had met Rick Rosenfeld and Larry Flax, who took over the dining room at Touché for a private party. They were the owners of California Pizza Kitchen and had just sold out to Pepsi for millions of dollars. They were left with one-third of the company so they could continue to expand the franchise.

It occurred to me that I had a unique concept in a combination nightclub/disco/restaurant. My idea was to build two more Touchés—one in Newport Beach, California, and one in Las Vegas. After I had those three stores, I would then attempt to go public and build a large chain of Touchés.

One of the main reasons that I wanted to expand was so that I could afford to hire a high-powered executive to oversee all three operations. I could not afford one with just one nightclub. I advertised in a national restaurant publication for the position offering to give him/her a piece of the business. I received twenty qualified résumés. The right people were definitely out there. If my business grew, so would the right person's wallet.

I made the rounds to various investment houses to raise the money to finance the additional two operations. My contribution would be the $1.3 million I put into the Rancho Mirage location. Assuming the two sites would cost the same to build, I needed to raise $2.6 million. Much to my frustration, I couldn't generate any interest in my idea.

What compounded my frustration was that there was a Southern California restaurant chain that had six stores and kept growing with investors' money despite the fact that each store they opened lost $300,000 a year. Here I was, a self-made guy, who ran all of these successful operations from the ground up with his own cash and had a proven track record, and I couldn't raise a dime. I was at my wit's end.

I had read about the Peter Principle in Dr. Laurence J. Peter's book of the same name. He wrote that "in a hierarchy, every person tends to rise to his level of incompetence." For example, in the restaurant business, the lowest point you start at is the dishwasher. If that person is any good as a dishwasher, you promote him to the pantry. If he excels there, then you would make the employee a cook. If that person is no good as a cook, then that's where he remains forever at his level of incompetence. Following that theory, everybody gets promoted to the next higher level until they get to a level where they are no good and that's where they remain. It's the same system in our government and military.

Peter's principle was a concept that hit me like a ton of bricks. I could have gone further with my business ventures, but the fact was I could no longer find good help. I've always felt it was my failure to be intuitive or insightful enough to hire the right people to expand with. I, Mel Haber, decided that my level of competence was one hotel and one restaurant.

I sold Touché in 1996, almost two years after opening. It didn't matter that I sold Touché for $250,000—almost a million dollars less than what I spent on constructing and furnishing the place. The stress of running Touché began taking its toll on me, and people noticed. One night a good friend wrapped his arm around me and said, "Mel, just remember that at our age stress is our enemy." I realized how right he was. I decided at that very moment that I would sell Touché and take whatever I could get. I wish I could say the stress ended there.

A local doctor wound up buying Touché but gave me a very rough time. With the summer approaching, I turned the keys to the property over to him as soon as we opened escrow. I gave him possession before the liquor license transferred and before I got my money, which turned out to be a big mistake. A few days later he started acting strange and accused me of stealing a vacuum cleaner. I simply sent one of my employees to buy him a new one. He then accused me of taking two cases of glasses, worth approximately fifty bucks. I sent him a check in the mail. But this was just a precursor of things to come.

The doctor intentionally delayed the closing of the escrow for several months. I found out that he did that because he was earning the interest on the quarter-million dollars while he had possession of the club and the income. He had control of his money and control of my restaurant at the same time. He claimed that his wife was his business partner and had to sign the papers, but that she was in the Middle East on a sabbatical.

After the sale finally closed, the doctor went to the State Equalization Board and claimed that of the $250,000 purchase price, the furniture, furnishings, and equipment were worth only $35,000. This was because the furniture, furnishings, and equipment are subject to state tax. The balance, he claimed, was goodwill because that was not taxable. The board was skeptical and told him that they knew I had spent $1.3 million on construction and the furnishing of Touché only two years earlier. How could everything be practically worthless? He went to work on the board with the precision of a surgeon, submitting an appraisal from a restaurant equipment company. The board had no choice but to go along with the appraisal.

What makes that story interesting is that six months later, Touché was "robbed" and the doctor claimed to the insurance company the bandits made away with $150,000 worth of merchandise. The last I had heard, he was sued by the insurance company for fraud.

Just another day in Palm Springs.

I got out of the saloon business for good and I never looked back.

I had a heck of a ride—I opened five restaurants and a hotel, befriended hundreds of celebrities and the Palm Springs elite, and met my wife, and along the way encountered wealth and success beyond all my wildest dreams.

Other than my family and the Angel View Crippled Children's Foundation, nothing mattered more to me than the Ingleside Inn and Melvyn's, my employees and customers. After more than thirty years, the two establishments were still thriving. In a way, I had come full circle and I was returning home to where it all started.

# CHAPTER 17

# Ten Things to Do
# While in Palm Springs

There's an old saying that when God closes a door, he opens a window. That most certainly was the case when Touché closed its doors for good. With the sale of Touché safely in the rearview mirror, I suddenly found myself with additional free time. I put it to good use, and the end result was that I wrote an anecdotal book called *Bedtime Stories of the Legendary Ingleside Inn*.

The book mainly focused on funny stories and misadventures involving the Ingleside Inn and Melvyn's. For years people had stopped me in the restaurant to tell certain stories, with Sir John topping everyone's Hit Parade. To do Sir John's story proper justice took anywhere from forty-five minutes to an hour. After so many requests, I dictated the story into a tape recorder and had it transcribed and copied at a local office supply store. People loved my twenty-page manifesto on Sir John's visit to the Ingleside Inn. Later, I added various amusing stories and called the book *Bedtime Stories*. I did it primarily to put copies on the nightstands in the hotel rooms. It turned out to be quite an entertaining read and was a journey in and of itself. It was really about what a "jerk" I was. The book had a dedication by Arnold Schwarzenegger. As of this writing I have sold almost 10,000 copies.

When *Bedtime Stories* first came out, I was contacted by two different groups to talk about my book. At that point I had never spoken publicly, but I was excited about the idea. I committed to the local Jewish temple and a group called Round Table West.

The temple talk was scheduled for a Sunday. When I arrived at the temple, there were about twenty people in attendance, and the average age seemed to be about eighty—fifteen of them were sleeping, and the other five were falling over and drooling. I didn't know what I had gotten myself into. I made up my mind that I would have to honor the other commitment, but that would be the end of my speaking career.

The Round Table West Group met once a month at the historic La Quinta Hotel in the desert. Their program always had four authors. When I entered the ballroom there were 300 beautifully dressed women. I spoke and was encouraged by their response. I stayed afterward and sold and autographed approximately 150 books, with a majority of the proceeds going to my Angel View Crippled Children's Foundation.

As a result of that appearance, I was invited to speak for Brandeis University. Following me on the program was the talented and prolific Steve Allen. I was the first speaker on the program, and as usual, told the Sir John saga that audiences loved. I received a big round of applause. When I finished speaking Steve Allen was introduced, and the first thing he said was, "I can't follow Mel Haber. I should probably give him my time." A higher compliment is not possible.

Another highlight worth noting: Someone sent producer and movie director Mel Brooks a copy of *Bedtime Stories*. He read it, loved it, and insisted on meeting me. I met him in Los Angeles at a place called Junior's Delicatessen, where we had a wonderful lunch and shared a few laughs. However, the most memorable moment was when an elderly Jewish lady came up to the owner, Marvin Saul, who was sitting with us, and blasted him about the location of her table.

"Marvin, if I vanted to sit in da kitchen, I vould haf stayed home," she said in a thick Yiddish accent. The scene could have been right out of one of Mel's movies.

But the accolades and wonderful experiences I received from *Bedtime Stories* was nothing compared to what happened next.

A committee for the Palm Springs Walk of Fame decided that my contribution to the city over the past two decades had been considerable, and they felt it was time to give me a star of my own. I was thrilled. The ceremony, which took place on October 24, 1996, was on my sixtieth birthday. My best friends flew out from New York for the occasion. The ceremony was attended by a big crowd of family, friends, customers, and well-wishers. Before the unveiling of the star, several people made comments about me, including Mayor William G. Kleindienst, who officially declared it as "Melvyn Haber Day" in Palm Springs. But it was my friend Jerry London who wrote and read a poem entitled: "When You're Big, You're Big." His funny and touching ode to me was a big hit with the crowd:

> *Mel Haber has a star on the "Walk of Fame,"*
> *That it isn't any bigger, is a low-down shame,*
> *Melvyn came from New York, working on "case-money,"*
> *Palm Springs, he found, was all milk and honey…*

> *He invested his dough, in a "landmark" hotel,*
> *And with Beverly's help, he fixed it up swell,*
> *The Ingleside Inn, is the name of the place,*
> *Melvyn's takes up quite a bit of the space…*

> *Then came Cecil's and a place called "Touché,"*
> *Then he sold out at Cecil's, and Touché went that way,*
> *Now Melvyn's back to just one good "store,"*
> *He could have saved lots of time, if he did that before…*

> *He's hosted a cadre of celebrity folks,*
> *Wrote an in-keeper's book of anecdotes,*
> *Had a couple of Rolls and a Cad or two,*
> *Not too bad a record for a poor New York Jew…*

> *Oy Melvyn, mine boy, you've come quite far,*
> *And now, on the sidewalk, you're getting a star,*

*Millions of people, some skinny, some fat,*
*Will walk down Palm Canyon and say, "Mel? Who's that?"*

*"Mel Haber," we'll holler, "You ignorant shmuck,"*
*He got here with chutzpah and a wee bit of luck,*
*He built up an empire on just food and drink,*
*You think it was easy? Is that what you think?*

*Well, you're wrong, you putz, it took lots of work,*
*Catering to you, and ten-thousand more jerks,*
*Now, today, the new STAR says, "Step up to the bar,"*
*"Pay attention, my son. You too, could go far"…*

*He's done "60 Minutes" and "The Rich and Famous,"*
*Palm Springs needs Melvyn, like Andy needs Amos,*
*Along with everyone here, Mel is quite quick to agree,*
*Palm Springs, been berry, berry good to me!*

—London, '96

It was around that time that the city of Palm Springs decided to make the Ingleside Inn an official historic site. The designation was not going to benefit me financially in any way, shape, or form. To be quite honest, I was not happy with the decision, because if I wanted to make any changes the city already had several layers of bureaucracy to wade through. Plans had to be approved by the municipality's architectural review committee, a planning and zoning committee, the building department, and, finally, the city council. Being an official historic site would just entail another level of bureaucracy that would have to approve any changes I wanted to make. There was always the distinct possibility that they might have ideas that clashed with mine.

I knew I couldn't fight city hall, but my wife Stephanie urged me to go down and explain my objections. I attended the next council meeting and made a very impassioned speech about the fact that I was the one who maintained the integrity and historical appearance of the Ingleside Inn over the past two decades. But more important, I was entitled to all the rights that existed on the property when I bought it. They had no right to take away any of the entitlements that came with the initial property. The council delayed the action item, and Stephanie said, "I told you that your appearance would make a difference." "Stephanie, they're only paying me lip service," I said in total frustration. "They will make the Ingleside Inn an official historical site at the next meeting." Sure enough, that's exactly what they did.

I decided to make the best of it, and we hosted a party in honor of the historical designation by inviting sixty people to what turned out to be a very lovely affair. Babs Rosen, the hotel manager, narrated a big-screen production on the history of the Ingleside Inn, which fascinated the intimate crowd. The night culminated with a special presentation by City of Palm Springs representative Richard Patenaude, who presented me with a bronze plaque that made our new status official.

With both honors, I was starting to feel like an old-timer. At that point I had only been in Palm Springs for a little more than twenty years, and already I had been dubbed "historic." But I guess everything is relative.

By the new millennium, many of Palm Springs celebrities who had made the town famous had passed on. Desert stalwarts Bob Hope, Frank Sinatra, Bing Crosby, Dean Martin, Liberace, Dinah Shore, and Lucille Ball were all gone. However, the city was infused with new life when the younger generation went through a retro movement and yearned for Hollywood's authentic glamour days. Many of Palm Springs's old haunts of the rich and famous are gone: Sorrentino's, Romanoff's on the Rocks, the Chi Chi Club, Ruby Dune's, Dominick's, Ethel's Hideaway, the Doll House, the Desert Inn, and the Racquet Club are all gone.

As a result, the Ingleside Inn and Melvyn's moved up on the list of places to see, and this new generation of hipsters has decided that Ingleside Inn and Melvyn's is the paragon of old Palm Springs charm. Today I have more young people in my lounge on a Friday and Saturday night than I have had in three decades of business.

As a result, we've become the center of the nostalgia movement. Or, as a desert reporter wrote in a recent article, there were ten things to do in Palm Springs, including visiting the Palm Springs Museum, going to the top of the Palm Springs Tram, and "getting your picture taken with Mel Haber."

It's become a strange ritual, but one I'm glad to fulfill. The fact that people think of me as some sort of celebrity is mystifying and somewhat of a hoot. During the height of the O.J. Simpson murder trial, Judge Lance Ito visited Melvyn's with his wife in tow. As he looked upon the celebrity wall in the lounge, he asked the maitre d' "do you think I can get a picture with Mel Haber?"

Sometimes, however, the joke is on me. Recently, a gentleman walked up to me at my table in the dining room of Melvyn's and said, "I understand you're the owner." I nodded my head in the affirmative and confirmed that indeed I was the owner. Then he asked, "How long ago did Mel Haber pass away?" For the first time in my life, I didn't have a comeback.

The snapshots of people and experiences I've accumulated over the past three decades are priceless and sustain me. They include:

- The night all three of actor Michael Landon's ex-wives ended up dining at the restaurant at the same time.

- The weekend visit by pint-sized *Diff'rent Stokes* star Gary Coleman, whose "Whatchu' talkin' 'bout?" attitude kept the whole staff on its toes one weekend.

- The day Goldie Hawn and Kurt Russell flew down in his new private plane just to have lunch poolside at the Ingleside Inn. They took a quick swim after lunch and then flew back to Los Angeles.

- The time that actor and comedian Richard Pryor invited me to accompany him to the Academy Awards after spending three nights hanging out with me at my various restaurants.

- When Rita Hayworth was released from a sanitarium in the

late seventies and insisted on recuperating at only one place—the Ingleside Inn.

- The day newspaper heiress and former Symbionese Liberation Army member Patty Hearst came to Melvyn's, with her aunt Rosalie Hearst, for a little R&R after she was released from prison.

- When Marlon Brando spent the entire weekend ensconced in his pickup truck in the back of the Ingleside Inn talking for hours on his CB radio.

- The special lyrics, set to the music of "My Way," that Paul Anka wrote for a black-tie affair at Melvyn's.

- The night I had dinner with studio mogul Darryl F. Zanuck, and his lovely wife, Virginia, at their home so he could show me his various awards.

- The time actor James Stacey, the talented Shakespearean actor who lost his left arm and leg in a September 1973 motorcycle accident, clubbed many of my patrons over the head with his crutches after he'd had one too many. Babs Rosen took control, made him her famous chicken soup, and ordered the thespian to go to bed.

- The weekend Tom Selleck filmed a commercial in the lobby of the Ingleside Inn. I can still see him adjusting his Stetson for the umpteenth time, walking down the steps and into a car where he drove out of the gates.

- Sly Stallone and a group of screenwriters staying up all weekend at the Ingleside Inn to rewrite *Rambo: First Blood Part II* because he decided the film needed to be punched up. Our staff kept feeding the crew round the clock and served them endless amounts of coffee to keep them going.

- Renowned artist Xavier Cugat giving me an original painting titled *Dining at Melvyn's* that characterizes some sixty different celebrities. The artwork still proudly hangs on my wall at home.

- The day a waiter accused Colonel Tom Parker of walking out on a check. Parker, who always paid in cash, was presented with the check a few days later by the same waiter. The colonel went ballistic and stormed out of the restaurant. He never came back.

- When musician Peter Cetera of the rock group Chicago discovered the desert and Melvyn's simultaneously. He eventually bought a house behind the Ingleside Inn so he could enjoy the cuisine at Melvyn's on a regular basis.

- The time actor David Hasselhoff, who was sunning by the pool, discovered a baby bird that had fallen out of a tree and gently deposited it back into its nest.

- The great singers who have walked into Melvyn's and entertained the crowds over the years. They include Frank Sinatra, Tony Bennett, Liza Minnelli, Natalie Cole, Jimmy Van Heusen, Paul Anka, Dinah Shore, and Frankie Avalon.

- TV personality Dinah Shore, the most gracious lady I ever met and who treated everyone like family when she walked into Melvyn's.

- The day Granny Rosen booked movie star Arnold Schwarzenegger into the hotel's crumbling annex five blocks down the street in order to punish him because he failed to cancel a prior reservation.

- Sir John's entire stay at the Ingleside Inn.

- The time actress June Allyson, after getting married at the Ingleside Inn, sent me a huge blown-up picture of her wedding party with the inscription: "Everybody should be married at the Ingleside Inn at least once in their lifetime."

- The drunk who wandered up to former First Lady Betty Ford in the restaurant and, right in front of her husband, former president Gerald Ford, and three Secret Service agents, planted a passionate kiss on her lips.

- Actress and comedienne Carol Burnett proudly giving her family a tour of the grounds of the Ingleside Inn as if it were her own home.

- Making arrangements with Frank Sinatra for his pre-wedding dinner and remarking, "What a great honor to have your party at Melvyn's." Whereupon, Frank said, "C'mon, kid, you're meshbugah!" (The Jewish word for family.)

- When Governor Arnold Schwarzenegger, in 2007, pulled up to the Ingleside Inn with a motorcade of Hummers while on a whistle stop. He got out of the car with five burly bodyguards and showed them the grounds. He was overheard by one of my staff members telling his daughter, "I just had to show you my favorite place in Palm Springs." Quite a compliment.

Thirty years is a long time to be rubbing elbows with the biggest names in show business, politics, and high society, and in that time and in that company a fellow can't help achieving his own kind of celebrity status, as well as becoming the friend and confidant of the rich and famous and keeper of their most intimate secrets. For whatever reasons, I have become the man with a million stories and the gatekeeper of old Palm Springs. And I have no intention of going anywhere.

Palm Springs is a wonderful place. When I opened the Ingleside Inn, I became a local celebrity. I had no money, but I was a star. In New York, in order to be big, you had to own a lot of real estate or a lot of factories. When I got to the West Coast, I discovered it was a totally different mentality. I never cared to meet the owner of a restaurant because it wasn't a big deal to me. To me, the real giants were the kings of industry. Out West it's just different. The owner of a famous restaurant, the head of a well-known hair salon, a doorman at a popular nightclub, the hot real estate broker, and the manager at Gucci were all celebrities. On the East Coast, you had to be really big to be a celebrity. Out here, you don't need to be such a big deal to be a big deal. I guess I've kind of grown accustomed to being a big fish in a little pond.

I'll be frank—I've seen many people die on the vine after they retire. I've had many customers who had made money and retired too early only to become alcoholics. For some reason, after they retired to the good life they could not get back into action or were not willing to work as hard as they once did. As a result, they were no longer able to function. There's an old cliché that I abide by: If you want to get something done, give it to a busy man. I have met many, many people at Melvyn's who retired too young. They lost the swing of things and were never able to get back into rhythm. Subsequently, they turned to whatever devices that got them through the day. Some turned to tennis or golf. Some did charity work or became volunteers. But a preponderance of the retired people I met who were once vital and energetic sadly turned to alcohol.

Today, at age seventy-two, I consider myself semiretired. I usually wake around 6 a.m., hit the gym for an hour, shower, shave, and go to work for a few hours every single day. (About 75 percent of the calls I make and receive are related to the Angel View Crippled Children's Foundation.) Then I head home, maybe play some golf, work on a few projects, or visit with some friends and read for several hours (I have a library of approximately 1,000 books) before my wife and I go out to dinner.

It's a nice life. But the fact remains that I still need the Ingleside Inn and Melvyn's, and they need me. Recently I was aggressively approached by a business group to sell the place. All kinds of things raced through my mind. What would I do on a Saturday night without my corner table? What's life without greeting old friends and breaking some bread? I have my entire life invested there; it's been wonderful to me, and I'm not ashamed to say that five minutes after I sell the place I would become "Mel who?" once more. Hanging out at my place is like watching a movie. I can't wait to see what's going to happen next. In talking to the buyers, I said something that even took me by surprise.

"If I had all the money in the world, I would like to own the Ingleside Inn and Melvyn's," I said. "Why then would I ever sell it?" That really summed it up for me.

In hindsight, I never knew I didn't have a chance. Knowledgeable people in the business said that a fifty-seat dining room and a hotel with twenty rooms were doomed to fail. Not only did I not fail—I became the hottest saloon keeper in the desert. I was too stupid to know that I had no chance, and that's probably why I succeeded. Sometimes ignorance is absolute bliss. Opening and operating a successful saloon is not a great contribution to society. There are people out there who have really given something to society, yet have been ignored. There are others who crave attention, but never get it. Why did God smile on a nice Jewish boy from Brooklyn? It just doesn't seem right to be that successful when you're having so much fun. They say a little knowledge is a dangerous thing. If I understood the obstacles and really knew the slim chances of my succeeding in a business I knew nothing about, I don't know what I would have done. Sometimes when you don't know the obstacles, you keep moving straight ahead and you manage to adapt and overcome.

I'll never forget the first time I went skiing. My lady took me to the highest mountain in Aspen despite the fact I had never been on skis. As you can pretty well imagine, I kept falling down. She kept encouraging me, telling me the bottom was not that far. It took me three hours to tumble down every inch of that mountain, but her constant encouragement made me get up, dust off the snow, and head toward the finish line. Had I known in reality how far I really had to go, I doubt that I would have tried and probably would have given up. There's something to be said about ignorance. What you don't know can't hurt you.

My success is a total accident. Whatever charm and magic exists at the Ingleside Inn, I did not create. There is a certain ambiance that exists there and is reinforced by the age of the place, and that cannot be duplicated. The only thing I'll take credit for is that I didn't destroy it, and that I worked very hard. It's like that old saying, "The harder I work, the luckier I seem to get." Any success requires putting in massive hours, and that was something I was never afraid to do.

One of the things I've found most difficult is staying on top of all the small details. After so many years, it's hard to see that the picture is crooked, there's a spot on the wall, the server has scuffed shoes, and the carpet is stained. After hearing the various complaints over the years, those things no longer seem as important. Those that have survived for many years have overcome the disease of mediocrity and managed to maintain their passion. Of course, employees are the key to maintaining that passion.

I have been very blessed over the years to have many faithful, loyal, dedicated, and good employees. The atmosphere at the Ingleside Inn and Melvyn's is wonderful and friendly. My maitre d', Brian Ellis, has been with me since the beginning. The same goes for Captain Bob Bouldoc in the dining room. The average tenure of all of my employees is between twenty-five to thirty years. That is unheard of in today's world.

I've shaken hands with President Ford, and with legends Frank Sinatra, Bob Hope, and Marlon Brando, and that they even knew my name still blows me away to this day. I've met almost every big celebrity in the world, and forgotten a few as well. One time, when I heard one of Barry Manilow's songs in Melvyn's dining room, I told Stephanie, "You know, I'd really love to meet Barry Manilow." She promptly took me by the hand, led me into my office, and showed me a picture of me shaking hands with Barry Manilow. Unfortunately, while I was running a hotel and five restaurants simultaneously, life sometimes became a blur, and I met a lot of great people I don't really remember that well. However, some of my fondest memories are of everyday customers who became friends of mine. I certainly look forward to the future and the many great experiences to come. It's been a great run, and I feel like I'm still the kid stuck in the candy store.

I'm also not ashamed to say that after three decades in the business, I still can't cook a steak, make a Bloody Mary or open a cash register.

But I hope my story is an inspiration to everybody because it shows that through tenacity and hard work, anyone can succeed.

If I can make it, anyone can.

# APPENDIX

## Guest List of the Ingleside Inn, Melvyn's, Cecil's, Doubles, and Touché

Don Adams
June Allyson
Edward Arnold
Armand Assante
Gene Autry
Lucille Ball
Joseph Barbera
Lita Baron
Rona Barrett
Tony Bennett
Jay Bernstein
Mr. Blackwell
Ward Bond
Sonny Bono
Ray Bradbury
Marlon Brando
Governor Jerry Brown
Hillary Brooke
Paul Burke
Carol Burnett
John Byner
Edd Byrnes
Jeanne Cagney
Milton Caniff
Hoagy Carmichael

Jack Cassidy
Peter Cetera
Cyd Charisse
Charo
Chevy Chase
Linda Christian
Cher
Joan Collins
Dennis Conner
Gary Cooper
Jackie Coogan
Cynthia Corning
Joseph Cotton
Norm Crosby
Xavier Cugat
Bill Cullen
Tony Curtis
Salvador Dali
Joan Darling
Geena Davis
Marvin Davis
Richard Dix
Brian Donlevy
James Doolittle
Kirk Douglas

Michael Douglas
Morton Downey Jr.
Buddy Ebsen
Don Felder
Fyvush Finkel
Eddie Fisher
Peter Folger
President Gerald Ford
John Forsythe
Zsa Zsa Gabor
Greta Garbo
Ava Gardner
Greer Garson
Barry Goldwater Jr.
Samuel Goldwyn
Linda Gray
Helen Gurley Brown
Jack Haley
George Hamilton
Phil Harris
David Hasselhoff
Goldie Hawn
Louise Hayward
Rita Hayworth
Patty Hearst
Sonja Henie
Katharine Hepburn
William Holden
Skip Homeier
Herbert Hoover Jr.
Bob Hope
Engelbert Humperdinck
Howard Hughes
Lee Iacocca
Marty Ingels
John Ireland
Reggie Jackson
Erich Johnson
Carolyn Jones
Jack Jones

Quincy Jones
Shirley Jones
Tom Jones
Sam Kinison
Kirk Kerkorian
Jack Klugman
Patrick Knowles
Andre Kostelanetz
Louis L'Amour
Michael Landon
Charles Laughton
Cyndi Lauper
Peter Lawford
Mark Lawrence
Barbara Leigh
Jack Lemon
Mervyn LeRoy
Jerry Lewis
Liberace
Guy Lombardo
Trini Lopez
Peter Lorre
Clare Boothe Luce
Joel McCrea
Darren McGavin
Jim McKay
Ali MacGraw
Patrick Macnee
Madonna
Barry Manilow
Marla Maples
Marty Martin
Zeppo Marx
Jackie Mason
Penny Marshall
Mary Martin
Patricia Medina
Ray Milland
Donna Mills
Liza Minnelli

George Montgomery
Richard Mulligan
Louis Nizer
J. J. Newbury
Richard Ney
Lloyd Noland
Margaret O'Brien
Donald O'Connor
Tip O'Neill
Jack Paar
Colonel Tom Parker
Gregory Peck
J. C. Penney
Bernadette Peters
Michelle Phillips
Papa John Phillips
Walter Pidgeon
Lily Pons
Victoria Principal
Richard Pryor
Claude Rains
Charlie Rich
Debbie Reynolds
John Ritter
Hal Roach
Harold Robbins
Tristan Rogers
Ginger Rogers
Linda Ronstadt
Charles Ruggles
Kurt Russell
Gunter Sachs
Morley Safer
Arnold Schwarzenegger
Tom Selleck
Sidney Sheldon
Brooke Shields
Dinah Shore
Sammy Shore
Maria Shriver

Frank Sinatra
Frank Sinatra Jr.
Elke Sommer
Jill St. John
James Stacy
Sylvester Stallone
Barbara Stanwyck
Elizabeth Taylor
Robert Taylor
Lowell Thomas
Cheryl Tiegs
Gene Tierney
Lily Tomlin
John Travolta
Claire Trevor
Donald Trump
Frankie Valli
Dick Van Dyke
Dick Van Patten
Lyle Waggoner
Mike Wallace
Joseph Wambaugh
John Wayne
Andy Williams
Cindy Williams
Esther Williams
Herman Wouk
Jane Wyman
Darryl F. Zanuck